Rectify

Rectify

The Power of
Restorative Justice
After
Wrongful Conviction

Lara Bazelon

Beacon Press
Boston

Beacon Press
Boston, Massachusetts
www.beacon.org

Beacon Press books
are published under the auspices of
the Unitarian Universalist Association of Congregations.

21 20 19 18   8 7 6 5 4 3 2 1

This book is printed on acid-free paper that meets the uncoated paper
ANSI/NISO specifications for permanence as revised in 1992.

Text design and composition by Kim Arney

Library of Congress Cataloging-in-Publication Data

Names: Bazelon, Lara, author.
Title: Rectify : the power of restorative justice after wrongful conviction /
    Lara Bazelon.
Description: Boston : Beacon Press, 2018. | Includes bibliographical
    references and index.
Identifiers: LCCN 2018001102 (print) | LCCN 2018004432 (ebook) |
    ISBN 9780807029190 (ebook) | ISBN 9780807029176 (hardcover : alk. paper)
Subjects: LCSH: Judicial error—United States. | False imprisonment—United
    States. | Restorative justice—United States. | Criminal justice,
    Administration of—United States. | Prisoners—United States. |
    Victims of crimes—United States.
Classification: LCC HV9950 (ebook) | LCC HV9950 .B39 2018 (print) |
    DDC 364.6—dc23
LC record available at https://lccn.loc.gov/2018001102

This book is dedicated to Kash Delano Register and Wilma Register, and was written in loving memory of my grandfather, the Honorable David L. Bazelon, the author of many groundbreaking and prescient judicial opinions, including the concurrence in United States v. Telfaire.

Contents

Author's Note

THIS IS A WORK OF NONFICTION. Names have been changed only where necessary to protect the anonymity of the sexual assault survivors who did not consent to have their full names or actual names used. In these instances, they are referred to by a first name only. Unless otherwise noted, the quotations and descriptions in the book come from interviews conducted by the author with the people who are described and quoted. Whenever possible, the information they provided was corroborated by individuals with personal knowledge of the events, court records, emails, photographs, letters, newspaper accounts, and media reports.

Why I Wrote This Book

I WENT TO LAW SCHOOL because I wanted to be a very specific kind of lawyer.

I wanted to be a public defender. The transgressions of the wealthy never interested me much because their privilege guaranteed them access to the best possible lawyers. It was the poor and resourceless who stood to lose the most because the deck was stacked against them and always had been. No matter how heinous the accusation, they needed a fighter.

When I was twenty-seven, I landed a job at the office of the federal public defender in Los Angeles. My first day was November 5, 2001. I showed up with my hair twisted in a tight knot, wearing the new suit my mother had helped me pick out. Stiff and awkward in too-tight heels, I did my best to look like someone who could walk into an austere marble courtroom and try a case. I had no idea what I was doing.

I gradually learned—sometimes painfully and in public. With time, I got better and, finally, even very good. For seven years, I represented men and women of every race, ethnicity, and nationality. Some of my clients came from Compton or Watts; others from countries I had never heard of, speaking languages I didn't know existed.

Before moving to Los Angeles, I pictured a city out of the pages of *US Weekly*: white beaches, sprawling estates, glittering movie premieres, and the possibility of a celebrity sighting at every Starbucks. Needless to say, that was not the world I inhabited. The packed, buzzing arraignment court where I spent most Monday mornings housed dozens of suspected criminals who were the city's hidden faces, the ones most of us take pains to avoid seeing.

When people asked me what I did for a living—at parties, waiting to board a plane at the airport, on a date—my answer was sometimes met with a look of barely concealed distaste. One law professor, after requesting that I speak to a class of first-year law students, opened the question-and-answer portion by asking: "How can you spend your days defending scumbags?"

Here is the answer: my clients were not all angels, but they were human beings just like the rest of us. They had husbands, wives, boyfriends, girlfriends, children, and grandchildren. For some of the younger men, the gang was their family and violence was a basic means of communication. Some had serious addictions to alcohol, drugs, gambling, or the thrill of getting over on other people. Others were mentally ill. Many had been abused. All of them were desperate. Whatever money or luck or goodwill they once possessed was long gone.

Their lives could not have been more different than mine or, I suspected, most of the law students the law professor had asked me to address that day. But what I tried to get across then—and believed to the marrow of my bones—was that there was a powerful connection between my clients and me. At the end of the day, it was just the two of us, up against the seemingly infinite resources of the government.

I loved my public defender life. The work felt important. It was also fast paced and exciting. The stakes were high. In the cases that went to trial, I worked constantly and thought of nothing else, inhabiting a closed-off world so fraught and churning it often made me physically sick. But as a moral matter, the universe was simple and binary. There are always—and only—two irreconcilable sides of the same story. Black/white. Right/wrong. Feller/fallen. Beginning/end. Next case.

I left the federal public defender's office in 2008. By then, I was in my midthirties and in a serious relationship. I wanted to have children. While many women in my office were able to strike that balance, I did not believe I could. For seven years, my job had consumed me. I did not know how to do it any other way.

It was five years before I returned to criminal defense work, this time as the director of the Loyola Law School Project for the Innocent in Los Angeles, a free legal services clinic founded by Professor Laurie Levenson and staffed by law students that is dedicated to freeing the falsely convicted. It was inspired by the Innocence Project, a nonprofit organization founded by attorneys Barry Scheck and Peter Neufeld in 1992. Based in New York City, the Innocence Project litigates wrongful conviction cases across the nation and has freed more than two hundred innocent men and women from prison. Its success has spurred the creation of a network of nearly seventy similarly named organizations around the world that are dedicated to the same mission. The transformational effect of this advocacy on individual lives and on the public's perception of the criminal justice system has created an innocence movement.[1]

At Loyola's Project for the Innocent, we had a client with the improbable name of Kash Register. In 1979, Register, who is black, was convicted by an all-white jury of murdering an elderly white man. Register was eighteen years old, with a new job and a baby on the way. He spent the next thirty-four years in prison for a murder he did not commit. Litigating his case, I slipped into my public defender mind-set: my focus was on how to marshal the evidence and arguments necessary to win in court. And we did win, by proving that a toxic combination of false testimony and misconduct by the police and prosecutors resulted in a conviction that was based on nothing but lies. After more than a year of litigation and a two-week evidentiary hearing, Register was exonerated on November 7, 2013.[2]

But unlike my public defender work, Register's case did not end. Yes, the legal wrangling was over, but then there was the rest of his life to consider. His mother, Wilma, a woman of unshakable Christian faith, remained in the apartment where they had lived together when he was arrested. But Wilma was in her late seventies, still working full-time selling concessions at LA's Staples Center and barely getting by. Register needed a job. He needed clothes. He needed to reconnect with his thirty-four-year-old daughter, who had been born while he was in jail, and meet her two children—his grandchildren. He needed good civil lawyers who would sue the police and the city for every dime they owed him. He needed to learn to navigate a world that was unrecognizable from the one that was snatched away from him in 1979. He needed to heal from the psychic damage of being locked away from society for most of his life when he had done nothing wrong.

A few months after the exoneration, I received an email from a man named Bob Pool. The message began, "I read of the liberation of Mr. Register with the help of your project. I am both elated for him and personally shaken. I was a member of the jury that voted to convict him so long ago. To find out that we were betrayed by the judicial system while tasked with one of the most difficult decisions in our (my) lives disgusts, sickens and saddens me." Pool said that his faith in law enforcement had been utterly destroyed. He concluded, "I am trying to come to a personal resolution about this affair."

· · ·

In March 2014, a Louisiana man named Glenn Ford was freed after serving thirty years in solitary confinement on death row. Like Register, he was African American and convicted of killing an older white man by an all-white jury. Unlike Register, he left prison in poor health, diagnosed with lung cancer that had spread to his bones and spine. He died a year later. After Ford's exoneration, the trial prosecutor, A. M. "Marty" Stroud III, wrote a public letter of apology that was published in the *Shreveport Times*, admitting that he struck every potential black juror and went out and celebrated at a bar with his colleagues after the verdict. Interviewed in 2015, Stroud told journalist Bill Whitaker on *60 Minutes*, "I've got a hole in me through which the north wind blows. It's a sense of coldness; it's a sense of disgust." He continued, "It was a train to injustice, and I was the engineer. Glenn Ford will be a part of me until the day I die."[3]

The damage inflicted by wrongful convictions is massive. Attending my first Innocence Network conference in May 2014, I met scores of exonerees. Some had been raped in prison. Some, like Ford, had spent decades awaiting their execution. The senselessness and the monstrosity of their suffering were unfathomable. Nor was the suffering limited to the exonerees, although clearly they had endured the worst. It included their mothers, fathers, husbands, wives, and children. It included the original crime victims who mistakenly identified them; the jurors, like Bob Pool, who convicted them; the police detectives who thought they were using the right methods to obtain a rock-solid identification. It included the prosecutors like Stroud who realized, too late, that their zeal to convict had gotten in the way of their ability to play by the rules. It included the witnesses who had not come forward because they had their own problems and because they were afraid.

I grew frustrated and restless. Direct advocacy was not satisfying in the way it had once been. I felt as if I was using my fingernails to tear down a boulder. The limitations of the criminal justice system were too blatant to ignore, as was its foundational rot. I found myself looking for different answers. I began writing about exonerations as part of a series for *Slate*, the online magazine. In the process, I stumbled upon a fledgling movement to apply something called "restorative justice" to wrongful conviction cases.

Restorative justice is a centuries-old practice of bringing together victims, offenders, and their respective communities to address the harm inflicted by a crime and agree upon a series of measures designed to repair that harm rather than meting out punishment. In the United States, restorative justice is best known as an alternative to juvenile court. Its most effective practitioners are able to convince police and prosecutors to consider victim offender dialogues and reparations as an alternative to the school-to-prison pipeline.

Now there is a growing movement to apply restorative justice practices in wrongful conviction cases. The best-known example is the case of Jennifer Thompson and Ronald Cotton. Thompson, raped by a stranger when she was in her early twenties, misidentified Cotton as her attacker after faithfully following faulty identification procedures that were standard at the time. Cotton was wrongfully convicted and served more than a decade in prison before he was freed.

After Cotton's release, he and Thompson had an emotional reunion and formed a lifelong bond. Practicing restorative justice without any awareness of what it was, they told their story to prosecutors, judges, and legislators, achieving major legislative reforms in North Carolina, where the crime occurred, and beyond. Among their achievements was convincing state lawmakers to pass legislation eliminating the suggestive eyewitness procedures that led Thompson to misidentify Cotton in the first place.

Their experience hints at broader, exciting possibilities. There are hundreds, if not thousands, of Thompsons and Cottons. They have their own stories, distinct and powerful. What if, like Thompson and Cotton, they could come together? What if their voices became a chorus that included not only other crime victims and exonerees, but also the many other people who inadvertently contributed to a catastrophic miscarriage of justice? That kind of emotional urgency would be difficult to ignore or dismiss. Now imagine if, connected and empowered, they shared their stories with each other, with crucial stakeholders, and with the general public, across the United States. As Thompson says, when she and Cotton speak, those in power "cannot *not* hear us."[4]

The innocence movement has challenged the conventional wisdom underlying the basic tenets of the American criminal justice system. We now know that witnesses like Thompson who were 100 percent certain can be 100 percent wrong. That prosecutors like Marty Stroud can let tunnel vision and blind ambition get in the way of their obligation to seek justice. That jurors like Bob Pool can convict based on evidence that turns out to be false. The exposure of these fault lines in our justice system is directly attributable to the brilliance, dedication, and sheer will of the wrongfully convicted and their advocates.

As with all movements, though, there is space for fresh ideas and methods to address harms that are deep and systemic. Restorative justice is one of them. It connects isolated individuals who might otherwise shy away from one another out of fear or resentment. The kind of suffering experienced by those involved in a wrongful conviction case varies greatly, but arises from a shared traumatic experience. This shared suffering means that very differently situated people can unite in a common cause. And they are uniting. In voices too raw and powerful to ignore, they are helping each other to heal and they are advocating collectively for badly needed reforms. *Rectify* tells their stories.

CHAPTER ONE

A Rapist in Richmond

IT WAS DAYBREAK ON January 3, 1984, and Janet Burke was opening the day-care center where she worked at East End Church in Richmond, Virginia. She was twenty years old, with pale skin and blue eyes, her long brown hair feathered in the style popular at the time.

A man broke the glass portion of the locked front door and walked inside. "Sometimes," Burke said, "it takes everything to fall into place the wrong way for it to work to someone's advantage." Normally, for safety reasons, two people opened the center together. But that morning, Burke's coworker had her own childcare emergency, and Burke was alone.

Burke never heard the glass break, or the man's footsteps in the hallway, and that inability to sense the horror that was coming would haunt her for the rest of her life. The man held a serrated knife to Burke's throat and forced her into the back office. He was black, dressed entirely in black, wearing a ski mask with the face ripped out. For a brief, futile moment, Burke held out hope that he just wanted her money. He raped her.

In terror and pain, Burke focused on protecting the babies and toddlers she knew would be arriving at any moment. Over and over again, she told the rapist, "The children are coming," as she begged him to leave. A parent buzzed the front door and the man left out the back. Burke could still see him there, standing just outside, watching her. Eventually, he disappeared. "I composed myself as best I could," she said, and went to open the broken door.

As it happened, Burke's boyfriend's grandparents lived across the street from the church. Burke was taken to their house, and the police arrived soon after. Even though Burke had not been able to see above the rapist's hairline, she had seen his full face. She knew how tall he was and his approximate build. She believed she could describe and identify him.

Burke's father drove her to the hospital, where the doctors did a thorough medical examination to create a rape kit, assiduously swabbing, scraping, and plucking to preserve as much physical evidence as possible. As this was happening, police asked Burke to describe every detail of the crime, with her mother sitting in the room. Hours long and utterly invasive, the experience, Burke said, was "almost unbearable."

Within a month, four other young women were brutally attacked in Richmond and neighboring Henrico County under similar circumstances. On January 21, 1984, Diane was robbed, held at knifepoint, and orally sodomized by a black man who matched the description of Burke's rapist. Six days later, a black man approached Linda, outside of her house. He was wielding a knife, saying he was going to rob and rape her. She managed to get back inside, slamming the door and immediately calling the police. He fled.

Eighteen-year-old Mary was not so fortunate. Three days after Linda's narrow escape, on January 30, at 8:30 p.m., a black man with a gun accosted her on the street. After forcing her to walk with him into the woods, he repeatedly sodomized and raped her for over two hours. The man told Mary that he had done the same thing to other women. But usually, he said, he used a knife.

Less than two days later, the rapist struck again, approaching another young woman, Tracy, as she was getting into her car to go to work at 6:30 a.m. on February 1. Brandishing a gun, he demanded money, threatened to sodomize her, and ordered her out of the car. With the weapon at her back, Tracy reentered her house as the man followed her inside. When she stepped into the hallway and turned off the light as the man instructed, her dog rushed at him. Tracy called out to her grandmother for help, and the man ran out.[1]

All of the crimes occurred within a one-mile radius, some mere blocks apart. All of the victims were white women, attacked when they were alone and vulnerable, in the dimness of the early morning or after dark. The police had a terrifying prospect on their hands: a serial rapist willing to use deadly force who was liable to strike again at any moment. The fact that the rapist was a black man attacking white women seemed to raise the stakes exponentially. The glare of the media spotlight was intense, as was the public demand for swift action.

At the same time, there was reason to be hopeful that the perpetrator would be caught. All of the victims believed they could make an identification either because, as in Mary's case, the attacks went on for an extended amount of time or because there was enough light to see the attacker clearly. And then, one of them did.

Mid-morning on February 5, 1984, the police picked up Thomas Haynesworth, an eighteen-year-old who was on his way to the store to buy sweet potatoes for dinner on orders from his mother. That day, Haynesworth—quiet, well-mannered, unfailingly considerate—had few thoughts other than getting home in time to watch *Gunsmoke*, his favorite TV western. A self-described "goody two-shoes and peacemaker," Haynesworth aspired to become a police officer and had no criminal record whatsoever. But Linda had seen Haynesworth as he was walking down the street and called the police, saying she recognized him. Haynesworth was stopped and immediately surrounded by more than a dozen officers. Linda was brought to the scene. She stared at Haynesworth. He was light-skinned, like her attacker, and his features were similar. Haynesworth saw her hesitate and then watched as one of the police officers whispered in her ear. Her identification was tentative, but it was enough to get Haynesworth arrested and photographed.

When the detectives called Burke to notify her, she had already gone back to work at the church. They explained that they had a suspect in custody and wanted to show her some pictures. Four weeks after she was raped, Burke was handed several plastic sleeves of Polaroid photographs to see if she could pick out the man who had assaulted her. The detectives did not give her any particular instructions, as far as Burke can recall. But an arrest had been made, and to Burke, that meant the rapist had to be among the array of faces. It was her job to pick him out.

She looked at the first sleeve of photographs and then the second. She saw Haynesworth's picture and knew instantly that he was the one. Quickly, she turned the page. "I remember thinking in my head, 'Do I really want to say that I identified him because it is going to mean going to court and seeing him? Am I really going to be able to do this? And then I decided, yes, I really did need to do this because I couldn't let it happen to anyone else. I have to make sure that this person isn't able to hurt anyone ever again.'"

Burke turned back to the second sleeve of photographs and pointed out Haynesworth to the detectives. "I was positive," she said. "I never second-guessed myself one bit." She described "this feeling in the room of, 'we are going to get this guy.'" Burke's confidence was buoyed when the detectives told her later in the legal proceedings that Haynesworth's blood test showed that he was a type O secretor, just like the rapist. What Burke did not know was that type O is the most common blood type in the United States—the blood type of nearly half of all African Americans—or that nearly 80 percent of the population is classified as secretors. Instead, this piece of information cemented Burke's certainty.

The other three victims also selected Haynesworth's picture. Mary, who described the rapist as "in my face, right, his face was up in mine" throughout her two-hour ordeal, said she had "no doubt." Like Burke, she had also been told that Haynesworth's blood type was a match. Tracy, too, was sure: "As soon as I saw the picture, I picked him out." Diane also identified Haynesworth.

He was charged in all five cases. The prosecutor told Burke that her case would be tried first because it was the strongest—of all the victims, she was the most certain, the most credible, and had the best opportunity to get a look at the rapist's face. Burke was terrified, but determined to see the legal process through to the end.

It was harrowing. In the weeks leading up to the trial, Burke received threatening calls at work. One man told her, "You have the wrong person. If you testify, we are going to kill you." At another point, a caller told Burke that if she showed up at a predetermined location, she would come face-to-face with the real perpetrator. The police acted on the tip, going so far as to dress one of the day-care mothers in a wig to look like Burke. She drove to the site with a police officer stowed away in the trunk. But no one showed up. The calls continued, sometimes twice a week or more: "We are going to blow up the day-care center." That time, Burke and her staff had to evacuate the kids. Attempts to trace the calls failed. Asked if she would have doubted herself if the caller had told her, in a nonthreatening way, "Look, you have the wrong guy. There is someone in the neighborhood who looks exactly like him," Burke paused to think. "I don't know," she said finally. "But the menace made me even more sure it was him."

When Burke saw Haynesworth in the courtroom at his preliminary hearing, her reaction was immediate and visceral: she collapsed. "The detective had to stand beside me and hold me up," she said.

Haynesworth, too, was terrified, albeit for a completely different reason. The charges were literally incomprehensible to him: his mother had to explain what "sodomy" and "abduction" meant. And he had no idea why these five women were so firmly convinced that he was the worst kind of sexual predator. He was innocent, he insisted. As the first trial approached, Haynesworth, who was still in jail, tried to remain hopeful that the jurors would believe his side of the story—that he was at home asleep on the morning Burke was attacked. A devout Christian, he prayed that Burke would realize she had made a terrible mistake.

None of that happened at the trial. "What stood out to me," Haynesworth said, "was that she said I had a face she would never forget. That she was positive. It hurt more than the actual accusation." Shock and disbelief gave way to anguish and despair. It was 1984, and he was a black teenager accused of raping a white woman who said she was 100 percent certain that he was guilty. If she had no doubt, how could the jury?

For Burke, the trial was a tortuous combination of shame and fear. She was forced to describe every foul detail of what the rapist had done to her in a courtroom full of people, including her mother, father, and numerous members of the media. All the while, the man she believed was responsible was just feet away, staring at her. Burke broke down in sobs on the witness stand. The judge called for a recess, and she was taken out of the courtroom before she was able to continue.

Haynesworth watched Burke closely as she testified. He remembers her saying, "I would bet my life," and thinking, "Well, you would lose your life then." And yet, listening to the broken young woman, who was a mere two years older than he was, tugged at his heartstrings. Sometimes he would find himself overcome with sympathy, only to be jerked back to the reality that the monster she was describing was supposed to be him.

On July 12, 1984, the jury found Thomas Haynesworth guilty of raping Janet Burke. Listening as the verdict was read, Haynesworth remembers being furious: "On what ground did they find me guilty? What evidence was there? I had an alibi. There were no fingerprints, no other evidence. It all turned on the testimony of the victim."

The judge sentenced him to ten years in prison.

Mary's case was next, and here it seemed that perhaps Haynesworth had a chance. After Mary, who was five feet eight, insisted that her rapist was "taller than me," Haynesworth's attorney asked her to step down from the witness stand. He had her stand beside Haynesworth to establish that, at five feet six and a half, he was actually the shorter of the two. But Mary did not back down, and the blood evidence collected from the rape kit appeared to back up her claim. As in Burke's case, the man who raped her was a type O secretor and so was Haynesworth. On August 10, 1984, the jury found him guilty of rape, sodomy, abduction, and using a firearm in the commission of a crime. This time, he was sentenced to thirty-six years.

In a strange twist, the prosecutor dismissed for lack of evidence the charges brought by Linda, whose sighting of Haynesworth on the street led to his arrest, the circulation of his mug shot, and the four subsequent victim identifications falling like dominoes. But Haynesworth was bound over for trial for the crimes committed against Tracy, and her identification proved ironclad. On October 11, 1984, Haynesworth was convicted of abducting her. For that offense, the punishment was twenty-eight years in prison. A different jury acquitted Haynesworth of the attack on Diane.

At the time, there was every reason to believe that justice had been done. There was, in Burke's and Mary's cases, the matching blood type. And most damning, there were five identifications, and three of them seemed rock-solid. What were the chances that *all* of these women would mistakenly pick the same man as their attacker? Haynesworth remembers a husband-and-wife minister couple coming to the jail to offer prayer and comfort. When Haynesworth told them that five different women had accused him of sexual assault, he said, "They cut the visit short and they never came back."

That's the One

An identification made by an eyewitness in open court is dramatic and damning. As the late Supreme Court justice William Brennan famously wrote, "There is *nothing more convincing* than a live human being who takes the stand, points his finger at the defendant, and says, 'That's the one!'"[2] Studies have shown that the impact on juries is profound; the more confident the witness, the more likely the jury will take the identification as conclusive proof of guilt. Burke, Mary, and Tracy were not merely confident that Thomas Haynesworth was the perpetrator; they were dead certain. Burke said, "I knew exactly that that's who it was."

Yet, the United States Supreme Court has long entertained doubts about the validity of eyewitness identifications. As early as 1927, Justice Felix Frankfurter wrote, "The identification of strangers is proverbially untrustworthy. The hazards of such testimony are established by a formidable number of instances in the records of English and American trials. These instances are recent—not due to the brutalities of ancient criminal procedure."[3]

In 1967, the United States Supreme Court decided the landmark case *United States v. Wade*.[4] In *Wade*, the justices put in place an important safeguard by giving defendants in live lineups the right to have their attorney present. The purpose was to ensure that the police did not—knowingly or unknowingly—engage in suggestive practices, such as subtly encouraging or discouraging a particular choice, or congratulating the witness afterward on "getting it right."

Thomas Haynesworth never stood in a live lineup. Instead, each of the victims selected his picture from a group of Polaroid photographs in a process shielded from external monitoring. Three years earlier, James Summitt had petitioned the US Supreme Court to have his rape conviction overturned under similar circumstances—where a victim identified him from an array of photographs at a police station when his lawyer was not present. The court rejected Summitt's argument that the trial judge was required, at a minimum, to hold a hearing outside the jury's presence to make sure the victim's identification was not the result of pressure or suggestive behavior by law enforcement. Instead, a majority of the court held that Summitt's ability to cross-examine the witness in open court was "the device best suited to determine the trustworthiness of testimonial evidence."[5]

But Brandon Garrett, a professor at the University of Virginia School of Law and one of the nation's top experts on eyewitness identification, says that years of empirical studies have cast serious doubt on that premise: "Once memory is contaminated there is no amount of cross-examination at trial that can change an eyewitness' altered memory. We also know through jury studies that it is very hard for defense counsel to convince juries that very confident witnesses could be wrong."

Burke recalls nothing suggestive or untoward in the way the police administered the lineup in her case. Haynesworth's attorney, Shawn Armburst, says that all these years later, "not much exists in terms of documentation" about what actually occurred when Burke and the other four victims made their identifications, leaving "a bit of a black hole." Assuming that the police did everything properly does not eliminate the possibility of suggestiveness either; studies have shown that the practices used by the Virginia police—practices that remain in place in Virginia today and in the majority of states—may have been suggestive in and of themselves.[6] These include having the investigating detectives administer the procedure—creating the risk of intentional or inadvertent signaling to the witness.

Studies have also shown that witnesses are more likely to pick out a suspect if they are shown pictures grouped in an array rather than sequentially.[7] And the detectives had told Burke a crucial fact: that there was a suspect in custody. Quite logically, she concluded that the guilty man was somewhere in those plastic sleeves of Polaroids; it was just a matter of finding him. With this preconception, the mind engages in what experts call "relative judgment," by contrasting each photograph against the others to see which one looks the most like the perpetrator. Indeed, Tracy testified that she engaged in precisely this practice, testifying that "I compared his picture to each picture to make sure it was the right one."

The Perils of Cross-Racial Identification

Also crucial to assessing the validity of the eyewitness identifications was the fact that Haynesworth was black and his victims were white. Numerous studies, some dating back to the 1970s, have revealed the perils of cross-racial identification.[8] Across race and ethnicity, human beings engage in what is known as "own-race bias," meaning that they are much more accurate when identifying members of their own racial group than those outside it. Experts have pointed to many possible explanations for this phenomenon, including the fact that many Americans have limited contact with people outside their own racial group, giving them less experience "encoding" features that distinguish one similar-looking person from another.[9]

Some high-ranking members of the judiciary had highlighted the problems posed by cross-racial identification long before Haynesworth's case went to trial, but the concerns they raised were not widely accepted within the legal community. In 1972, the chief judge of the United States Court of Appeals for the District of Columbia wrote a concurring opinion in a case called *United States v. Telfaire*, which addressed the issue head-on: "The available data, while not exhaustive, unanimously supports the widely held commonsense view that members of one race have greater difficulty in accurately identifying members of a different race." He advocated that trial judges educate juries about this issue and proposed an instruction of his own as an example.[10]

In the decades that followed, a small number of state and federal courts adopted the so-called *Telfaire* instruction—or a variation on the same theme. In the 1999 case *New Jersey v. Cromedy*, the state's highest court reversed a black man's conviction for raping a white woman because the jury had not been instructed about the problems with cross-racial identification, the woman's testimony was critical, and her identification was not corroborated by other evidence.[11] In 2017, New York State's highest court held in *People v. Boone* that in cases where the victim and the defendant were of different races, an instruction on cross-racial identification was required if requested by counsel, stating that "the near consensus among cognitive and social psychologists that people have significantly greater difficulty in accurately identifying members of a different race" required this safeguard to mitigate against "the risk of wrongful convictions."[12]

But *Boone*, *Cromedy*, and *Telfaire* have remained the entrenched minority position, even though the data show that mistaken eyewitness testimony played a role in 77 percent of the first two hundred DNA exonerations, nearly half of which involved cross-racial identifications. In 2008, relying "especially [on] the jury instructions in *Telfaire* and *Cromedy*," the American Bar Association crafted a model cross-racial identification instruction of its own, and also suggested that the government provide funding for expert testimony to further explain the issue to jurors.[13]

Currently, cross-racial identification instructions for juries have been adopted—either in mandatory or advisory form—in only eight states and the District of Columbia: California, Georgia, Hawaii, Maryland,

Massachusetts, New York, Utah, and Washington.[14] Virginia, where Haynesworth was tried, routinely upholds convictions where judges refuse to allow this kind of expert testimony or give a cautionary instruction about the problems inherent in identifying people outside one's racial group.[15] No such evidence or judicial instruction was provided in any of Haynesworth's four trials.

Perhaps equally important was the specter hanging over each of the cases against Thomas Haynesworth, or what University of Michigan Law School professor Samuel Gross has called "the incendiary relationship" between race and rape. Dating back to slavery, white Americans have been fixated and terrified by the idea, Gross said, "that Black male sexuality is wanton and bestial, and that Black men are wild, criminal rapists of white women."[16] In the pre–Civil War era, Virginia law—the state where Haynesworth was tried and convicted—provided for the death penalty if a black man was found to have raped a white woman; if the rapist was white, the punishment was ten to twenty-one years.[17]

Until the middle of the twentieth century, black men accused of raping white women were routinely lynched before their cases ever reached a courtroom. While the practice of lynching had slowed to a trickle by the 1950s, so-called legal lynching—that is, the lack of due process afforded black defendants accused of raping white women—was all too common.[18] Perhaps the most famous instance of legal lynching was the "Scottsboro Boys" case, in which nine young African American men were convicted of raping two white women in 1931. Angry mobs gathered outside the courthouse daily demanding vigilante justice. The threat of violence became so great that the National Guard was dispatched. All of the defendants were quickly convicted and eight were sentenced to die, a punishment that the Alabama Supreme Court upheld as appropriate for this "most foul and revolting crime." (The following year, the US Supreme Court later overturned the convictions because none of the defendants had been given a lawyer at their trials.)[19]

Fifty years later, the chances that a black man could receive a fair trial for such a historically fraught crime—particularly in the South—remained dubious. The likelihood of conviction was far greater than if the defendant was white. The sentence was likely to be more severe as well, even though the laws, post-Reconstruction, were race neutral.[20]

Most chillingly, there was the increased likelihood of convicting the wrong man. According to the National Registry of Exonerations, which has documented every known exoneration from 1989 through the present day, a disproportionately "huge" percentage of black men have been wrongfully convicted of rape. "[A] black prisoner serving time for sexual assault is three-and-a-half times more likely to be innocent than a white assault convict," according to the National Registry's 2017 report, *Race and Wrongful Convictions*. In most of these wrongful conviction cases, the victim was a white woman.[21] When Burke's case went to trial in 1984, her race and the race of her rapist were factors that weighed heavily against Haynesworth.

"You Should Be Proud"

Eight months and six days after he was first arrested, Haynesworth—a teenager who had never received so much as a traffic ticket—had been convicted of being a repeat, violent sexual predator and sentenced to a total of seventy-four years in prison. He was nineteen years old.

Burke felt a sense of relief. Her rapist would, in all likelihood, die in prison. And she said she took some small measure of comfort in knowing that "I played a part in making sure that this didn't happen to anyone else."

Throughout the legal proceedings, Burke's family supported her as best they could. But as Burke explained, "People don't know what to do with you. They don't know what to say to you. They don't know what to do for you. And you are not in a position to say what you need. You don't even know."

Ironically, it was a total stranger who offered her the greatest solace. Eric Allan, a newsman for a local television station, wrote Burke a letter as he sat in the courtroom. It read:

Janet,

As a reporter my job is to just state the facts. I'm not here to make any judgments or conclusions in a case such as yours. Publicly, I won't.

But watching you testify affected me strongly and I wanted so badly to do something to make you feel better.

That's why I am writing this note.

I want you to know I admire your courage for trying to bring your assailant to justice. I'm a man, so I cannot know your pain. But I'm also a good judge of emotions, so I could see it.

People like you won't make the sick any less sick but you will make them think twice. You are part of a growing number of women who are standing up for your rights and you should be proud.

I hope you don't hate all men. If you do, I surely understand. But please try to remember there are good people in the world and you have the rest of your life ahead of you to find them. I'm sure you will.[22]

Burke put the letter in her wallet. She never showed it to anyone. Not her parents, not her closest friends or, later, her husband. As the years went by and one wallet replaced another, the letter remained, tucked inside. "There is nothing about the process that is not humiliating," Burke said. But the letter made her feel stronger. It reminded her that she had been brave and had done the right thing by facing her attacker and, in the process, protecting other women. More than anything else, Eric Allan's words gave Burke hope. "That letter," she said, "was a lifeline for me for a long time."

Twenty-seven years later, Burke received news about Haynesworth's case that was so shattering it upended the life she had worked so carefully to rebuild. Burke took the letter out of her wallet, feeling that she no longer fit the description of the woman it depicted.

CHAPTER TWO

Convicting the Innocent

THE NATIONAL REGISTRY of Exonerations is a small, nonprofit research project founded in 2012 by University of Michigan Law School professor Samuel Gross and Rob Warden, then the executive director for the Center on Wrongful Convictions at Northwestern University School of Law. What the project lacks in manpower it makes up in zeal, documenting every known exoneration dating back to 1989, the first year that DNA exonerations were recorded in the United States. Two staff members—Klara Stephens and Pulitzer Prize–winning journalist Maurice Possley—collect detailed information about each case from court documents and news reports, provide a comprehensive narrative about the case, and break down the data into numerous categories, including gender, race, geography, crime of conviction, factors that contributed to the wrongful conviction, and whether the case involved DNA. The registry's website provides detailed graphs that set out the cause or causes of the wrongful convictions and chart their frequency over time.[1]

On March 7, 2017, the registry released a report summarizing the data it had documented since its founding: 1,994 exonerations. (The number is now above 2,100.)[2] Seventy-eight percent of the exonerations did not involve DNA evidence. This finding surprises many people, as it seems at odds with the way that crime is prosecuted on popular television shows and in movies, where the perpetrator inevitably leaves behind a tiny but undeniable bit of himself. Skin follicles are collected from under the victim's fingernails, blood or semen is retrieved from a stain, a trace of saliva is lifted from a soda can or cigarette butt. In fictionalized accounts, diligent detectives and technicians rapidly collect and analyze this trace DNA evidence. More often than not, when the episode concludes, the bad guy has been conclusively identified, apprehended, and locked away.

The reality is much messier and more complicated. Even when DNA exists, backlogs and bureaucracy mean that it can take months, if not years, to test. Crime labs also come to erroneous conclusions, often because the technicians are incompetent, overwhelmed, or even corrupt. In 2010, at a San Francisco crime laboratory, a technician stole some of the cocaine she was supposed to be testing, resulting in a scandal that led to the dismissal of seventeen hundred pending criminal cases. Five years later, in the same laboratory, two other bad apples—a technician and her immediate supervisor—were discovered to have committed misconduct so serious it required the San Francisco district attorney's office to review fourteen hundred criminal cases. Both employees had failed DNA proficiency testing examinations administered by a national crime lab accrediting agency a year earlier, but had kept their jobs. At least one found conclusive DNA matches where none existed.[3]

San Francisco is just one example. Similar and worse corruption has been exposed in Massachusetts. In April 2017, state authorities overturned twenty thousand convictions after a crime lab technician was caught falsifying test results; in November of the same year, another six thousand convictions were thrown out when it was discovered that a lab technician in a different laboratory was on drugs when she performed the testing.[4]

But most crucial, and most fundamentally misunderstood, is the fact that there is no DNA to test in the vast majority of criminal cases. What this means is that even if DNA evidence is competently collected and properly tested in every case where it exists, it will do little to stem the rising tide of false convictions.

And it is a tide—a rising one. In 2014, a record-setting 147 people were exonerated. That record was broken in 2015, when 160 people were freed. It was broken again in 2016, when the number rose to 168, an average of more than three people per week.[5] In a 2017 report, the National Registry of Exonerations came to this sobering conclusion: "Exonerations used to be unusual; now they are commonplace." Yet, "the record numbers of exonerations we have seen in recent years have not made a dent in the number of innocent defendants who have been convicted and punished."

The Tip of an Iceberg

Experts believe that the men and women who have been exonerated are only a small fraction of those who deserve to be. Many wrongful convictions remain hidden or, if known, unprovable. According to the National Registry of Exonerations, "By any reasonable accounting, there are tens of thousands of false convictions *each year* across the country." A 2015 study by the University of Michigan found that 4.1 percent of those on death row were falsely convicted, and conservative estimates in noncapital cases range from 2 to 5 percent.[6] According to the federal Bureau of Justice Statistics (BJS), in 2015—the most recent year that BJS data were available—there were approximately 1,530,000 people in prison in the United States.[7] Using the most conservative estimate of wrongful convictions—1 percent—means that on any given day, 15,300 innocent people are sitting in prison. If, as with death row inmates, it is 4 percent, that number climbs to 61,200, which is roughly the capacity of Soldier Field, the stadium where the Chicago Bears play professional football.[8]

Lies

In 2015, the National Registry of Exonerations released a comprehensive report titled *The First 1,600 Exonerations*, which analyzed the data by crime, causation, race, gender, and geography. Fifty-five percent of the first sixteen hundred exoneration cases involve false testimony—not mistaken identifications, like Janet Burke's—but flat-out lies. Witnesses lie for many reasons: some to protect themselves or someone else, some because law enforcement has coached, coerced, or promised them a reward. Some witnesses lie out of plain malice. Lying under oath is perjury, which is a state and federal crime, though it is among the least prosecuted.

Hannah Quick is one jarring example. In 1981, three Hispanic men—William Vasquez, Amaury Villalobos, and Raymond Mora—were convicted of burning down a Brooklyn building Quick owned. Left inside to die were Elizabeth Kinsey and her five small children. The night of the fire, Quick told the jury, she was awakened by the whispers of Vasquez, Villalobos, and Mora outside her door. Through her bedroom window, she watched them leave the building. Quick said that she heard an explosion and ran from the building as it burst into flames.

Quick was a shady character. A drug addict and known liar, she herself had been charged with using her apartment—located on the first floor of the same building—as an opium den where people came to use the heroin she sold them. And Quick had every incentive to deflect attention away from herself. She could have been held liable for the unsafe conditions that likely had led to the fire: what the *New York Times* described as "an illegal hookup to the electrical grid" and allowing the addicts who used her apartment to light candles when they got high.[9] But the jury believed her. On November 24, 1981, Villalobos, Vasquez, and Mora were each convicted and sentenced to twenty-five years to life.

In 2014, on her deathbed, Quick confessed to her daughter that she lied about what she saw and sent three innocent men to prison. Vasquez (blind from untreated glaucoma) and Villalobos had been released on parole two years earlier, after more than three decades behind bars. At sixty-six and seventy years old, respectively, they celebrated with their families at their exoneration hearing, held on December 16, 2015. Mora could not. He had died in prison in 1989. His widow and daughter came in his stead, holding a framed photograph taken of him before he was sent away. Collectively, the three exonerees had served seventy-one years in prison.[10]

Mistakes

An additional 34 percent of wrongful convictions among the first sixteen hundred arise from good faith but mistaken eyewitness identifications. Like Janet Burke's, these often occur in rape cases. While many involve cross-racial identification, not all do. On June 7, 1998, Clarence Elkins and his wife, Melinda, were living in Barberton, Ohio, with their two young sons when they received horrifying news. Melinda's fifty-eight-year-old mother, Judith Johnson, had been beaten, raped, and murdered in her home, and Melinda's six-year-old niece, Brooke Sutton, had been raped and beaten to the point where she lost consciousness. But Brooke survived and told police that the killer "looked like Uncle Clarence."[11] Based on Brooke's statement, Elkins was arrested. In 1999, after Brooke identified him in court, he was convicted of both rapes, Judith's murder, and given a life sentence.

Brooke's identification was the only evidence against Elkins, and there was reason to doubt its validity from the outset. Not only was Brooke a small and traumatized child, but the police had interviewed Judith's neighbor, convicted felon Earl Gene Mann, shortly after arresting Elkins. According to the detectives' notes, Mann asked, "Why don't you charge me with the Judy Johnson murder?"[12] In 2002, three years after Elkins was sent to prison, Mann was convicted for raping three girls, all under the age of ten.

But in a stroke of luck that followed years of unending years of misery, Mann landed in the same prison as Elkins. Melinda, who had long suspected Mann, urged Elkins to collect any evidence he could find. In 2005, Elkins retrieved one of Mann's discarded cigarette butts and mailed it to his attorneys at the Ohio Innocence Project at the University of Cincinnati College of the Law. The DNA on the cigarette butt matched the DNA left at the crime scene. Brooke Sutton had long since recanted, stating that the police had coached her testimony. But the local prosecutor dug in and refused to agree to Elkins's release. Under pressure from the Ohio attorney general—the top prosecutor in the state—Elkins was released on December 15, 2005.[13] Three years later, in 2008, Mann pleaded guilty to aggravated murder, attempted murder, burglary, and rape in the crimes against Judith Johnson and Brooke Sutton. He was sentenced to life in prison without the possibility of parole.

Elkins and Melinda divorced shortly after his release. "The media expected us to be happy," she told reporters, "but it was at that point that I started grieving for my mom." Elkins, who told the US Senate Judiciary Committee in a written statement that, after several stints in solitary confinement, "I pretty much lost my mind," won several settlements in the millions of dollars, but most of the money went to Melinda, their sons, and his attorneys.[14] Elkins has remarried. After suffering periods of unemployment and setbacks from post-traumatic stress disorder, he is trying to start a new life.[15]

Police Misconduct

A shocking 45 percent of the documented sixteen hundred wrongful convictions are the result of bad acts or omissions by police and prosecutors.[16]
This misconduct turns what is supposed to be a level playing field into a
ski slope, with the state gliding to victory by running over the defendant's
right to a fair trial. It includes, but is not limited to coercing, coaching,
or threatening witnesses; physically beating defendants until they give
false confessions; neglecting to turn over exculpatory evidence or actively
hiding it altogether; making false representations to the court and to the
jury; and committing perjury. The percentage of false convictions arising
from official misconduct often overlaps with percentages involving perjury; that is, many wrongful convictions are due, at least in part, to false
testimony that is coerced or partially fabricated by the police.

Consider Debra Milke. In 1989, she was a divorced single mother
living in Phoenix, Arizona, with her four-year-old son, Christopher, and
roommate James Styer. On December 2, 1989, Styer left their apartment
with Christopher, ostensibly to take him to the mall to see Santa Claus.
Instead, he picked up his friend Roger Scott. Styer and Scott drove the
little boy deep into the desert where they shot him three times in the back
of the head and left him in a ravine. They reported Christopher missing, but under questioning by the police, Scott confessed and led them to
Christopher's body. The lead detective, Armando Saldate Jr., suspected
that Milke was involved after Scott apparently implicated her in one of
his statements.

Milke was taken to a police station and put in a cell. Saldate entered, placed her under arrest, and proceeded to interrogate her. No one
else was present in the room or observed the interview. Ignoring the
instructions of his supervisor, Saldate did not tape-record it. According
to Saldate, Milke waived her right to remain silent and her right to an attorney before providing a full confession, stating that she masterminded
her son's murder.

Because there was no physical or other evidence linking Milke to the
crime and no independent way to verify Saldate's account, the trial boiled
down to "he said, she said." Saldate testified to Milke's confession, but
neither Styer nor Scott would implicate her. Milke denied any involvement in her son's death, testifying that Saldate had ignored her requests

for a lawyer and fabricated her confession. The state's case was dependent on Saldate's word, so it was crucial to bring out any facts that might show he was an unreliable witness. Milke's trial lawyer subpoenaed Saldate's personnel file, but the trial prosecutor refused to provide it and the trial judge quashed the subpoena. In the end, the jury believed Saldate's account. Milke was convicted of murder, conspiracy to commit murder, child abuse, and kidnapping. In 1990, the judge sentenced her to death.

Years later, after spending thousands of hours searching old court records, Milke's lawyers were able to show that Saldate was a liar and a reprobate long before and well after Milke's trial. In 1973, internal affairs for the Phoenix Police Department had disciplined Saldate after he released a female driver with a possible outstanding warrant in exchange for sexual favors and then lied about it to his superiors. In 1986 and again in 1989, Saldate lied to a grand jury, which forced the judges in both cases to dismiss the indictments.

In 1990—the same year Milke was convicted and sentenced to die—a judge threw out another case after Saldate admitted that he lied under oath and continued to question the defendant after he invoked his right to remain silent. That same year, a different judge threw out a confession that Saldate had obtained through "flagrant misconduct." In 1984 and 1992, Saldate obtained so-called confessions from defendants who were in the hospital, semiconscious and seriously injured. In one case, the defendant did not know his own name, the year, or the name of the president of the United States. In the other case, even Saldate admitted that the suspect was "in pain" and possibly had not responded to the reading of his Miranda rights "because of the medication he was on."

The jury in Milke's case knew nothing about Saldate's lengthy history of doing whatever it took—including perjuring himself—to obtain so-called confessions from the men and women in his custody. In 2013, twenty-three years after Milke was sent to death row, the Ninth Circuit overturned her conviction.[17] Even then, the state vowed to retry her, deterred only when the Arizona Court of Appeals forbade it, calling the case "a severe stain on the Arizona justice system."[18] Saldate, now retired, has never been charged or convicted of any crime. According to Phoenix City records, he was collecting a monthly pension in excess of $4,300 as recently as 2014.

Prosecutorial Misconduct

Prosecutors also commit misconduct. Often, it is the result of overzealousness, inadvertence, or negligence, as win-at-all-costs prosecutors are often rewarded with promotions and many offices lack the resources to properly train them in their constitutional and ethical obligations. But sometimes prosecutorial misconduct is calculated and even malicious. The two most notorious cases in recent memory—and perhaps not coincidentally, among only a handful in which the prosecutor faced consequences—targeted innocent white men.

In 2006, Michael B. Nifong, then the district attorney for Durham, North Carolina, indicted three Duke University lacrosse players for raping an African American stripper who had danced at a team party. When the woman was unable to identify her attackers, Nifong showed her photographs only of lacrosse players, an extremely suggestive practice that violated the guidelines of his own office. The players all had strong alibis, which Nifong discounted. When the DNA evidence did not point to the defendants, Nifong withheld it from them. Even after the woman changed her story, Nifong insisted on going forward with the kidnapping charges.

The case made national headlines from the start because of the salaciousness of the crime and the fact that the defendants were white and largely came from wealthy families. This distinguished them from the vast majority of people accused of serious, life-ending crimes. The money bought them excellent lawyers, who diligently investigated the allegations and were able to disprove them, sparing the men the horror of convictions that could have sent them to prison and labeled them lifelong sex offenders.

The case remained in the spotlight for months, and political pressure on Nifong mounted. Before the defendants could be brought to trial, Nifong was forced to turn the case over to the state attorney general, who concluded that all three lacrosse players were innocent and Nifong was a "rogue prosecutor." After the charges were dropped, the North Carolina state bar brought charges against Nifong and disbarred him. Then Nifong was himself prosecuted for withholding DNA evidence from the defense and lying about it in court. He received a one-day jail sentence.[19]

Most people do not have the resources the Duke lacrosse players had. For Michael Morton of Williamson County, Texas, justice proved elusive for twenty-five years. In 1985, Ken Anderson, then the district attorney and a former Texas Prosecutor of the Year, charged Morton with the murder of his wife, telling the jury that Morton masturbated over her dead body before leaving the house to go to work. Morton was convicted and sentenced to life in prison.

Anderson obtained the conviction by withholding crucial evidence that showed Morton was not the killer. He never told Morton's attorneys that Morton's young son, Eric, told his grandmother that a "monster with a moustache" had killed his mother while his father was not home, or that the victim's mother told police in a recorded phone call that Morton could not have committed the crime after recounting Eric's statement. Other vital leads—the sighting of a stranger and a green van, the use of the victim's credit card in the days after the murder—were never followed up. In 2011, Morton was released after Scheck and Neufeld's Innocence Project demanded the retesting of a bloody bandanna found a hundred yards from the crime scene. The results matched those of the true attacker, Mark Alan Norwood, who had gone on to murder another woman under similar circumstances. For most of his life, including when he killed Morton's wife and at his arrest decades later, he had a droopy horseshoe-shaped moustache.

Meanwhile, Ken Anderson had become a judge. At the insistence of Morton's lawyers, a special court of inquiry was convened to investigate Anderson. At the end of the process, a judge ruled that Anderson had broken state law and committed perjury by lying to the court. After Anderson was convicted and sentenced to serve ten days in jail, his license to practice law was revoked and he resigned from the bench.[20]

While it is true that Nifong and Anderson were disgraced and prevented from practicing law, their respective one- and ten-day jail sentences are paltry in comparison to the massive damage they caused, particularly Anderson. Yet, these are exceptional cases because there was any punishment at all. The majority of prosecutors who commit misconduct are never disciplined, much less disbarred or charged with crimes.[21]

Junk Science

Nearly one quarter of the sixteen hundred exoneration cases involve what we now know to be "junk science"—that is, methods of analyzing physical evidence to implicate a specific person or diagnose a particular type of crime that are deeply flawed and, in some cases, are based on little more than guesswork and conjecture.[22] Junk science—usually physical in nature and often explained by seemingly well-credentialed experts—is a particularly pernicious kind of evidence because it is so persuasive to jurors, who are fed a steady diet of crime-show procedurals that portray these methods as unfailingly accurate and central to catching the bad guy.

Examples of junk science include expert testimony that bite marks on a victim's body were almost certainly made by the defendant's teeth; that a hair found at a crime scene can be examined under a microscope and linked to a particular person; or that fire patterns inside a burned building point to arson rather than an accidental fire. After decades of its use in state and federal courtrooms across the country, much of this "science" has been called into question as error-prone, empirically unverified, and based on false assumptions or outright speculation. Yet junk science has led to convictions that haunt the public as wrongful.

Take Cameron Todd Willingham. So-called arson experts were used to convict Willingham of setting a fire that killed his three small children in Corsicana, Texas, in 1991. Year later, lawyers for Willingham were able to present compelling evidence that these "experts" had no idea what they were talking about. But the state declined to review the case. All of Willingham's appeals were denied, and he was executed on February 17, 2004, at the age of thirty-six. Questions about his case continue to swirl. In August 2009, the *Chicago Tribune* reported: "Over the past five years, the Willingham case has been reviewed by nine of the nation's top fire scientists—first for the *Tribune*, then for the Innocence Project, and now for the [Texas] commission. All concluded that the original investigators relied on outdated theories and folklore to justify the determination of arson."[23] (The state also relied on a jailhouse snitch, who told the jury Willingham confessed. He later recanted.)

The most recent and dramatic unraveling of junk science has been in the area of hair analysis, that is, expert testimony that hair found at the scene of the crime is similar to or indistinguishable from the defendant's hair based on characteristics such as its color, texture, and length. (This is different from DNA evidence retrieved from a hair follicle, which embeds the hair in the skin and can point conclusively at a single perpetrator.) In the 1990s, the United States Department of Justice undertook an investigation into allegations that some of the hair analysis work by an FBI crime lab was error-ridden.

Over the years, the investigation expanded, morphing into an indictment of an entire system of collecting, testing, and relying on so-called hair science evidence. In April 2015, the *Washington Post* published this shocking disclosure by the Justice Department: "Of 28 examiners with the FBI's Laboratory's microscopic hair comparison unit, 26 overstated forensic matches in ways that favored prosecutors in more than 95 percent of the 268 trials reviewed so far."[24] In thirty-two of the cases, the defendants received the death penalty. By the time the news became public, fourteen of them had been executed or died in prison. Experts believe that there are at least twenty-one thousand additional cases—state and federal—that used this discredited science and therefore must be reexamined.[25]

That is what happened with Kirk Odom's case in 2009. A black man, he was convicted in 1981 of raping, robbing, and sodomizing a white woman in Washington, DC, and then sentenced to a minimum of twenty years in prison. Odom, who was raped in prison and contracted HIV, was paroled in March 2003, but forced to register as a sex offender, which placed severe restrictions upon where he could live, work, and travel.[26]

As in Thomas Haynesworth's case, the victim identified Odom, but here the state bolstered the conviction with what appeared to be irrefutable forensic science. An FBI special agent told the jury that a hair found on the victim's nightgown was microscopically indistinguishable from Odom's hair and that he had found such matches only ten times over decades of performing thousands of such tests. Not only was the FBI agent's testimony grossly exaggerated, it was unsupported by his own notes, which identified the nightgown hair only by color, length, and the part of the body it appeared to come from.[27]

Once the federal investigation into the FBI lab became public, Odom's lawyers demanded that the evidence collected at the crime scene, including the offender's semen and the supposedly indistinguishable nightgown hair, undergo rigorous DNA analysis. The retesting resulted in a genetic profile of the rapist that categorically excluded Odom and pointed to another man. A judge exonerated Odom and signed a certification proclaiming his innocence on July 13, 2012. It was Odom's fiftieth birthday. More than thirty years had passed since his conviction, twenty-two of which he spent in prison. Because the statute of limitations had long since run out, the real perpetrator could not be prosecuted.[28]

In the case of Villalobos, Vasquez, and Mora—convicted of starting the Brooklyn opium den fire because of Hannah Quick's perjured testimony—prosecutors also relied heavily on junk science to convince the jury that the fire had been deliberately set. Adele Bernhard, the lawyer who advocated successfully for Villalobos, retained an expert named John Lentini to pore over the old forensic evidence. Lentini explained, "The science of fire dynamics was poorly understood in 1980, and much of what was believed by well-meaning investigators was, unfortunately, false." He concluded, "If today's standards and knowledge of fire dynamics were applied to this investigation, the results would have been significantly different."[29] Bernhard and her co-counsel approached prosecutors at the Brooklyn County district attorney's office. After reexamining the case, they came to the same conclusion: the fire that Quick testified the men had set deliberately was almost certainly an accident. It wasn't a question of having convicted the wrong people, the district attorney explained, but rather convicting them of "a crime, which did not in fact occur."[30]

False Confessions

Thirteen percent of the first sixteen hundred exonerees falsely confessed to crimes they did not commit.[31] Understandably, this statistic is difficult to accept. "Innocent people do not confess," prosecutors often tell juries, an assertion that carries enormous weight because, as a matter of logic and intuition, it makes perfect sense. What sane person would ever admit to committing a heinous crime unless he was guilty? Yet, people do.

There is no single explanation for this phenomenon, but many of the people who give false confessions are vulnerable to police coercion because they are young, unsophisticated, poorly educated, of below-average intelligence, or some combination of the four. The law allows police to lie to suspects, and many suspects admit to wrongdoing after being told they will be allowed to go home, avoid charges, or plead to a minor offense.

A recent example involves the notorious Central Park jogger case. In 1989, five young black and Latino teenagers, ranging from fourteen to sixteen years old, confessed to raping a young white woman out for a nighttime run in New York's Central Park, then beating her and leaving her for dead. At trial, the defendants insisted that they were innocent. Their lawyers argued that the boys' admissions were the result of hardball tactics by detectives desperate to make an arrest in a city convulsed with fear over images of marauding groups of black and brown youths out to wreak havoc and assault innocent civilians.

All five teenagers were convicted and sentenced to lengthy prison terms. In 2002, DNA retested from the jogger's rape kit identified a single unrelated suspect who then confessed, stating that he acted alone. The defendants, now adult men known as "the Central Park Five," were exonerated. They sued the city of New York and, in 2014, received a global $40 million settlement.[32]

Police coercion usually involves psychological tactics that prey on a vulnerable suspect, but it can also be physical. Severe beatings that detectives in the Chicago Police Department administered to black suspects throughout the 1980s and 1990s under the direction of Lieutenant Jon Burge were so common that the state of Illinois set up the Torture Inquiry and Relief Commission to investigate them. One victim was Shawn Whirl, who, in 1990, was arrested and charged with the murder of a cab driver on Chicago's South Side. Whirl explained that he had jumped into the victim's cab after being chased by gang members after falling and scraping his leg; the cabbie, he said, dropped him off at his girlfriend's house. The torture commission found that a detective working under Burge's direction handcuffed Whirl to the wall, gouged at the open wound on his leg with a car key, hit him repeatedly, used racial epithets, and put a bag over his head to drown out the sound of his screams.

But the torture commission did not issue its finding until 2012. In the interim, Whirl, charged with first-degree murder and facing the death penalty, had pleaded guilty and received a sentence of sixty years. His first three petitions to overturn his conviction were denied for lack of evidence. In 2015, the Illinois appellate court granted Whirl relief. At that point, Burge had been convicted of lying under oath about denying the existence of his torture regime and was serving his own prison term. The detective who had interrogated Whirl, meanwhile, invoked his privilege against self-incrimination when asked about the tactics he had used to secure the confession. Whirl, who had no criminal record before his arrest, was released after serving twenty years in prison.[33]

No Defense

In 2012, the National Registry of Exonerations found that 17 percent of non-DNA exonerations involved poor defense lawyering. According to Samuel Gross, the cofounder of the registry, the actual percentage is likely much higher: "[W]e believe that many of the exonerated defendants—perhaps a clear majority—would not have been convicted in the first instance if their lawyers had done good work."[34]

Most exonerees were represented by public defenders or other court-appointed lawyers. It is no secret that indigent criminal defense in this country is in crisis and has been for decades. In December 2004, the American Bar Association published a groundbreaking, comprehensive study entitled *Gideon's Broken Promise: America's Continuing Quest for Equal Justice*. The report, which was written to coincide with the fortieth anniversary of the Supreme Court's landmark decision establishing the right to counsel in *Gideon v. Wainwright*, is a stunning indictment: "[G]laring deficiencies in indigent defense services result in a fundamentally unfair criminal justice system that constantly risks convicting persons who are actually innocent of the charges lodged against them."[35]

As the fifty-fifth anniversary of the *Gideon* decision approaches, little has changed. Indeed, it is arguable that the problems afflicting the delivery of indigent defense services are even more dire. Derwyn Bunton, the chief district defender for Orleans Parish in New Orleans, instructed his deputies to stop taking serious felony cases in January 2016. By requiring Bunton's staff of fifty to handle twenty-two thousand filings a year, the state had made it impossible to investigate any of the cases, much less mount a defense. Instead, the public defenders at Orleans Parish resembled workers on an assembly line that swiftly delivered poor people— mostly African Americans—to prison regardless of guilt or innocence.[36]

In an opinion editorial for the *New York Times*, Bunton said that his decision came after a troubling development in a particular high-profile case. Following a mass shooting in Bunny Friend Park on November 22, 2015, that left seventeen people injured, police arrested thirty-two-year-old Joseph "Moe" Allen, based on eyewitness identification. Allen was jailed, and bail was set at $7 million. His family was able to hire a lawyer and investigator who retrieved a video from a Walmart in Houston, Texas, which showed Allen and his pregnant wife shopping for baby clothes when the crime occurred. The prosecution dismissed the charges, and Allen was released after spending twelve days in jail.

Reading about the case, Bunton realized Allen would have faced far greater jeopardy had he been assigned one of his public defenders, who lacked the time and funds to obtain the video footage before Walmart would have erased it in the regular course of business. Bunton wrote, "That would have left an innocent man to face trial for his life for what was labeled an act of 'domestic terrorism' by the mayor of New Orleans."[37]

Allen was lucky, considering the circumstances. Having an alibi and the means to corroborate it meant he was not convicted. Unfortunately, for defendants who lack access to paid attorneys, the price of freedom is set too high. In April 2017, with Bunton's prohibition still in place, nine of the Orleans Parish public defenders were interviewed by Anderson Cooper on *60 Minutes*. When Cooper asked, "How many of you believe that an innocent client went to jail because you didn't have enough time to spend on their case?" every single hand went up.

Consider Alabama, which has no statewide public defender system and largely leaves the representation of the poor to the discretion of individual judges, who decide whom to appoint and what to pay.[38] The results can be catastrophic. Anthony Ray Hinton was charged in 1985 with robbing and killing two convenience store clerks in Birmingham, Alabama. A third clerk, who was shot and survived, identified Hinton in a lineup. Police detectives collected two bullets from each crime scene. A search of the home Hinton shared with his mother turned up an ancient .38 caliber gun she stored under her mattress. Forensic experts from the Alabama Department of Forensic Sciences concluded that all six bullets from the three crimes were fired from Mrs. Hinton's revolver.

The linchpin of the state's case was the forensic evidence. Seeking to counter the prosecution's experts, Hinton's court-appointed attorney asked for money from the court to hire his own expert. The trial judge gave him a thousand dollars, stating that "if it's necessary we can go beyond that." But Hinton's attorney made no additional motions. Instead, he used the thousand dollars at his disposal to hire the only expert who would testify at that price. The cross-examination was withering. The witness had little expertise in bullet comparisons. Because he had only one eye, he had to get help from the prosecution experts when operating the microscope to perform the necessary tests.

On September 17, 1986, Hinton was convicted of both murders. In December 1986, he was sentenced to death. Decades later, Hinton's post-conviction lawyers retained three renowned firearms experts to review the evidence against Hinton. All three found that there was insufficient evidence to conclude that any of the six bullets had been fired from Mrs. Hinton's revolver. In 2014, the US Supreme Court reversed Hinton's conviction and death sentence due to the poor performance of his trial attorney.[39] In preparing for the retrial, experts retained by the prosecution came to the same conclusion as Hinton's postconviction experts: there was no match. On April 2, 2015, almost thirty years after he had been convicted and sentenced to die, the state of Alabama dismissed all of the charges against Anthony Ray Hinton and he was freed.

Too Late

Then there are exonerees who died before their names could be cleared. In addition to Raymond Mora—one of the men exonerated in the opium den fire case—there are at least thirteen people on record who have been exonerated posthumously. One of them was Timothy Cole, an African American army veteran who was a student at Texas Tech University in Lubbock, Texas. A white rape victim named Michelle Mallin picked his photograph out of an array that was highly suggestive. Cole's photograph was the only Polaroid picture; the others were mug shots. Cole was the only suspect facing the camera; the others were in profile. In 1986, Cole was tried and convicted based on evidence remarkably similar to that used to convict Thomas Haynesworth: the victim's positive in-court identification and an expert's testimony that his blood type, A, matched the blood type of the rapist. Cole was convicted and sentenced to serve twenty-five years in prison.

Nine years later, Jerry Wayne Johnson, a prisoner who was serving ninety-nine years for two rapes, wrote letters to the police and prosecutors in Lubbock County in which he admitted to raping Mallin. Johnson's confession was corroborated by the striking similarity between his rape convictions and what had happened to Mallin. His letters were ignored.

In 1999, Timothy Cole died in prison due to complications from asthma. Johnson then wrote to a judge, making the same confession. The judge also ignored the letter, but it eventually made its way to the Innocence Project, which successfully sought DNA testing on the Mallin rape kit. The DNA was a match to Johnson. Mallin, shattered by the news, worked with Cole's attorneys to ensure that his name was cleared. Cole was posthumously exonerated in 2009 and officially pardoned by Texas governor Rick Perry in 2010.[40]

Group Exonerations and the Role of Race

The registry keeps a second, parallel list of "group exonerations," which occur when a single corrupt police officer or a gang of officers systemically plant evidence, perjure themselves, and commit other crimes to frame innocent people.

In 2017, the registry released a report, *Race and Wrongful Convictions in the United States*, which found 15 group exonerations totaling more than 1,840 people in 13 cities and counties in the United States.[41] The best-known group exoneration is the Rampart scandal. From 1990 to 2000, a gang of Los Angeles police officers in the Rampart division routinely framed innocent people and then lied in court to convict them. In some instances, this occurred after the defendant had been shot and wounded by an officer; the evidence was then planted at the crime scene to suggest that the suspect had been the aggressor. When the officers' crimes were brought to light, 156 convictions were thrown out and the Los Angeles Police Department was placed under a federal consent decree.

The most egregious group exonerations, however, are also among the most obscure. These include two separate group exonerations in Philadelphia—one in 1995–1998 and another in 2013–2016—in which corrupt police officers targeted a total of 1,042 innocent people.

Group exonerations are alarming for three reasons. First, they are underreported; according to the National Registry of Exonerations, "[T]here are clearly many more false convictions of drug defendants who were framed by police than we have identified in these 15 groups."[42] Second, it is profoundly disturbing to realize that individual or small-group misconduct can have such exponential impact. It is difficult enough to comprehend a single case of wrongful conviction involving a corrupt police officer. It is quite another to be told that some police officers are serial predators, returning over and over again to the communities they were charged with protecting to extract new victims.

Third, the group exoneration population is overwhelmingly black and Latino, leading to the inescapable conclusion that the targeting is racially motivated. Corrupt police officers train their sights on people of color for a number of reasons, including that they are more likely to be poor and disbelieved. But the main reason, according to the registry, is that law enforcement efforts concentrate disproportionately on minority populations. African Americans, who constitute only 13 percent of the US population, make up the majority of group exonerees and nearly 50 percent of exonerated individuals. "Race is central to every aspect of criminal justice in the United States," the registry reports. "The conviction of innocent defendants is no exception."[43]

Big Picture

In the vast majority of cases, the criminal justice system gets it right. The witnesses who lie or make mistakes, the police and prosecutors who commit misconduct, the defense lawyers who fall down on the job, the experts who testify using junk science are a small percentage of the men and women in these professions who ably perform their jobs.

Yet, the number of exonerations, the reasons why they happen, and the people to whom they happen reveal grotesque and shameful problems with the way that we administer justice in the United States. The average time spent by an innocent person behind bars is nine years and three months; a significant number of exonerees have spent decades in prison. Wrongful convictions are not isolated instances. They happen in every state; they happen multiple times a week. In 2015, the National Registry of Exonerations' report *The First 1,600 Exonerations* delved into the data it had collected on more than a thousand exonerations.[44] As a group, the exonerees in the report were imprisoned for more than 14,750 years. According to report author Samuel Gross, since the year the report was published, more than four hundred men and women have joined the list.

We say we have the best criminal justice system in the world. But like any system, it fails, and when it does, the failures are spectacular. The work of the innocence movement has exposed many of these failures and provided the narratives and propulsive energy behind many important reforms. But there is more work to be done, and not by the lawyers. Too often, the voices of the harmed go unheard, and they speak a brutal truth that should not be ignored, both as a matter of justice and public policy.

CHAPTER THREE

A Broken System

THE INNOCENCE MOVEMENT has been tremendously successful in free-ing the innocent and alerting the public to the alarming frequency of the problem. Twenty-five years ago, the very notion that an innocent person could spend years in prison was unthinkable. In 1993, the late Supreme Court justice Antonin Scalia rejected the idea that a prisoner could bring a constitutional claim based on factual innocence with these words: "With any luck, we shall avoid ever having to face this embarrass-ing question again."[1]

Now the conviction of the innocent is an established fact. Yet many states, including those considered solidly blue and purple on the electoral map, have been slow to adopt much-needed reforms designed to prevent wrongful convictions in the first place and make them easier to undo on the back end. Only a small minority of states have adopted methods de-signed to ensure that suggestiveness and bias do not infect eyewitness identifications. The majority of police departments do not record the in-terrogations of suspects and witnesses to capture exactly what was said and done by everyone in the room, a procedure designed to reduce the number of false confessions and damning statements made as the result of threats or undue coercion. Many states routinely destroy biological and physical evidence after a conviction, which makes future testing impossi-ble if that conviction is called into question years later.

More than 225 innocent people have been released through the co-operative efforts of prosecutors assigned to conviction integrity units or conviction review units, known as CIUs or CRUs. These integrity units, set up at the discretion of the county's chief prosecutor, are supposed to take an objective look at old cases where there is evidence suggesting that a terrible injustice occurred. But they exist in only twenty-nine counties, encompassing a mere 17 percent of the population, and many, if not most, exist in name only: understaffed, under-resourced, without publicly available contact information or a single exoneration to their name. Eighty-five percent of conviction integrity unit exonerations were the result of work done by just four offices.[2]

Eighteen states have no law that provides exonerees with money or services, leaving them on their own to find work and a place to live, and to cope with severe physical and mental health problems, many the direct result of the years spent in prison. An exoneration is often compared to a rebirth, but for many, the metaphor applies only in the most raw and literal sense: naked and defenseless, exonerees are made to confront a world they do not recognize.

While thirty-two states, the District of Columbia, and the federal government have passed laws that provide some form of compensation for the wrongfully convicted, those laws vary greatly when it comes to how much money they award and what evidence exonerees must provide to qualify for it. Some statutes are relatively generous, providing high five-figure amounts for every year of imprisonment, as well as access to education, counseling, and health services; other states cap the total amount as low as $20,000, regardless of the length of the sentence.[3]

Some state compensation laws come with an asterisk, barring awards to those who pleaded guilty or confessed—even to avoid capital punishment or because their age or mental disability made them vulnerable to police lies, threats, or trickery. Louisiana, like several other states, denies compensation to anyone found to have "contributed" in some way to his or her own conviction. A judge made that finding in Glenn Ford's case, despite the public plea of Marty Stroud, the prosecutor who confessed in writing and on national television to his own responsibility for what had happened.[4] Ford, a terminally ill man who spent three decades in a small, dark cage on death row, died a pauper, forced to spend the remaining year of his life, postexoneration, relying on charitable donations.

There is extreme variation in how states address issues surrounding wrongful convictions. As a result, whether prisoners seeking to prove their innocence have a legal means to do so, whether they will receive compensation if they succeed, and whether they can have some assurance that reforms will be put in place to prevent their tragedy from visiting itself upon others depends largely on geography. The contrast between the rights and remedies available in Texas and Pennsylvania attests to this disquieting reality.

Texas

Ironically, it is blood-red Texas, which proudly touts its ability to execute the greatest number of criminal defendants at the fastest clip, which leads the way in wrongful conviction reform. Conservative Republicans, who have occupied the governor's mansion and dominated the state legislature for decades, have enacted an impressive list of laws designed to address breakdowns in the criminal justice system and make amends for those that occurred within its jurisdiction.

Texas has the most generous wrongful compensation statute of any state, awarding $80,000 for each year of imprisonment, an annuity, and an additional $25,000 for every year spent on parole or on a sex offender registry. The state pays for 120 hours of job training or education at a state-run school and enables exonerees to sign up for health insurance on its public employee health plan. Texas also has a law that requires eyewitness identification procedures to conform to best practices, and the state's chief law enforcement body, the Texas Law Enforcement Management Institute, has a model policy that many police departments use.

In 2016, the Texas Forensic Science Commission recommended that the state ban the use of bite-mark expert testimony because it was junk science and unreliable. The recommendation, and a second recommendation urging prosecutors to reopen old bite-mark cases, came after a six-month investigation, which included a study showing that most board-certified dentists could not even agree that a particular injury *was* a bite mark, much less inflicted by a particular person's teeth.[5]

These reforms are fueled in part by the sheer number of innocent people that the Texas criminal justice system has failed catastrophically—the number of exonerees in Texas exceeds three hundred and continues to rise.[6] But that is not the whole story. The wrongfully convicted are a small, marginalized group without a powerful constituency in a state with a population of close to twenty-seven million. The wherewithal to enact these reforms in Texas shows that not all conservative lawmakers can be conveniently pigeonholed as knee-jerk, pro-prosecution advocates.

A sizable number of Republicans classified as "far right" on issues like gun control, climate change, and abortion also hold a fiercely pro-liberty stance and a deep-seated suspicion about the competence of oversized, publicly funded bureaucracies. If there is good reason to doubt the government's ability to regulate firearms, health care, and the environment, why not apply the same skepticism to the government's ability to justly enforce the laws, particularly if there is stark evidence that fundamental miscarriages of justice can and do occur?

Texas is also a role model when it comes to conviction integrity units. The first one, established by former Dallas district attorney Craig Watkins in 2006, has had a hand in more than three dozen exonerations. In 2015, the Texas CIU in Harris County—which encompasses Houston and its environs—made headlines when its lead prosecutor, Inger Chandler, uncovered scores of old cases in which defendants had pleaded guilty to crimes that did not occur. In each case, the county had obtained a narcotics conviction based on field tests performed by police officers, a method so unreliable as to "routinely misidentify everything from Jolly Ranchers to chalk to motor oil as illegal drugs," according to the National Registry of Exonerations' report.[7] When results from the crime laboratory—which trickled in long after the cases had concluded—proved the items seized from these defendants were innocuous, Chandler and her successor took the legal steps necessary to undo the convictions. At last count, there were more than 125, and the number is expected to rise.[8]

One of the more alarming aspects of the Harris County cases is how common they may be. In many state courtrooms across the United States, particularly in large cities, what passes for justice is churned out on an assembly line. As the breakdown in the public defender system in New Orleans so powerfully demonstrates, some innocent defendants plead guilty to serious felonies. Represented by overworked and underpaid attorneys, they face a terrible choice: endure months in custody and the risk of trial and years in prison if convicted, or get out immediately by admitting to something they did not do. Given that more than 90 percent of all criminal cases result in guilty pleas, and that most defendants lack the time, resources, or money to challenge the state's evidence, it is hard to believe Harris County is an outlier.[9] More likely, the difference lies in the diligence and dedication of one CIU unit in righting the wrongs after the fact.

Pennsylvania

Pennsylvania ranks eighth in the nation when it comes to the total number of wrongful convictions per state, according to statistics compiled by the National Registry of Exonerations in 2016.[10] But although Pennsylvania is widely considered to be far more politically progressive than Texas, voting twice for Barack Obama and electing Democratic governor Tom Wolf in 2014, it lags far behind when it comes to enacting wrongful conviction reforms and, perhaps more distressingly, to recognizing the need for those reforms in the first place.

No Defense

One major cause of wrongful convictions is bad lawyering, which is much more likely to happen when defense attorneys are overwhelmed and ill compensated. You get what you pay for, and Pennsylvania pays nothing at all—standing alone among the fifty states in its steadfast refusal to allocate money for indigent criminal defense. Instead, each individual county designs and pays for a system to provide legal representation to the poor. Not surprisingly, the performance is uneven: Philadelphia's public defender office, set up as a nonprofit, is known for its well-trained and diligent attorneys. But in other parts of the state, there is no public defender at all. Instead, judges appoint lawyers on an ad hoc basis, at an hourly compensation that is shockingly low.

The woeful underfunding of lawyers who represent the poor and criminally accused extends to cases in which Pennsylvania's district attorneys seek the death penalty. According to Marc Bookman, who directs the Philadelphia-based Atlantic Center for Capital Representation, many of these court-appointed lawyers are poorly trained and completely unprepared to litigate a case of that magnitude. Unless a defendant is acquitted, every death penalty case is actually two separate trials: one to determine guilt and the other to determine punishment. This second trial, known as the penalty phase, is often far more extensive. It is necessary to undertake an investigation to uncover mitigating evidence—for example, a defendant's history of severe mental illness, developmental disabilities, physical or sexual victimization in childhood, in short, any fact that will convince the jury to spare his life. The top defender offices in the country, well funded and staffed by highly experienced attorneys, routinely spend months, if not years, preparing for a penalty phase trial.

More than 250 death penalty verdicts have been thrown out over the years in Pennsylvania, the majority because of atrociously poor representation by defense counsel. It is, Bookman said, "a bigger reversal rate than any state in the country." In 2011, Bookman filed a petition for a writ of mandamus—an extraordinary remedy for cases of "immediate public importance"—in the Pennsylvania Supreme Court.[11] He sought to have the compensation rates for court-appointed lawyers in Philadelphia County capital cases declared unconstitutional. (Bookman targeted solo practitioners, not the Philadelphia public defender, which began accepting capital cases in 1993 and has never had a client sentenced to death.)

Capped at $2,000 to investigate and prepare the case pretrial, and at $400 per day to try the case, the rates were the lowest in the nation by several standards of deviation. "Of course, some jurisdiction has to be last," Bookman wrote, "but Philadelphia County is not even close," lagging well behind far poorer states like Mississippi and Arkansas.[12] Bookman's legal theory was novel but grounded in common sense: no competent lawyer would take a death penalty case for so little money.

Mid-litigation, Philadelphia County raised the cap for pretrial preparation in capital cases to $10,000, which, according to Bookman, was still "absurdly low" given the amount of work involved and the hourly rates provided in other states. There is widespread agreement on this front. The trial court judge assigned to review Bookman's lawsuit and issue a report recommended an hourly rate of $90.

Bookman pressed on with his lawsuit. In 2014, he lost, in a 4–3 ruling by the Pennsylvania Supreme Court. The majority dismissed the case without explanation. One of the dissenting judges lamented his colleagues' refusal to "address a systemic challenge amidst much evidence that Pennsylvania's capital punishment regime is in disrepair." He characterized the county's recent adjustments to its fee structure as "modest," adding, "Petitioners reasonably question the adequacy of such changes."[13]

Powerful statistics suggest that the past and current fee schedules in Philadelphia County, which indicts most of the capital cases in the state, continue to dissuade all but the worst defense lawyers from taking capital cases. A local Philadelphia paper, the *Reading Eagle*, examined 312 capital cases in Pennsylvania dating back to 1980, most of them prosecuted in Philadelphia. The results, published in 2015, concluded that almost one in five of the defendants were "appointed attorneys with drug and alcohol addictions, who suffered from depression, have had a history of mishandling clients' cases or were convicted felons." The fact that these attorneys had faced professional discipline—often multiple times—did nothing to stop judges from appointing them. Over 80 percent of the defendants they represented were either African American or Latino.[14]

Six men sent to death row in Pennsylvania are now free after their convictions were overturned.[15] The list includes William Nieves, who was given the death penalty following his 1995 conviction for shooting a drug dealer three times in the back. Nieves paid his court-appointed attorney, Thomas Ciccione, a total of $2,500 to defend him in the guilt and penalty phase trials, approximately what Ciccione would have earned had he been appointed by the state.

The central evidence against Nieves consisted of the eyewitness identification of a jailhouse snitch and a prostitute with five outstanding warrants. At the scene, the prostitute told police that the shooter was a short, slim, black male. Nieves, a Latino, was six feet tall and stocky. At trial, Ciccione, a divorce lawyer who had never tried a capital case, did not impeach her with these statements. Nieves was determined to take the stand and proclaim his innocence. Ciccione advised against it, telling Nieves that his prior drug and firearms convictions would be used against him. As it turned out, the law precluded the state from introducing them. Ciccione called no witnesses, even though there were two people who would have corroborated the description of the shooter as a short, slim, black male. On July 26, 1995, Nieves was sentenced to death.[16]

Desperate to free her son from death row, Nieves's mother approached Jack McMahon, a former prosecutor turned Philadelphia defense lawyer.[17] McMahon, a bald man with a thick white moustache and black-framed glasses, knew his way around a courtroom: from 1978 to 1992, he had been an assistant district attorney, mainly trying homicide cases. And a hard charging one. The *New York Times* reported that, in 1986, McMahon made a training tape advising new prosecutors not to select black people from disadvantaged neighborhoods to serve on juries because "they are less likely to convict."[18] (The tape surfaced in 1997, when McMahon ran for district attorney against the incumbent, Lynne Abraham. He lost.)

McMahon said that he left the Philadelphia district attorney's office in 1992 because he "fell into this psychological position of everything on the other side of the table is evil and everything on my side of the table is good. I lived and breathed it 24/7. What passes for success is winning. I moved up rapidly within the trial division because I was winning. I got into major crimes, into homicides, because I won. The guys who didn't win, they didn't go to homicide. The theoretical premium is justice but the real premium is winning and at times, winning at all costs so justice gets lost at times."

As an attorney in private practice, McMahon turned his zeal toward criminal defense. When he met Mrs. Nieves in the summer of 1995, he was well known, with a formidable track record. Though Mrs. Nieves had very little money, McMahon felt sorry for her and unsettled by the case, so he slashed his rates, preparing and arguing the appeal for $10,000. On February 17, 2000, the Pennsylvania Supreme Court reversed the conviction based on Ciccione's deficient performance and granted Nieves a retrial.[19] At that point, Mrs. Nieves was out of money, but McMahon was so convinced of his client's innocence that his attitude was, "I would have paid *them* $10,000 if I had to. I said, 'Let's win this thing, let's get him home.'"

At the retrial, McMahon impeached the prostitute with her inconsistent statements and called the two other witnesses who had seen a completely different person commit the crime. Ironically, McMahon never called Nieves to the stand; there was no need to, he said, because the prosecution's case had been so thoroughly "obliterated" already. The jury acquitted him on October 20, 2000; after spending six years on death row, Nieves was set free.

But while he was in prison, Nieves was diagnosed with hepatitis C, which, according to McMahon, the prison failed to treat properly. A few years later, McMahon got an alarming call from Nieves's mother. He drove to her modest row house in North Philadelphia to find Nieves bedridden and skeletal, his skin a sickening yellowish green. Nieves told his lawyer, "I just wanted to see your face one more time." Telling the story, McMahon's voice caught. "And I said, 'of course you did, a good-looking guy like me.'" The two men talked for several hours about Nieves's activism against the death penalty, which had taken him as far as Ireland while he was still healthy enough to travel. "He was a gentleman," McMahon said, "and I enjoyed his company." But it was more than that. "When you pull someone out of the grave and out into the world there is a connection there that will never go away." McMahon was both sad and angry at what happened to Nieves, who died on October 8, 2005, several weeks before the fifth anniversary of his release.[20] "There is no question in my mind that if he had gotten treatment, he damn sure would have lived a lot longer."

Pennsylvania has seen more than sixty-five people released from prison due to wrongful convictions since the National Registry of Exonerations began keeping track, using records dating back to 1989.[21] But Pennsylvania has no statute that provides these men and women with any kind of compensation, monetary or otherwise. When Nieves died, he was living with his mother, wholly dependent on her. Asked if his client ever received an apology from the Philadelphia district attorney's office for the years he spent on death row, McMahon gave a short, bitter laugh. "For what? They still think he's guilty."

When it comes to implementing best practices in police procedures designed to guard against convicting innocent people, Pennsylvania also lags far behind other states. It has no law requiring that the police record interviews with suspects to rule out the possibility of a coerced or false confession. Nor does Pennsylvania have a law setting guidelines for police to follow when conducting eyewitness identifications. Until 2014, defense attorneys in Pennsylvania were barred from introducing expert testimony to explain to jurors the reasons to doubt the reliability of eyewitness identifications, reasons that are counterintuitive and contrary to public perception. Now such testimony is permissible, but only in cases that hinge on identification testimony and only at the discretion of the trial judge.[22]

Turning a Blind Eye

In Pennsylvania, which has a population of nearly thirteen million people, there is only one prosecutor's office with a unit designated to investigate and remedy wrongful conviction cases. It opened to much fanfare in 2014 by Philadelphia district attorney R. Seth Williams, who declared, "This is the right thing to do."[23]

But Williams dedicated only one lawyer to what he called the conviction review unit or CRU: Mark Gilson, a longtime homicide prosecutor. Gilson had other responsibilities, including trying complex high-profile cases. Two and a half years later, in November 2016, the *Philadelphia Inquirer* ran an exposé called "Justice on Hold," which described the CRU as having a "perfect record." It had exonerated no one. It was not for lack of meritorious cases, advocates said. Gilson, the CRU—and Williams's office more generally—appeared to have little appetite for second-guessing old convictions, no matter how compelling the new evidence.[24]

In the late summer of 2016, Anthony Wright's case emerged as the symbol of the intransigence and apparent irrationality of Philadelphia prosecutors when it came to claims of innocence. Wright had been convicted in 1993 for the rape and first-degree murder of an elderly African American woman named Louise Talley, based in large part on a confession written out by police. Wright said he signed it only after the interrogating officers threatened to "poke his eye out" and "skull fuck" him. He was twenty years old, alone and terrified. "I was in there crying," he said. "I wanted my mother. I had no idea what these people would do to me." Wright, who was given a sentence of life without parole, never saw his mother again outside of a jail cell. In 1998, she died at the age of forty-four. The cause, Wright said, was "complications from diabetes and a broken heart. My mother cried for me every day until the day she died."

In 2005, Wright caught the attention of New York–based Innocence Project lawyers Nina Morrison and Peter Neufeld. Along with local pro bono counsel Sam Silver and Rebecca Lacher, they succeeded in getting DNA testing in 2013, over the steadfast opposition of the Philadelphia district attorney's office.

The tests showed the rapist's sperm matched deceased crack addict Ronnie Byrd, who was known to hang around the victim's block. Clothes that police claimed they found after searching Wright's house, and which they testified he wore to kill the victim, came back without any trace of Wright's DNA. Not only that, but the clothes were not his size, and DNA found in the elbows and knees, as well as the victim's blood, suggested that they were the victim's clothes and that the police had planted them. Witnesses who testified against Wright came forward to say that they had been threatened with prison themselves or promised leniency in their own cases.

In 2014, the Philadelphia district attorney's office conceded that the DNA evidence entitled Wright to a new trial. But rather than admit the obvious—that Wright was innocent—prosecutors revoked Wright's bail and retried him in 2016, this time under a different theory of the crime. In 1993, relying on Wright's recanted confession, they argued he had acted alone. Twenty-five years later, prosecutors told the jury that Wright and Byrd—who have no known connection to one another—committed the rape, robbery, burglary, and murder together. Under the state's new theory, Wright murdered the victim and Byrd raped her, anally and vaginally, after she was dead.[25]

Wright, who spoke to the jurors afterward—they came back to the courthouse the next day to meet him in person, embracing him and posing for pictures—said it took five minutes to reach a verdict: not guilty on all counts. They had not wanted to go back to the deliberation room at all, agreeing only after being told that sandwiches had been preordered for lunch and not to waste the food. On August 23, 2016, after spending two additional years in jail following the disclosure of the DNA test results, Anthony Wright was finally free.

The forewoman, Grace Greco, told the media at a packed press conference, "I'm angry that this case was ever retried, but thrilled that we were able to release Tony from this nightmare of twenty-five years."[26] The Innocence Project's Neufeld called the prosecutors' actions "unconscionable and unacceptable." The district attorney's office doubled down, insisting in a publicly issued statement that Wright was guilty and that "the verdict only shows that the jury did not find that his guilt was proven beyond a reasonable doubt."[27]

Corruption

But to find a wrongful conviction case that most powerfully symbolizes the profound and lasting damage caused by the failure to provide justice, correct errors, punish blatant corruption, and remedy harm, it is necessary to look to Fayette County, a rural community at the opposite end of the state. David Munchinski's tortured path through Pennsylvania's legal system has spanned thirty years and multiple trips to state and federal courts.[28]

The saga began in the early morning hours on December 2, 1977, with the discovery of two dead bodies in Bear Rocks, a rural, sparsely populated area in western Pennsylvania. Two white men, James Alford and Raymond Gierke, had been shot multiple times, and the forensic evidence strongly suggested that they had been raped. In 1979, a convicted thief and con artist named Richard Bowen reached out to the authorities from his prison cell, claiming that a man named Leon Scaglione confessed that he was the killer. Three years and a dizzying number of stories later, Bowen added a second perpetrator: Munchinski, a twenty-five-year-old local drug dealer known for his flame-red hair and fiery temper. Bowen said he drove Scaglione and Munchinski to the crime scene and witnessed a drug-related robbery and double-rape that ended in the victims' violent execution.

Bowen supplied the only evidence placing Munchinski at the crime scene, and it was his narrative alone that the state relied upon in telling the jury about the horrors that happened there. Yet, Bowen had a history of lying and cheating, and there was no reason to believe he was telling the truth now. To the contrary, his numerous statements contained gaping discrepancies, internal inconsistencies, and obvious lies—for example, Bowen claimed that he drove the defendants in Scaglione's green Ford Torino, a car that Scaglione did not buy until six months after the crimes had occurred.

Fayette County's top prosecutor, Gerald Solomon, assigned his assistant Ralph Warman to take the case to trial, and in 1986, Munchinski was convicted of two counts of the first-degree murders of Alford and Gierke and sentenced to two consecutive terms of life in prison. But in 1991, the case began to unravel: Bowen had reached out to the FBI and recanted his trial testimony, later stating under oath that the police told him if he did not implicate Munchinski, they would blame the crimes on him. According to Bowen, Solomon told him to go ahead and lie, explaining, "We have to put somebody there to say they seen them."

Based on these new allegations, Munchinski was granted a hearing, but after the prosecutors threatened to charge Bowen with perjury, he recanted his recantation on the witness stand. Warman, now the head district attorney for Fayette County, and Solomon, now a Fayette County judge, stoutly denied Bowen's allegations. But what they did admit to was nearly as bizarre: excising an entire paragraph of an early statement Bowen made to police and pasting the remaining paragraphs together to conceal the tampering. Still, the judge ruled against Munchinski, concluding that he had not provided enough evidence to warrant a new trial.

Munchinski fought on, convinced that Solomon and Warman had not turned over all of the records in his case. The practice in Fayette County was to send a complete copy of every police file to the Pennsylvania State Police Repository in Harrisburg, the state's capital. Munchinski and his daughter, Raina, prevailed upon his court-appointed lawyer, R. Damian Schorr, to serve a subpoena on the repository, not only for Munchinski's file, but for Bowen's.

Schorr finally served the subpoena in 2001, and four case files were delivered: three for Bowen, and one for Munchinski. The contents were jaw-dropping: a dozen pieces of exculpatory evidence that Warman, Solomon, and Kopa had squirreled away. Included in the long list: a statement from Bowen's girlfriend placing Bowen in Oklahoma on the night he claimed to have witnessed the murders, written promises by the prosecution to give Bowen money and a break for his own criminal acts in exchange for this testimony, and an addendum to the autopsy with test results that excluded Munchinski as the source of blood in Alford's rectum, the victim Bowen said Munchinski had raped.

But Schorr's representation came to an end without the opportunity to use the new information. Munchinksi's family reached out to numerous lawyers to take the case pro bono, and finally one of them agreed. Noah Geary was not yet thirty and only four years out of law school, running a small practice with his father in Washington County, which neighbors Fayette. Geary knew he might pay a price. Solomon and Warman were now both judges in Fayette, powerful men who were well known and respected in the legal community. But the sheer injustice filled him with outrage. "They committed crimes," he said. "Four different times they went to court over a span of twenty years and lied to convict an innocent man. That's as evil as it gets."

And taking on the power structure appealed to the iconoclast in Geary.[29] He remembers thinking, "Wow, who in their legal career gets to put sitting judges on the witness stand and work them over. I thought that would be just so fun." Geary ultimately did get Solomon and Warman on the witness stand, after yet another judge determined that Munchinski was entitled to a new hearing.

At the conclusion of the hearing, the judge ruled for Munchinski, labeling Solomon's and Warman's behavior as "anathema to our most basic vision of the role of the Commonwealth in the criminal process."[30] But Munchinski's victory proved short-lived. In 2005, a Pennsylvania appellate court reversed the decision, and the state's highest court issued a one-sentence opinion, upholding that opinion.

Out of options in state court, Geary turned to a federal trial judge in a last-ditch effort to get his client out of prison. Geary was sure he was right on the law: in 1963, the Supreme Court ruled in *Brady v. Maryland* that the prosecution must turn over any evidence that tends to show either that a criminal defendant did not commit the crime or that the witnesses against him were lying. If the state failed to do so, and the suppressed evidence was "material"—important—to either guilt or punishment, the defendant's conviction had to be overturned. It was hard to imagine evidence more material than the pile of documents Solomon and Warman had held back.

Geary's problem was a stringent federal statute making it nearly impossible for a federal judge to hear Munchinski's legal claims at all. The odds of winning were long, and at times, Geary said, he would ask himself, "What the hell am I doing?" Not surprisingly, there had been significant blowback in the local community. Geary could not point to a particular case in which one of Solomon's or Warman's judicial colleagues had been unfair to one of his other clients, but the reception in Fayette County's courtrooms was inevitably chilly. The lawyers were less subtle; some even crossed the street to avoid speaking to him.

And dealing with Munchinski himself was not easy. "The most proactive client in the history of the American legal system," according to Geary, Munchinski regularly wrote him three letters a day. Munchinski was brilliant, Geary said, "pretty much as good as a lawyer. He's on the money 85 percent of the time." But he could also be mercurial and obnoxious, criticizing Geary with "volcanic intensity" and constantly threatening to fire him.

In 2009, Munchinski did exactly that, filing a motion demanding that Geary be removed, which Geary discovered only after his investigator called and read him the headline in the local paper. At that point, Geary had put ten thousand hours into the case, nearly all of it unpaid. But if there was an irony in trying to fire a lawyer who had spent the better part of eight years working thirty-five hours a week for free, Munchinski did not see it. "I have joked half-kiddingly to close friends that my motivation to get him out was so I could personally stalk and kill him myself with my bare hands," Geary said.

Finally, in 2013, Geary prevailed, convincing both the federal trial and appellate judges that the state's misconduct was so extreme, and the wrongful conviction so undeniable, that they had no choice but to intervene. "The scope of the *Brady* violations here is staggering," the Third Circuit Court of Appeals wrote, going on to say that "the murders *could not* have happened" as Solomon and Warman argued at trial. Worse, they both knew it. "Munchinski has demonstrated his actual innocence by clear and convincing evidence," the judges wrote, and voided his conviction.

During the course of the federal litigation, while the state appealed the lower court's decision, Geary was able to get Munchinski out on bail.[31] On September 30, 2011, at the age of fifty-nine, David Munchinski walked through the prison gates a free man. A quarter of a century had passed, and the moment was bittersweet. Eight years earlier, he had developed Parkinson's disease, which the prison had failed to treat properly. "He looked like a ghost," Geary said, "so aged and gray." He left the state correctional institution in Pittsburgh a sick man in late middle age without two dimes to rub together.

Shortly afterward, Geary filed a civil lawsuit against Solomon and Warman, arguing that they should be forced to pay Munchinski $50 million as punishment for their wrongdoing. Geary also lobbied the US attorney's office and the attorney general to indict Solomon and Warman for perjury and evidence tampering. Of those efforts, he says, "I could have had a more fruitful conversation with a mannequin." Unprosecuted and undisciplined, the two judges continued to preside over their courtrooms until 2012, when Warman retired and Solomon took part-time status as a senior judge.[32]

Years passed, and as the civil case dragged on, Munchinski's health went from bad to worse. Geary described his client as "having one foot in the grave and the other on a banana peel." Today, Munchinski lives in Florida, surviving on welfare payments of $700 per month, the Parkinson's affecting his speech to the point where he can be incomprehensible.

In 2015, Geary won an extraordinary victory when the Third Circuit ruled that, for some of the claims, Solomon and Warman should be stripped of the complete immunity that nearly all prosecutors are entitled to claim in civil lawsuits alleging misconduct.[33] They responded by filing a motion in the trial court to dismiss Munchinski's lawsuit. In June 2017, the trial judge issued a forty-five-page order that allowed Munchinski to have a jury hear most of his claims.[34] The judge also ordered Solomon's and Warman's lawyers to sit down with Geary at a settlement conference in early August.[35] One week before the conference, Solomon and Warman appealed the judge's findings, in what Geary characterized as a "bad faith" move designed to "delay the case."[36] The trial judge put the proceedings on hold to await a decision from the higher court. Solomon and Warman, Geary said, are simply waiting for Munchinski to die, a strategy that may well pay off.

On Their Own

As extreme as Munchinski's case is, he is not the only exoneree left destitute and irreparably damaged in Pennsylvania. Pennsylvania is one of the minority of states that has no statute providing compensation for the wrongfully convicted. Drew Whitley, a black man with a history of petty crimes, was falsely convicted in 1989 of murdering Noreen Malloy, a twenty-two-year-old white woman. The crime occurred during a botched robbery of the McDonald's where Malloy worked as the night manager. The case against Whitley turned on a single mistaken eyewitness identification and the testimony of a jailhouse informant. The informant, awaiting execution for raping and murdering his stepdaughter, was taken off death row in exchange for his testimony that Whitley confessed to shooting Malloy.

When the jury came back with a guilty verdict, Whitley said, "I didn't know whether I was coming or going. My lawyer had told me, the case they have against you is no case at all." The judge sentenced him to life without the possibility of parole. Whitley spent the next eighteen years in prison, freed in May 2006 after a DNA test conclusively proved he could not have been the killer.

For a while, Whitley had lived in a cramped studio apartment in a small town in western Pennsylvania. Then he was evicted. Like Munchinski, he survives on the $700-per-month welfare disability check. His civil attorney argued that the state turned a blind eye to other viable suspects and ignored evidence that pointed away from Whitley. A federal judge acknowledged that the detectives' "reckless investigation was outrageous and rose to the level of a constitutional violation," but threw out the case because it failed to meet the highly technical standard requiring that officers be "on notice" that their conduct violated the Constitution.[37]

Whitley said his nerves are shot. The steady diet of Valium and sleeping pills he takes does little to relieve his fear, anxiety, and profound sense of hopelessness: "Every time I hear a siren, I turn around and think they are coming for me. If it happened once it can happen again. Sometimes I wish I was back in prison because I am more depressed out here than I was in there."

Pennsylvania exoneree Lewis "Jim" Fogle is also struggling to survive after spending thirty-four years in prison for raping and murdering a fifteen-year-old girl based on the testimony of three jailhouse snitches. Fogle, a white man with a history of petty crime who dropped out of school in the eighth grade, was exonerated by DNA in 2015. He was sixty-three years old. Standing outside the prison where he had spent more than half his life—bald and bespectacled, his face covered by a bushy white beard—Fogle told local reporters, "They have halfway houses for people who committed a crime but don't have a dang thing for people who didn't commit a crime. They just threw me out here and expected me to survive." He added, "I am just existing, one day at a time."[38]

Gridlock

If Munchinski, Whitley, and Fogle had been wrongfully convicted in a courthouse across the river in New Jersey, their lives would be radically different today. New Jersey has had thirty exonerations to Pennsylvania's sixty-eight but has passed a raft of reforms similar to those in Texas.[39] In addition to new laws meant to improve eyewitness identifications, evidence preservation, interrogations, and access to DNA testing, New Jersey has a relatively generous compensation statute. Exonerees receive $50,000 for each year of imprisonment, or twice the amount of their income in the year before they were imprisoned, whichever is higher, provided that they did not plead guilty. They are also eligible for job training, tuition money, counseling, health insurance, and assistance in finding a place to live.[40]

How can it be that Pennsylvania, a state more politically liberal than Texas, with more than twice the number of the exonerees as New Jersey, has implemented no wrongful conviction reforms? One important factor is the decentralized, sprawling nature of Pennsylvania's government. There are more than a thousand different police agencies and sixty-seven counties in Pennsylvania, each with its own police chief and elected district attorney, according to Rebecca Brown, who is the director of policy at the Innocence Project and works closely with other innocence organizations across the country to lobby for reforms. Unlike the vast majority of states, Pennsylvania remains a commonwealth, meaning it does not centralize command over these diffuse agencies in one state body. In New Jersey, by contrast, the attorney general mandates a top-down, uniform set of law enforcement policies that all police and prosecutors must follow.

Another important factor is the size of the Pennsylvania legislature, the largest in the United States, with 253 members, dwarfing those of Texas and California, which have only 181 and 120 members, respectively. Fractious and unwieldy, it is dominated by conservative Republicans. Jay Costa, who leads the Democratic minority in the Pennsylvania State Senate, said both chambers have become more extreme in recent years, with moderates on each side choosing retirement over the daily engagement in the partisan warfare that has played out in recent years. Thoughtful compromise has become more difficult with increasing polarization.

Costa's more liberal Democratic colleague, Senator Daylin Leach, said that part of the problem is the opposition posed by the Pennsylvania District Attorneys Association, a statewide organization with a powerful lobbying arm and over twelve hundred members. The PDAA keeps close tabs on the criminal justice legislation moving through the Pennsylvania State Senate and House of Representatives, and it directly communicates its concerns to lawmakers. Tom Hogan, the district attorney of Chester County and a member of the PDAA's executive committee, says that no organization "has a bigger platform" to advocate for or against legislation, in part because "no one wants to be on the wrong side of the DA." When the PDAA expresses opposition to a proposal to amend the criminal justice system, there is almost no likelihood of it getting to the floor for a vote, much less enacted into law. Leach said that the PDAA has not been shy about wielding this de facto veto power, adding that while "there are some very good district attorneys who view their jobs as keeping the streets safe in a thoughtful way, there are others who are against any reform of the system. There is a lot of indifference to lives that are ruined."

CHAPTER FOUR

The Road to Damascus

WITHOUT A DOUBT, the current landscape in the Pennsylvania legislature is bleak when it comes to wrongful conviction reform. But that is not the whole story. There have also been some important breakthroughs. Leading the charge is an unlikely warrior: Stewart Greenleaf, a seventy-eight-year-old Republican state senator who has represented Montgomery County—a moderate-leaning suburban area outside of Philadelphia—since 1978.

Tall and lean, with silver hair and a polite, patrician bearing, Greenleaf played basketball for the University of Pennsylvania and, after graduating from law school, spent his early career in the district attorney's office. There, he prosecuted violent felonies, including robbery, rape, and murder, before ascending the ranks to become the chief of the appellate unit. When he became the chairman of the Pennsylvania senate's judiciary committee, a post he has held for twenty-nine years, Greenleaf brought a prosecutorial mind-set, convinced that he was "on the side of justice."

Greenleaf was frank when discussing the legislation he passed during his first two decades heading up the committee: "It was pretty draconian." He authored a bill imposing mandatory minimum sentences for drug offenders, under the impression that it would only be used to target drug kingpins. He cosponsored Pennsylvania's three-strikes-and-you're-out law. And he wrote the state's version of Megan's Law, which mandates the lifelong registration of defendants convicted of sex offenses, including juveniles. He firmly believed that all of these bills would help reduce crime by meting out the stiffest possible punishments to those who most deserved them.

In the late 1990s, as DNA testing became more common, advocates came to Greenleaf with claims that this new science could conclusively prove that some of Pennsylvania's prisoners—including those on death row—were actually innocent. Greenleaf's initial reaction was disbelief; his experiences as a prosecutor, in his words, "disproved" what he was being told: "I said, no way we had done that." Greenleaf had always been an avid supporter of capital punishment, and he was proud of having authored Pennsylvania's lethal injection bill.

In 2000, Greenleaf held hearings in the judiciary committee about DNA testing and wrongful convictions, confident that his vision of the justice system would be vindicated. "Prove me wrong," he told his challengers, "I am not afraid of the truth." Sitting at the head of a conference table in his office on an unseasonably warm day in early February 2016, Greenleaf shook his head at the memory: "Well, they did." Greenleaf had demanded facts, and the facts presented to him were undeniable. DNA proved that eight Pennsylvania prisoners were not responsible for their crimes. A problem solver by nature, Greenleaf wanted to pass laws to stop it from happening. Interested in the root causes of wrongful convictions, he met with John Rago, a professor of criminal law at Duquesne University and an expert on the subject.

Rago's interest in wrongful convictions began by happenstance, when exoneree Kirk Bloodsworth gave a speech at the law school in 1999. Bloodsworth, the first death-row inmate to be freed by DNA testing, nervously told his story to a packed room of three hundred people. Rago recalls Bloodsworth breaking down as he described the pain and frustration he felt when his mother died five months before his release: "She always knew I was innocent and she never saw me a free man again." Listening to Bloodsworth speak, Rago said, "I did not know whether to applaud or jump out of the window."

Rago decided to do some research. In the law library, he picked up a book called *Convicting the Innocent*. Written in 1932 by Yale Law School professor Edwin Borchard, it documented sixty-five cases of wrongful conviction due to errors such as mistaken eyewitness identification, false confessions, police misconduct, and perjured testimony. Reading Borchard's case studies more than fifty years later, Rago realized, "Nothing had changed. It was the same patterns, the same mistakes." If anything,

DNA had made it clear that breakdowns in the criminal justice system were far more frequent and extensive.

Rago studied the eight known cases of DNA exonerations in Pennsylvania. In 2006, he published a law review article titled "A Fine Line Between Chaos & Creation: Lessons on Innocence Reform from the Pennsylvania Eight." Rago argued that these cases provided a compelling reason "to act on our basic and decent instincts 'to do justice.'" Rather than wait any longer, he wrote, "Pennsylvania should join with other states, such as Wisconsin, Illinois, and North Carolina, among others, in leading the nation on the rising road to critical innocence reforms."[1]

Greenleaf read the article. At first, he balked at Rago's explanations. The idea that standard police identification procedures were suggestive and unreliable was deeply troubling. So, too, was the concept that entire fields of expert testimony were not based on real science. Greenleaf had routinely deployed these evidentiary missiles to convict the defendants he prosecuted, and no judge or defense attorney had ever challenged him. With a chill, Greenleaf remembered a burglary case from years before. He had called an expert to testify that tool markings found on the victim's property were a match to a tool found in the defendant's possession. The markings were a key piece of evidence in identifying the perpetrator, and Greenleaf had told the jury with full confidence that they were "120 percent accurate." Now he knew otherwise.

Greenleaf's conversion from tough-on-crime crusader to criminal justice reformer was dramatic. He called it his "road to Damascus." All those years, he realized, "It wasn't only justice we were doing. It was injustice, too." In 2006, he passed a resolution in the Senate to create a wrongful convictions advisory committee to look at wrongful convictions from arrest through sentencing. To carry out this mandate, the members were directed to study DNA exoneration cases in Pennsylvania, identify the causes, and propose model legislation and criminal justice policies designed to prevent similar miscarriages of justice in the future.

The Wrongful Convictions Advisory Committee

At Greenleaf's suggestion, Rago chaired the advisory committee, which was made up of fifty-two judges, prosecutors, defense attorneys, victims' rights advocates, and experts. Rago said that the members were divided from the outset—literally. At the first meeting, which took place on March 7, 2007, Rago looked out into a room he described as parted "like the Red Sea." There were prosecutors on one side, with the police behind them, and defense attorneys on the other side.

The advisory committee was scheduled to issue its full report in 2008. But the deadline came and went. Months of delay became years. Like a miniature version of the legislature that established it, the committee members had become sharply adversarial. The diversity of political, professional, and personal experiences created irreconcilable worldviews, with an angry minority of prosecutors and victim's rights advocates insisting that the majority was wildly exaggerating the problem of wrongful convictions and badly overreaching in its proposed solutions.

The advisory committee finally issued its report in late September 2011, a doorstopper at 328 pages.[2] Delving deeply into nearly every aspect of the criminal justice system, it identified systemic problems with numerous law enforcement and prosecution practices and characterized the defense bar as chronically unable to effectively challenge the state's evidence "due to underfunding of public defender offices and substantial underpayment of appointed counsel representing indigent defendants."

The report was also chock-full of findings and proposals. Among them, a model statute requiring the recording of interrogations and the blind administration of eyewitness identifications to ensure that the police officer instructing the witness had no involvement in the case so as to eliminate any bias. Other proposed statutes sought the preservation of biological evidence and provided compensation packages for exonerees. The committee also called for increased funding for indigent defense counsel and for prosecution offices to raise their ethical standards and discipline those who violated them. In the preface, the authors emphasized the immediacy and magnitude of the problem, stating, "There is every reason to believe that mistaken identifications, false confessions, inadequate legal representation, and other factors underlying wrongful convictions occur with comparable regularity in criminal cases where DNA is absent."

While some of the reforms were not as extensive as those adopted by Texas, the report was a remarkable document nonetheless. What it proposed was no less than a major overhaul of the system, restructuring and even jettisoning practices that had been relied upon to investigate and prosecute crime for decades. But the report's influence was diluted when fourteen committee members, including the district attorneys of Montgomery, Philadelphia, and Allegheny counties, as well as several chiefs of police, the representative from the state Attorney General's Office, and a number of victim's rights advocates, refused to sign on. On the day that the advisory committee report came out, the PDAA issued a press release denouncing it as a "roadblock to justice" that would "primarily benefit the guilty."[3]

The PDAA press release included a link to an "independent report" authored by fourteen committee defectors.[4] The advisory committee's report, they wrote, was "a Trojan horse carrying a long-awaited slate of new laws to help the criminal defense bar." The model statutes were unnecessary and destructive, making it harder to convict guilty people and protect public safety. Of the eight DNA-based exonerations under study, the independent report disputed seven, insisting that the guilt of those individuals remained "compelling." According to the independent report, of the more than five million prosecutions that had taken place in the state since 1970, only one had resulted in the conviction of a plainly innocent person.

Dug In

Richard Leo has a name for the dissenters: "innocence deniers." A law professor at the University of San Francisco, Leo is one of the country's foremost experts on the causes of wrongful convictions. He made this analogy: "It is like after we discover that the world is round, you have this minority of people insisting it is flat." Marissa Boyers Bluestine, the legal director of the Pennsylvania Innocence Project, called the independent report "one of the most mean-spirited and close-minded documents that I have ever seen." She continued, "The idea that we don't convict innocent people is just astounding, like there is some magical pixie dust coming down from the Allegheny Mountains that protects Pennsylvania against the errors of wrongful convictions that infect every other state in this country."

Greenleaf, too, was taken aback. An ardent student of American history, he was inspired by the founders who wrote criminal justice protections into the Constitution and believed fervently in Benjamin Franklin's famous saying: "That it is better 100 guilty persons should escape than one innocent should suffer." When the independent report was issued, Greenleaf discovered the maxim has been "switched completely around and now we think it is better to convict an innocent person than to possibly free a guilty person." Still, he thought that a compromise could be reached. He tried to persuade his colleagues to vote to enact the model statutes. Not a single one of them became law.

Greenleaf had also been unsuccessful in amending Pennsylvania's DNA testing law, which was enacted in 2002. It excluded from eligibility people who had already served their time, and it limited testing to certain categories of crimes. People who pleaded guilty were also disqualified, because Greenleaf's congressional colleagues firmly believed, he said, that "innocent people do not plead guilty. Innocent people do not confess." These mantras, recited with dogmatic intensity, were all too familiar to Greenleaf—he had once said the same things himself. Still, he pressed on, hoping to convince others in the legislature that despite their best intentions, "there were collateral consequences that we never anticipated." He tapped the stack of bills in front of him during our interview. "I put the same energy into criminal justice reform that I put into the tough-on-crime stuff." But he got nowhere.

An Unlikely Team and a New Strategy

Greenleaf decided to take a different approach. It was vital, he said, "for all of the people in the justice system to get on board." In an effort given crucial momentum by the Innocence Project's policy director Rebecca Brown, Bluestine, and Rago, he embarked on an education and advocacy campaign. Working in tandem, they brought in police, prosecutors, and experts from other states to meet with the skeptics in Pennsylvania to convince them that the wrongful conviction reforms proposed in the advisory committee's report were worth a second look.

In 2010, Bluestine asked for a meeting with H. Charles Ramsey, the commissioner for the Philadelphia Police Department. A close friend had spoken highly of the Pennsylvania Innocence Project, and Ramsey agreed to the meeting. Ramsey, who is African American, had a national profile: well respected and admired, he served as president of the Major Cities Chiefs Association and later as the cochair of President Obama's Task Force on 21st Century Policing.

Ramsey was also well aware of Philadelphia's sordid history when it came to policing. In the late sixties and early seventies, under the leadership of Frank Rizzo, who went on to become the city's two-term mayor, police officers were indoctrinated into a culture where beating suspects into submission to extract confessions was not only tolerated but encouraged.[5] Though Rizzo was long gone, many of his recruits remained and, as Wright's case demonstrated so profoundly, carried on with their brutal tactics well into the 1990s.

After hearing from Bluestine and several exonerees, Ramsey was on board: "One innocent person is too many." The reforms that Bluestine was proposing, he said, "just made sense. We have an obligation to protect the rights of all people, including the accused. That is the responsibility of the police and prosecutors and the courts as much as it is the public defenders. I want to go to bed at night knowing that I did everything I could to get the right person."

Ramsey readily acknowledged that the Philadelphia Police Department, which did not record interrogations and had not updated its eyewitness identification procedures for decades, was "behind the times." But reform would require more than acceptance from high-ranking officers. Every member of his police force of 6,600 would need to be retrained, and a top-down directive would never work without buy-in from the rank and file.

Together with Brown, Ramsey and Bluestine organized a training in best practices for Ramsey's department at Temple University with the Pennsylvania Municipal Officers Training and Education Commission in 2010. Police officers from other states did much of the training on eyewitness identification and suspect interrogations. Cops like to hear from other cops, Ramsey said. Presentations from academics and other experts "tend not to go over too well."

They consulted with Jim Trainum, a homicide detective in Washington, DC, who once obtained a false confession that sent an innocent woman to prison. As Trainum has described in interviews that have appeared in *Serial* and *This American Life*, his moment of reckoning came after watching a videotape of his seven-hour interrogation of Kim Crafton. The video made it clear that—without realizing it—Trainum and his partner were feeding Crafton most of the incriminating information she later provided. After seventeen hours, she confessed to a murder she did not commit. Ten months later, Crafton was released from jail after records from the homeless shelter where she was living conclusively proved her innocence.

Trainum said that getting law enforcement to honestly assess itself can be difficult. Unlike the fields of medicine or aviation, for example, which approach failures "with an autopsy mentality," the nature of the adversarial system puts people on the defensive and "tends to force mistakes underground." And there is a certain false sense of confidence at play. "Cops think we are natural lie detectors. We're not. We think we know who is guilty and who isn't, but we don't," he said.

Crafton's case, he said, is a perfect example. Trainum and his partner never deviated from the techniques they had been trained to follow. Observing them the entire time was a representative from the US attorney's office and Crafton's own lawyer, who believed she was guilty and wanted her to cooperate with the police to get leniency. No one second-guessed Trainum and his partner, because every admission they obtained by spoon-feeding it to Crafton just proved what they all believed in the first place: she was guilty.

Trainum does not doubt that there are bad actors in the system, like the prosecutors-turned-judges in Munchinski's case. But more often, he says, wrongful convictions occur because of a cascade of human error. Faulty techniques, however well intentioned and long used, must be jettisoned and replaced with more accurate and effective methods. Ramsey said that police officers who heard from their own—men like Trainum— were receptive. Encouraged, Ramsey continued his education campaign. In 2014, the Philadelphia Police Department adopted double-blind, sequential eyewitness identification practices. In 2015, it imposed the requirement that all interrogations in homicide cases be recorded. By the time the reforms went into effect, there was almost no resistance within the department, and they have remained in place following Ramsey's retirement in January 2016.

In an ironic twist, some of those who have adopted similar reforms in other parts of Pennsylvania were the same people who signed onto the independent report that once condemned them. Most prominent was Pittsburgh-based Allegheny County district attorney Stephen Zappala, the chief law enforcement officer for a jurisdiction of 1.3 million people.

Working closely with Greenleaf and Rago, Zappala "reevaluated how we do business."

Zappala said that a key turning point came between 2012 and 2013, when the Pittsburgh Police Department arrested the wrong men—two black, one white—in three unrelated robbery cases, all based on mistaken eyewitness identifications. The three men were jailed. Two were able to get the charges dismissed after convincing police they had ironclad alibis. The third, who spent nearly a year behind bars, was acquitted in fifteen minutes. All three filed federal lawsuits charging the Pittsburgh Police Department with wrongful arrest, malicious prosecution, and false imprisonment.

Zappala was careful to say he did not believe the police committed misconduct. Instead, they were using eyewitness procedures that resulted in sincere but mistaken identifications. Realizing that the practices had to change, Zappala partnered with the Pennsylvania Chiefs of Police Association and the Western Pennsylvania Chiefs of Police Association to institute double-blind, sequential eyewitness identification procedures, the recording of interrogations, and the preservation of biological evidence.

Zappala took a lot of heat, but he said that with "all the criticisms, we have not lost a case" since the changes were implemented. Speaking before the Pennsylvania Senate Judiciary Committee in 2015, Zappala told Greenleaf and his colleagues, "I want to thank you for helping us to articulate together that anytime somebody is arrested for something they did not do and certainly if somebody is convicted for something they did not do, that is a tragedy, and we should address that and we should look at that in a fashion where we can avoid that in the future."[6]

The new protocols in Philadelphia and Pittsburgh have changed the way that the justice system functions for the millions of people living within these jurisdictions. Rebecca Brown is confident they will remain in place: "Voluntary compliance does not get undone. People see it works and that their concerns—that they won't be able to convict guilty people anymore—have not come to pass." The key, though, is moving beyond these voluntary, ad hoc reforms to statewide mandates that will ensure that justice is administered uniformly across Pennsylvania.

CHAPTER FIVE

Life After Conviction

THOMAS HAYNESWORTH SPENT the ten months that passed between his arrest, trials, and convictions locked up in the Richmond city jail. Meanwhile, the rapes, abductions, robberies, and stabbings in Richmond and Henrico counties continued. The rapist had become emboldened, proclaiming himself the "Black Ninja" to the victims he held at knifepoint and brutalized. Between March 5, 1984, and December 13, 1984, there were eleven additional victims. Two were fifteen-year-old girls.[1]

On December 14, 1984, the police arrested Leon Davis Jr., a young, light-skinned, clean-shaven black man. Davis's arrest was a media sensation, and his mug shot was plastered everywhere. An inmate at the Richmond city jail threw a newspaper on Haynesworth's bed and told him, "They got the guy who did what you're in here for." Davis adamantly protested his innocence, and he, too, was held at the Richmond city jail while he waited for his day in court.

The guards at the jail were constantly mixing up the two men, and Haynesworth got used to hearing Davis referred to as his "twin." Davis did not share a cellblock with Haynesworth, but they ran into each other periodically. The first time Davis saw Haynesworth, he said, "I told the police what they did to you was wrong." Haynesworth stood still, his heart beating fast.

"Really?" he managed.

"Yeah," Davis replied. "I told them they locked the wrong dude up."

Haynesworth tried to keep his cool, hoping that if he could keep Davis talking, without being confrontational, he might actually confess. He never did.

Instead, the next time they met in the hallway, Davis had a favor to ask. His first trial was approaching, and he wanted to bring Haynesworth into court to sit beside him at the defense table when it was time for the victim to point out her attacker. Davis reasoned that she would never be able to confidently make an identification; it was simply too difficult to tell them apart, particularly for a white girl. And, Davis pointed out to Haynesworth, if she did pick him, what did it matter? He had already been sentenced to die in prison.

In the winter of 1986, Haynesworth was sent to the Southampton Correctional Center, a prison about seventy miles south of Richmond near the North Carolina border where he remained off and on for the next twenty-two years. It took about twelve months to adjust. When he first arrived and was marched past the open prison yard, the inmates took one look at him—short, skinny, unable even to grow facial hair—and yelled, "Fresh Meat."

A counselor at the prison in charge of Haynesworth's orientation warned him that he would be a target. The fact that Haynesworth was a convicted rapist only made it worse: in the prison hierarchy, sexual offenders are considered one of the lower life forms, only slightly above child molesters. Haynesworth never discussed his case with anyone. He recalls only two occasions in nearly thirty years of prison life when other inmates called him out for being a rapist. As it turned out, both men had been convicted of similar crimes themselves.

Haynesworth knew that the bigger, more violent inmates were plotting to turn him into their sexual property, and he was determined not to let that happen. For months, Haynesworth watched quietly, taking note of who picked fights and who ran his mouth. "Prison is like a world inside a world," he explained. "There are rules and regulations, places you can't go, people you can't associate with. Just like in society." Haynesworth avoided the troublemakers and kept to himself as much as possible, declining proffered gifts like cigarettes and items from the prison canteen, knowing they were being used as bait.

"Don't borrow what you can't pay back" was a lesson others learned too late. Teenage inmates who came to Southampton often got sucked into the game, accepting five packs of smokes and then being unable to come up with the ten packs required when the loan came due. While most of the inmates frowned on homosexual activity, some did not. Haynesworth saw what could happen when a borrower was empty-handed. Two "big cats" would come to a young man's cell. One would stand at the door, while the other went inside and raped him. Then they would trade places. After something like that, Haynesworth said, the big cats owned their victim, body and soul.

Haynesworth focused his mind and energy on two distinct goals: getting an education and getting into the best physical shape possible. Pursuing goals was important because it both kept him busy and made him useful, which reduced the chance that he would be transferred. Haynesworth was the baby of the family, and his mother and three older sisters came to visit regularly, taking the prison bus that picked up family members in Richmond and dropped them off outside the institution ninety minutes later. But his family had neither the money nor the means to see him if he was sent to an institution hundreds of miles away.

Haynesworth got a job in the recreation department under corrections officer Donald Lee, making sure that the gym ran smoothly, signing people in and out, and keeping the place clean. He worked out constantly and participated in every team sport on offer: football, baseball, and basketball. Haynesworth was a good athlete, and other inmates wanted him on their team. Lee came to like and trust Haynesworth. Over time, Haynesworth became his right-hand man, supervising fifteen other inmates.

Haynesworth said, "One thing I always said to myself was, as bad as it was inside, I was gonna be better coming out." He enrolled in a GED program where he met an instructor who was impressed by Haynesworth's work ethic and encouraged him to take college classes. Haynesworth fell in love with learning, taking a particular interest in his business and communications classes. Ironically, prison gave Haynesworth the opportunity to get an education he never would have pursued otherwise. He knew no one who had gone to college and had no plans to do so himself.

Haynesworth also made it a mission to learn as many vocational skills as possible. He enrolled in and completed six-month programs in brick masonry, auto mechanics, welding, cooking, carpentry, and roof maintenance. With nearly every trade, Haynesworth stayed on for months afterward, determined to hone his skills. Haynesworth lived by the mantra "You have to do the time; you can't let the time do you." He learned quickly that an idle moment—even an idle thought—could prove disastrous: "If you sit around doing nothing, you will get caught up in something. You have to keep moving." When it was time to go back to his cell, Haynesworth read the Bible and wrote letters.

Haynesworth did the best he could to remain stoic, but at certain moments, his frustration over the rank injustice of his situation was almost unbearable. Sometimes, when he was working outside in the rec yard, he would look up at the barbed wire fence around him, mindful that it was all that separated him from society—that and the phalanx of armed guards who had the right to shoot him on sight if he tried to escape. His freedom was right there; he could see the blue sky and even a bit of the horizon just beyond the walls, and yet it was maddeningly out of reach. Over the years, Haynesworth wrote hundreds of letters to Scheck and Neufeld's Innocence Project, to newspapers, to *60 Minutes*, to anyone who he thought might pay attention to his case and try to help him prove his innocence. No one responded.

Eventually, Haynesworth let down his guard enough to make a few close friends. One of them was Marvin Lamont Anderson, who had come to Southampton several years before Haynesworth. Like Haynesworth, he was African American, convicted at the age of eighteen for raping a white woman based almost entirely on her eyewitness identification. The crime had been particularly brutal and horrific: the victim had been raped twice, sodomized, beaten, urinated on, and forced to eat feces.[2]

Anderson was targeted as a suspect after the victim told police her rapist had bragged to her that he had been with a white woman before. It was 1982, and Anderson was the only local man they knew who had a white girlfriend. Even more brazenly, he was living with her. But Anderson had no criminal record and, therefore, no mug shot. The police went to his employer and obtained a color photograph taken for work. They placed it in an array of possible suspects and asked the victim if she could identify anyone. Every other picture was a black-and-white mug shot.

It was common knowledge in the local community that another man was likely responsible. The victim reported that her attacker lured her by sitting next to his bicycle, holding his knee and feigning injury. The bicycle was traced to a black man, John Otis Lincoln, who had stolen it shortly before the rape occurred. Indeed, the police had put Lincoln's picture in the photo array that they showed the victim. But she picked Anderson instead, telling the jury, "There is no doubt in my mind, whatsoever."

An all-white jury convicted Anderson, and he was sentenced to serve 210 years in prison.[3]

In the summer of 1988, Lincoln confessed to the rape under oath in a state court hearing, providing details that backed up his involvement in the crime. But Anderson's trial judge was unmoved and refused to overturn his conviction. At that point, Haynesworth had been incarcerated for four years; Anderson, six. A sense of hopelessness descended. If the real perpetrator's sworn confession was not enough to win a prisoner his freedom, what was?

Haynesworth and Anderson had another friend, James Thomas, who had been convicted of murder and was known throughout the prison as R.I.P. The three men would play sports, study, and spend their free time together. "We was like brothers," Anderson said. In a world full of brutality, backstabbing, and ever shifting alliances, Haynesworth was one of a handful of people Anderson knew he could trust: reliable, honest, and "always willing to help somebody." Anderson said that he made a crucial decision early on, one that his friends mutually reinforced and supported: "We did not allow ourselves to become institutionalized. You see people come into the system and allow that to happen and when it happens it makes a person do crazy things."

The close friendship between Haynesworth, Anderson, and R.I.P. was as important for security reasons as it was for their psychological well-being. Anderson explained, it meant "we would not be left out there by ourselves, in case something were to happen." Several years after Haynesworth arrived at Southampton, something did happen. The prison had an open shower area, where the prisoners soaped up side by side under four showerheads. One day, Haynesworth, Anderson, and R.I.P. were taking a shower after playing sports in the gym. Another inmate was rinsing off under the spigot by the far wall. Haynesworth and R.I.P. were in the middle, with Anderson to their right. Suddenly, the bathroom door opened and another inmate came in. He was fully dressed, wearing boots instead of shower shoes. Behind him, another man shut the bathroom door and locked it.

Haynesworth, Anderson, and R.I.P. immediately knew something horrible was about to happen. The man came toward them, his hand closed around a gray metal combination lock to his storage locker wrapped tightly in several pairs of white gym socks. Holding the heavy object high above his head, he turned toward the naked inmate standing in the shower stall next to Haynesworth and swung hard. The lock smashed against the inmate's skull. The man screamed, and there was a sickening sound of crunching bone as his skull fractured and blood splattered over the tiled walls and floor.

Having exacted his revenge, the attacker fled. As soon as his accomplice released the lock on the door, Haynesworth and his friends wrapped their towels around their waists and left the shower room, walking calmly back to their cells as if nothing had happened. Eventually, guards were called in and the victim was taken to the hospital. Haynesworth never saw him again.

"It terrified me," Haynesworth said, but he knew better than to say anything. Clearly, there had been some kind of dispute: over money or drugs or someone disrespecting someone else. Haynesworth did not know exactly what had fueled the violence, and he made it his business never to find out. A few days later, the attacker came up to Haynesworth and R.I.P. in the rec room and offered a personal apology. "It was not my intention to disturb your shower," he told them. Haynesworth's response was equally magnanimous: "I told him I just had to get cleaner faster." They parted on good terms. The necessary respect had been paid, and there would be no snitching.

·   ·   ·

Janet Burke's rape tore a hole in her traditional family. Her upbringing was modest, but comfortable and sheltered. Her mother did not drive, and most of the places she went with her brother—the dentist, the pediatrician, elementary school—were within walking distance from their house in Sandston, a small, nearly all-white community just outside of Richmond. Once a year, the family would take a trip together on the bus to a big department store in downtown Richmond or to her grandmother's house in Verona in her dad's car. It was only a ninety-minute drive, "but felt like the other side of the world for us." Until Burke went to community college, she had never crossed the James River, which runs along the southern border of Richmond less than a twenty-minute drive from her house.

Burke remembers her parents taking her to the hospital on the day the rape happened, her father driving the car, her mother next to him, Burke hysterical in the backseat. Her father looked at her in the rearview mirror. "You need to stop crying," he told her.

"It was not to be mean," Burke explained. "It was just his way of handling things. Looking back, I think he believed that if I could just stop crying, I would not be hurting anymore and it would be easier for me. And I am sure it had to be incredibly hard on him and on my mother. I can't imagine what they were feeling as parents. But to this day I remember that moment in the backseat, just kind of sucking in my breath and trying to pull myself together."

Before the rape, Burke had been on a clear path. In high school, she took a childcare elective during her senior year and "immediately fell in love with the little ones." A strong student, Burke was accepted into the early education program at the University of Virginia. When financial reasons prevented her from attending, Burke enrolled in the local community college, where she was taking classes part-time while also continuing to work with kids. She received her associate's degree in May 1983.

After Burke got her job at the East End Church day-care center, she decided to attend Virginia Commonwealth University School of Education part-time while she got the center up and running. She completed her college application in the late fall of 1983, planning to turn it in early in the new year. But, she said, "The rape happened instead." Afterward, Burke felt at a strange remove from the world, the life plans she made suddenly devoid of meaning. She never got her bachelor's degree. "For a few years," she said, "I merely existed."

Burke's high school sweetheart was a neighborhood boy, Dwayne. They had planned to get married and would have, but the relationship fell apart after the assault. It was impossible for Burke to be intimate with anyone, and Dwayne, without meaning to, could make comments that were deeply wounding. When he first saw Haynesworth in the courtroom, Dwayne looked at Burke, surprised, saying, "He's really not that big." Hanging in the air, unspoken, was the undeniable implication of those words: *Why didn't you fight back?*

Still, Burke was devastated when the relationship ended. She no longer had Dwayne to lean on, and her family could not bring themselves to discuss what had happened to her. And as far as telling other people, "It's just a downer." Burke found herself with no one to talk to. She became withdrawn and depressed, living each day as though she were half-dead.

One year after the attack, Burke hit bottom, drinking excessively and trying out a series of casual relationships that ended badly. The alcohol numbed her feelings, but only to a certain degree; midway through what was supposed to be a lighthearted date, Burke sometimes found herself sobbing. "I was pretending to have a normal life, but it wasn't normal," she said. The despair could be physically incapacitating, particularly around the anniversary of the attack. During what she called her "pity days," Burke lay motionless in bed, unable to eat, sleep, or even watch television, the rape playing on an endless loop in her mind.

Then came a turning point. Driving by a gas station one day, Burke saw Paul, a guy from her high school. He and Burke dated briefly before Dwayne, but Burke's parents disapproved because he was four years older. Burke had heard that Paul had gotten married, but she decided to strike up a conversation anyway. She pulled into the station and approached him with the excuse that she needed directions, even though she knew exactly where she was going. He called a couple of weeks afterward, and after telling Burke that he was divorced, asked her out. "He came over the next day and I don't know that we have been apart since then," Burke said.

Like everyone else in the community, Paul was well aware of what had happened to his girlfriend. He was not a big talker, but did his best to understand and be supportive. Most importantly for Burke, "he wasn't scared off. He stuck around." Still, the rape was a difficult subject. Burke said, "We did not talk about it."

One year after they began dating, Paul and Burke got married. One year after that, they had their first child, a boy they named Paul Jr. Five years later, they had a daughter, Emily. The pity days came to an end, as spending a full day lying catatonic in bed was impossible with two small children. But Burke's trauma and fear remained with her, no longer in the foreground, but present nonetheless. She said, "To this day I tell my husband, without getting into details, that if he had not come along when he did, I am not sure where I would be today. I was afraid to be left alone— what if I don't hear something?" It was hard not to think back to that fateful morning and her total unawareness that, within seconds, her life would be hanging in the balance, as she would be subjected to a violence and debasement beyond her worst nightmares.

Every January, on the anniversary of the rape, Burke "went through a downtime," which repeated itself each time the state called with news that Haynesworth was once again eligible for parole. But she did her best to hold it inside, just as she had that day in the backseat of her father's car.

Paul took a job with the Henrico parks and recreation department, while Burke continued to work with children. In 1992, a friend contacted Burke about an opening at a nonprofit that focused on children who were the victims of poverty, abuse, and neglect by working within their communities to help strengthen and support their caregivers, who were often grandparents or more distant relatives.

Excited about the chance to make more of an impact, Burke joined the organization, which was later renamed Childsavers. The work was draining but gratifying: Burke spent her days out of the office and in the community, working with mental health professionals, police, first responders, and the Virginia Department of Social Services. Much of her work focused on helping children who had been traumatized by sexual assault to build resiliency.

Some of Burke's friends were worried that she was taking too many risks. After everything that had happened to her, why would she voluntarily go into these terrible neighborhoods, potentially putting herself at risk? It wasn't safe. But Burke was determined not to live in fear. At times, she said, "I pushed more toward taking chances because I wanted to prove my point. That I was going to live my life." With her own children, Burke fought against the urge to be overprotective "because I wanted to make sure that my fears did not live in them." She never told them about the rape. She said, "I was always waiting for the right time and there was never a right time. There is never a right time to explain something like that."

CHAPTER SIX

The Path to Exoneration

DNA TESTING DID NOT EXIST when Marvin Anderson and Thomas Haynesworth were convicted in the early 1980s. DNA, deoxyribonucleic acid, is present in bodily fluids such as blood, saliva, and semen. It consists of twisting, self-replicating double strands of molecules that contain genetic information unique to each individual. Because no two people possess the same DNA sequencing except identical twins, it is possible to match DNA found at a crime scene to the DNA of the perpetrator with a degree of accuracy that is virtually unchallengeable—above 99 percent. By the late 1980s, while the technology was still in its infancy, a few prosecutors had begun to use DNA evidence in criminal cases as incontrovertible proof of culpability.

Barry Scheck and Peter Neufeld, two criminal defense attorneys based in New York, were among the first to realize the profound implications of DNA testing—not for the guilty, but for the innocent. In cold cases where biological evidence had been preserved, DNA held the power to prove beyond a shadow of a doubt that thousands of people locked away in prisons across the United States had been wrongfully convicted. In 1992, Scheck and Neufeld founded the Innocence Project at the Cardozo School of Law in New York City. A nonprofit legal clinic, the Innocence Project was almost entirely staffed by law students charged with sifting through the thousands of letters they received from prisoners desperate to have their cases reopened. Less than a decade later, the organization had played a role in freeing more than ninety people using DNA testing.

In 2001, Virginia passed a law allowing any person convicted of a felony to petition the trial court for DNA testing. But it seemed at first that the new law would do little to help prisoners in Virginia. Statewide, the practice of Virginia's crime labs was to destroy any biological and physical evidence after a conviction was obtained. When inmates and their advocates asked for DNA analysis in old cases, the authorities routinely said there was nothing left to test. But the unorthodox practices of one forensic scientist proved them wrong.

Mary Jane Burton, tall and taciturn, her salt-and-pepper hair cropped no-nonsense short, had worked for years in crime laboratories across Virginia as a serologist analyzing samples of blood and other bodily fluids. A widow with no children, Burton was devoted to her job, regularly working nights and weekends. But she played by her own rules. Instead of returning all of the evidence to the police after testing, she saved bits and pieces. Using strips of tape, she painstakingly attached Q-tips, slivers of stained bed sheets, and swatches of clothing to the inside of her case files. When called to testify at trial, Burton would bring the evidence to court to use as an exhibit when explaining her testing methods. It was Burton who was assigned to determine the blood type of the biological evidence used against Marvin Anderson in 1982.[1]

After serving fifteen years in prison, most of them spent with Thomas Haynesworth, Anderson was paroled in 1997. But because he received a sentence of 210 years, he would be a parolee for the rest of his live. Worse, he was required to register as a sex offender with the state police, readily identifiable as a rapist and effectively barred from many jobs, housing options, and public spaces.[2] Anderson chafed under the restrictions conferred by a shameful label he had done nothing to deserve. Determined to clear his name, he wrote a letter to the Innocence Project, which eventually made its way to Peter Neufeld, who took on his case in 1994. After meeting with Anderson, the law students who worked with Neufeld became completely convinced of his innocence.

The Innocence Project quickly determined that neither the courthouse nor the police department had preserved any biological evidence from Anderson's case. It also asked the state's crime lab to check, only to be told repeatedly that the practice was to return all of the evidence it tested to the police. Burton had died two years earlier, and apparently so had any institutional knowledge of her unusual methods. But the law students kept pushing. Finally, in 2001, shortly before the DNA testing statute was passed, they prevailed upon Dr. Paul Ferrera, then the director of Virginia's Division of Forensic Science, to retrieve Anderson's case file himself. When Ferrera opened the file labeled *Commonwealth v. Marvin Anderson*, he was shocked to find a Q-tip from the victim's rape kit. The DNA came back as a match to John Otis Lincoln, the man who had confessed to the rape thirteen years earlier. On August 21, 2002, Virginia's then governor Mark Warner issued a full pardon to Anderson.[3]

The magnitude of the discovery inside the Anderson file hit state authorities hard once they realized there could be hundreds, possibly thousands, of other files just like it. After all, Burton had been a forensic scientist for the state of Virginia from 1974 to 1988. In 2004, Warner decided to order DNA testing in a random sampling of thirty-one additional Burton case files. Two more men were exonerated in rape and sexual assault cases; one had served eleven years in prison, the other twenty. In 2005, Warner issued a second directive, this time for the testing of all the case files handled by Burton.[4] While there was no predicting how long it would take or how much money it would cost, Warner said in a public statement that "a look back at these retained case files is the only morally acceptable course, and what truth they can bring only bolsters confidence in our system."[5]

More than six hundred cases were selected for retesting.[6] Among them was Janet Burke's and, inside the file, snippets from her rape kit. But years passed until the state retested the evidence. Haynesworth got the news in prison, where he had served twenty-five years of his life sentence. In a letter he received in February 2009, state authorities informed him that the biological evidence taken from Burke's body excluded him as the perpetrator. Haynesworth called his cellmate over. "I was reading it and reading it and reading it and I asked him, 'Tell me if this says what I think it says,' and he said, 'Yeah, that's what it says.' I said, 'Okay, now, alright, finally somebody believes me.'"

Several weeks later, the police came to Burke's house with news that was simply beyond her belief. Thomas Haynesworth had not raped her. Leon Davis had.

Burke protested, reminding them that she had been told in 1984 that a different test had backed up her identification of Haynesworth. The police explained that the technology available then could reveal only that Haynesworth and Davis had the same blood type, as did millions of other Americans. This new DNA testing was different and definitive. There was no chance, not one in 6.5 billion, that the rapist was anyone other than Leon Davis.

Burke's denial gave way to shame, horror, and despair. She was both a crime victim and in some way, she felt, a perpetrator. Her mistaken identification had contributed to multiple miscarriages of justice that had ended up costing an innocent man twenty-five years of his life. The police had little to offer in the way of help or advice. "It is not that they were insensitive; it was just, I am not sure that they knew what to do with me," Burke said. "They were very nice people, but they both said, 'These two men are both not great men, so just put this behind you.'"

How, Burke wondered, would she ever be able to do that?

An Unlikely Team of Advocates

By the time Haynesworth's innocence in Burke's case became clear, Scheck and Neufeld's Innocence Project had grown exponentially in size and influence. Former federal prosecutor John Douglass, who served as the dean of the University of Richmond law school from 2007 to 2011, said that Scheck and Neufeld created "one of the most profound and powerful criminal justice movements certainly of my lifetime." In state after state, similar nonprofits were popping up like dandelions, forming a loose network that often partnered with the Innocence Project to litigate DNA cases across the country. One of them, the Mid-Atlantic Innocence Project (MAIP) opened its doors in 2000. The executive director, who had done similar work while a journalism student at Northwestern University, was Shawn Armbrust.

Armbrust, a slight young woman with porcelain skin, blue eyes, and long, red-blonde hair, bears an unmistakable resemblance to the actress Amy Adams. And like many of the characters that Adams plays, Armbrust manages to be both sweet and steely: smart, determined, indefatigable. Haynesworth had written to Armbrust directly once he was informed that DNA testing would be conducted in his case, and this time, he got a response. In early 2009, Armbrust met Haynesworth in prison and came away impressed: poised and soft-spoken but emphatic, he was utterly convincing in his assertion of innocence. But when MAIP agreed to represent Haynesworth in partnership with the Innocence Project and the pro bono assistance of a prominent DC law firm, Hogan Lovells, Armbrust knew it would be an uphill battle.

It quickly became clear to Armbrust that Leon Davis—Haynesworth's "twin"—had committed all of the crimes for which Haynesworth had been accused and convicted. On September 18, 2009, using the DNA results from Burke's rape kit, Armbrust and her team were able to obtain a writ of actual innocence in Burke's case from the Virginia Supreme Court—the first ever issued in the statute's eight-year history. Armbrust and her team won another victory when they successfully petitioned for DNA testing of Diane's rape kit—the sole case where Haynesworth had been acquitted. On June 17, 2010, the test results came back, once again excluding Haynesworth and matching Davis. But when Armbrust sought DNA testing for Haynesworth's two remaining convictions, the attacks on Mary and Tracy, she learned that all of the evidence had been destroyed. There was no way to prove conclusively that Davis had committed those crimes as well.

Rather than battling the state to clear Haynesworth's name, his legal team decided to adopt a collaborative approach. Shedding her traditional adversarial role, Armbrust worked to turn Haynesworth's staunchest adversaries into his advocates. With some trepidation, Armbrust went to see Burke, hoping that she might be willing to help but bracing for a cold reception. To Armbrust's surprise, Burke was eager to talk; in fact, she was desperate for information. No one from the police or prosecution had spoken to her since the initial notification about the DNA test results.

Burke wanted an explanation. At the same time, she wanted to explain herself. During the attack, Burke told Armbrust, she had had the wherewithal to pay attention to her rapist's face, his features, his skin tone. She had diligently followed the directives of the police and the prosecutor in making her identification, first out of the photo array and then in the courtroom. Burke was not a liar or a racist: she believed, to the marrow of her bones, that Haynesworth had raped her. How was it possible to do everything right, only to be proven absolutely wrong? Armbrust talked to Burke at length about how and why eyewitness misidentifications occur, particular those involving people of different races. Delicately, Armbrust broached the subject of Burke speaking to the press about the case, while retaining her anonymity as a victim of sexual assault. She gave Burke the contact information for Frank Green, the *Richmond Times Dispatch* reporter who had covered the Haynesworth and Davis cases for nearly three decades.

In early August 2010, Burke reached out to Green. A week or so later, the two sat down at a picnic table in a park. Across the street was St. John's Church in Richmond, where Patrick Henry had stood more than two centuries earlier to urge his fellow Virginians to rise up against the British Army in the War of Independence. He famously declared, "Is life so dear, or peace so sweet, as to be purchased at the price of chains and slavery? Forbid it, Almighty God! I know not what course others may take; but as for me, give me liberty or give me death!"

Green remembers that it was a warm day, and that Burke was "quite nervous at first." As Green later reported in an article that ran in the *Times Dispatch* on August 15, 2010, Burke's overriding concern was for the people that Davis had harmed, first by committing more than a dozen horrific sexual assaults and then by letting an innocent man take the fall for five of them. Haynesworth, she told Green, "is as much a victim in this as the rest of us."

Burke's quiet advocacy continued; in the months that followed, she gave more interviews with Green and talked to reporters from other news outlets, including the *Washington Post*.[7] As a rape victim, Burke was able to maintain her anonymity, and her shunning of the spotlight and ability to cogently explain how she had come to confuse Haynesworth and Davis made her very credible. Armbrust said, "She was a really important part of the case."

Armbrust also asked for a meeting with Richmond's commonwealth attorney, Michael Herring, who now presided over the office that had prosecuted Haynesworth for attempting to rob and sodomize Tracy. African American and whippet thin, with chiseled features and an unassuming manner, Herring was highly regarded for his intellect, experience, and progressive vision for the office. In 2005, Herring, who had been both a prosecutor and a defense attorney, unseated his predecessor, a college friend who was also African American. (He went on to become a judge.)

Herring had entered the race motivated by a belief that new leadership was necessary to boost morale, recruit talented young prosecutors, and aim higher than the headline-of-the-day. He said, "It was my thought that the office serves an important role in the city, which is, at an initial level, to prosecute cases. But my goal was never just that. I figured if I could get into the office and stabilize it, bring in a good team and reshape it, then I could turn to what was most interesting to me, which was shifting the policy." Newly elected to his second term, Herring was itching to get started on his bigger goals.

Yet, sitting down with Armbrust, Herring was skeptical. He had carried out his responsibilities under Warner's directive, reexamining cold cases when a prisoner or his lawyer made a request. Each time, the lab test results came back confirming guilt. But Haynesworth's story was different from the outset: DNA irrefutably proved the real perpetrator was Leon Davis in two of the four cases that had gone to trial. As Armbrust described the physical resemblance between Haynesworth and Davis, as well as the modus operandi of the attacks Davis was known to have committed long after Haynesworth was incarcerated, Herring listened intently.

On September 10, 2010, Herring met with Haynesworth in person. It was, he said, "the turning point." In the course of his career, Herring had prosecuted and defended scores of guilty people. Haynesworth was nothing like them. Short and dense with muscle from his daily workouts, Haynesworth was polite, forthright, and sincere. And he was dead serious, readily agreeing to a polygraph test. Herring said, "Afterward the examiner came out and said to me, in so many words, 'You got the wrong guy.'"

Herring went to Wade Kizer, the commonwealth attorney in Henrico County, where Haynesworth had been convicted for abducting and raping Mary. Kizer, too, carefully examined the evidence, assigning a cold-case investigator to reinterview witnesses. On October 26, 2010, Haynesworth took and passed a second polygraph. Herring and Kizer, now convinced of Haynesworth's innocence, faced the challenge of finding a legal way to free him.

Herring decided to see if he could get the support of the state's top law enforcement official, newly elected Republican attorney general Kenneth Cuccinelli II. It seemed unlikely. A longtime state senator already rumored to have his eye on the governor's mansion, Cuccinelli had made a national reputation for himself as unflinchingly conservative on nearly every issue. And he did not mince words. In 2003, after the US Supreme Court struck down Texas's anti-sodomy law on equal protection grounds, Cuccinelli had voted against a state bill amending a similar statute explaining that "homosexual acts are wrong" and "don't comport with natural law."[8]

Earlier in 2010—the same year that Herring and Kizer had come to the conclusion that Haynesworth was innocent—Cuccinelli had solidified his reputation as a Tea Party champion. In March, minutes after President Obama signed the Affordable Care Act, Cuccinelli filed a federal lawsuit to have it declared unconstitutional.[9] One month later, as part of what the *New York Times* called a "one-man war against the theory of man-made global warming," Cuccinelli sued the Environmental Protection Agency, claiming that it had no basis for concluding that greenhouse gas emissions were causally related to climate change.[10] A devout Catholic and the father of seven children, Cuccinelli believed in home schooling and was fiercely opposed to abortion. And it was not just on social and environment issues that Cuccinelli jackknifed rightward. He was a law-and-order guy, elected on a gun-rights platform and a promise, much like that of the late Supreme Court Justice Antonin Scalia, of "defending the Constitution as it was written."

Nonetheless, Herring was hopeful. Cuccinelli was extremely conservative, but he was principled. Herring knew this from personal experience, having overlapped with Cuccinelli at the University of Virginia, at one point living in the same dormitory. They had struck up a friendship that had endured for twenty years. Herring believed that the attorney general—whom he, like many others, affectionately referred to as "the Cooch"—would give Haynesworth's case a hard look.

In late autumn of 2010, Herring sat down with Cuccinelli in the attorney general's executive conference room. Cuccinelli said, "He gave me a general outline, and he said this guy may be innocent. He asked me if I would be interested in looking at the evidence, and I said, 'Show me what you got.'" Herring sent the files over.

Cuccinelli, who obtained a degree in engineering before going to law school, describes himself as "a left brain guy. I am about the data." For the next several months, he worked with Assistant Attorney General Alice Armstrong on nights and weekends, reviewing the files of more than a dozen violent sexual assaults that occurred in Henrico County and the city of Richmond between January 3 and December 13, 1984. Together, Armstrong and Cuccinelli made detailed charts of the five cases where Haynesworth had been identified as the rapist, including the two in which DNA testing had later revealed the true perpetrator as Davis. Then they created more charts, analyzing the evidence in the multiple rape, robbery, and abduction cases for which Davis had been convicted—all crimes that took place long after Haynesworth had been locked up.

The charts were so large that it took a six-foot printer to generate them. Cuccinelli and Armstrong continued to add information and then placed the charts next to each other in chronological order. Eventually, they covered an entire wall of Cuccinelli's office. Stepping back to take it all in, Cuccinelli was stunned. It was not a question of glancing similarities. The geographical clusters, the details of the physical violence, and the wording of the threats issued to the victims formed an unmistakable pattern.

To Cuccinelli, the black-and-white mug shots taken of Haynesworth and Davis before they entered the penitentiary in 1985 were the most powerful evidence. When the pictures were placed side by side, he said, the resemblance was remarkable. The two men appeared to have the same coloring, the same light facial hair on their upper lips and chins. Their eyes, noses, and lips were also very similar in shape.

Looking at the photos together, Burke analogized the likeness to the way she feels about some siblings: when she sees them at different times in different places, it is easy to mix them up. Only when she sees them together can she appreciate the differences. But when Burke made her initial identification, she never had that opportunity, nor did any of the other victims. Linda pointed out Haynesworth on the street; the others were shown photo arrays that contained only Haynesworth's picture, not Davis's. Add in the fact that all five cases were cross-racial, and the quintuple mistaken identification of Haynesworth—which had seemed statistically impossible in 1984—suddenly became understandable, if not obvious. Armstrong held a similar view. To check her own instincts, Armstrong would show the mug shots one at a time to friends who knew nothing about the cases. More often than not, she said, the reaction was, "Oh my God."

As far as Cuccinelli could tell, the only significant physical difference was in height: Davis was five feet ten; Haynesworth was far shorter at five feet six. But the victims had no way of knowing that just by looking at pictures of faces, and by the time the cases got to trial, it was too late. Even when Mary had been forced to stand next to Haynesworth and concede that he was shorter than she was—not taller, as she had originally stated—she never wavered. Mary was not lying; she genuinely believed a falsehood. The image of Davis, the man who subjected her to the worst trauma of her life, had long ago been replaced in her mind by the image of Haynesworth shown to her by police months before.

Long Odds

Haynesworth's case kept Cuccinelli awake at night. He remembered a colleague telling him, "We have so many systems in place to catch mistakes and this one walked through all of them. How many innocent people get nailed twice, never mind three times, for attacking three women in totally unrelated cases?" But it had happened, and if something were not done, Haynesworth, who was now finishing his third decade in prison, would likely die there.

Every time Haynesworth came up for parole—most recently in June 2010—he was asked to admit to his crimes. He steadfastly refused. Though Haynesworth was a model inmate in every other respect, his lack of remorse so troubled the parole board that it always voted against his release. In December 2010, Cuccinelli went to the governor, Republican Bob McDonnell, and urged him to pardon Haynesworth. McDonnell insisted that the legal process move forward.

That meant trying to overturn Haynesworth's remaining two convictions. Cuccinelli and Armbrust had hoped that Mary and Tracy would recant their identifications. But while the DNA evidence in Burke's and Diane's cases had shaken their confidence, neither woman was willing to conclude that she had been wrong. In early February 2011, Haynesworth's team of lawyers filed two petitions in the Virginia Court of Appeals seeking writs of actual innocence in the cases involving Mary and Tracy; Herring and Kizer publicly stated that Haynesworth had their full support. Cuccinelli, whose job it was to respond to the petitions, agreed with the state prosecutors in theory. But taking the extraordinary step of joining publicly with the defense team in the litigation meant more than admitting to a horrible series of mistakes. The statute demanded a very high level of proof in support of Haynesworth's innocence. The legal route to exoneration was not a pathway; it was a knife's edge.

Virginia law was strict and unforgiving: "All final judgments, orders and decrees, irrespective of court, shall remain under the control of the trial court and subject to be modified, vacated, or suspended, for twenty-one days after the date of entry, and no longer."[11] Designed to uphold the finality of convictions, the rule barred judges from considering any evidence brought to light more than three weeks after a defendant's conviction became official—the shortest window of any law in the country.

The twenty-one-day rule contained only two exceptions, enacted to give judges the power to grant "writs of actual innocence" to "those individuals who can establish that they did not, as a matter of fact, commit the crimes for which they were convicted." One statute, passed in 2001, permitted a writ based on DNA evidence; the other statute, passed in 2004, by newly discovered nonbiological evidence.[12] Both laws contained identical language making it clear that the writ was an extraordinary remedy, granted only in cases where the new evidence was so compelling that no rational person would have voted to convict had it been presented at trial.[13]

In the years since the laws had been enacted, only one person had prevailed under that test: a man convicted of illegally possessing a firearm that later tests proved to be inoperable and therefore not a "firearm" within the plain meaning of the statute. In other words, the man had been convicted of conduct that was not a crime. Haynesworth's two convictions would be much harder to undo. There was no question that both Mary and Tracy had been violently assaulted, and neither had gone back on their identification of Haynesworth as the perpetrator.

Armstrong was tasked with writing the attorney general's response to Haynesworth's petitions. A few weeks later, she filed paperwork declaring that the state was firmly on Haynesworth's side. Armstrong relied on the exonerating DNA test results from Burke and Diane, as well as the consistencies between the other rapes for which Haynesworth had been convicted and the string of subsequent attacks for which Davis was serving a life sentence. Any rational person, she argued, would conclude that only one man—the serial rapist Leon Davis—was responsible for terrorizing all of these women. The alternative explanation bordered on preposterous: two very-similar-looking black men who lived only blocks apart were sexually assaulting white women in the same geographical clusters, using the same weapons, threats, and physical violence, with Davis adopting Haynesworth's modus operandi after Haynesworth went to prison.[14]

The case took another dramatic turn on March 21, 2011, when Haynesworth was finally released on parole after serving twenty-seven years, due in part to the governor's request that the parole board reconsider its previous denials. It was his forty-sixth birthday. Outside the Greensville Correctional Center, still in his prison uniform, Haynesworth wrapped his mother, Dolores, in an embrace, his face pressed tightly against hers. "I am glad my mother is alive, that she can see this," he said.[15]

Haynesworth and Armbrust sat down the next day with Cuccinelli, who choked up as he apologized: "I told him, 'I wasn't here thirty years ago or however long it was, but I am the attorney general, and I represent Virginia. The state messed up in a way that abused you. There is no taking that back, and there is no making up for it. I am so sorry.'" Haynesworth, he said, did not say much, but he was "gracious." There was a job opening in Cuccinelli's office, in the mailroom. Cuccinelli did not mention the job specifically, but he did tell Haynesworth to call if he ever needed anything, and he held the position open.

Nine days later, on March 30, 2011, Haynesworth was back in court, this time in a new suit and tie. He watched from his seat in the front row with his mother, sisters, and niece as Innocence Project cofounder Peter Neufeld and Armstrong, named as opposing counsel on the legal pleadings, prepared to make what was essentially the same argument. Armstrong, who had been a law clerk to the former chief judge of the Court of Appeals, had argued dozens of cases in this courtroom. "I feel good in that court," she said. "That's my turf." But Haynesworth's case was different. The chief deputy of Armstrong's office sat beside her at counsel table—"we don't usually have a phalanx of lawyers sitting with us"—and the courtroom was packed with media and spectators; extra chairs had to be brought in, and many people were turned away.

Armstrong said that the questions from the three-judge panel were "really tough." The statute making an exception for relief based on newly discovered nonbiological, forensic evidence had been in place only six years, and there was no precedent for what the state was asking the court to do. It was historically the governor's job, one judge pointed out, to decide whether to pardon someone. If the governor refused to do it, why should the court step in and usurp his authority, particularly where the two victims sincerely believed that Haynesworth was guilty? Couldn't a rational juror convict today, simply based on their eyewitness identifications? Indeed, how could the state not prosecute such a case—wasn't that in essence telling these women that they were not to be believed?

When it was over, Armstrong said, "I felt like I had been through the wringer." The months of nonstop work on the case, and the skeptical nature of the court's questions left her exhausted and uncertain, replaying every exchange and wondering what she could have said differently. But the case was now under submission, and there was nothing to do but wait.

For Haynesworth, the next few weeks were excruciating. The exhilaration he felt leaving prison proved short-lived. He was no longer physically shackled, but he was not free. As his friend Marvin Anderson had been, Haynesworth was a convicted felon on parole, forced to register as a sex offender, and the constraints on his life were a nightmare. A heavy ankle monitor was attached to his leg at all times, a walkie-talkie always in his pocket so that his probation officers could track his every move. Perversely, he said, "I had more freedom in prison than I had on the street. There were so many places I could not go, so many things I could not do. I could not be near a playground; I could not be around my nieces and nephews without supervision. On holidays like Halloween, I had to be in the house from five p.m. until the next morning at eight. I could not come out." He had no job, no money, and no dignity.

Armbrust felt sickened watching Haynesworth suffer and decided to take Cuccinelli up on his offer to help. In early April, several weeks after Haynesworth's release, she called him. Cuccinelli told her to come to his office with Haynesworth. Armbrust assumed that Cuccinelli would offer to make a few phone calls to see about the possibility of getting Haynesworth a job. But when they arrived, Cuccinelli told Haynesworth he already had a job: in the Attorney General's Office. The work was not glamorous—Haynesworth would mainly be sorting and delivering the mail. But it came with a decent salary and excellent benefits. As Haynesworth sifted through a stack of new employee paperwork, Armbrust started to cry: "He had never filled out a tax form. He had no employment history, no social security, no employment prospects." In the space of a few minutes, Haynesworth's life had changed dramatically for the better.

Cuccinelli described his decision to hire a registered sex offender to work in his office as "not without controversy." Armstrong was more direct: "To say there was pushback would be an understatement. There was a lot of resentment." Many of Cuccinelli's colleagues disagreed with the attorney general's decision to take Haynesworth's side in court; having a convicted rapist present every day in their workspace, they believed, posed a real public-safety issue.

Cuccinelli acknowledged the stakes, citing Massachusetts governor Michael Dukakis's decision to furlough Willie Horton and the disaster that followed, both for Dukakis's 1988 presidential campaign and, far worse, for the woman Horton raped during the brief period he was free. But Cuccinelli responded with his typical absolutism: "I said if I had one shred of concern I wouldn't do it." Not to hire Haynesworth, he thought, amounted to moral hypocrisy. Cuccinelli believed that Haynesworth was innocent and that nearly three decades of his life had been stolen. In some ways, offering him a job in the mailroom was the least he could do. In the end, Cuccinelli said, it was Haynesworth who won over the dissenters. The nature of Haynesworth's job required that he come into contact with the entire office on a near daily basis—no matter what rank or division, everyone got mail. "Thomas," Cuccinelli said, "is a spectacular human being in his own right and that comes through. They met him. And that did it."

In July 2011, Haynesworth's advocates received an unwelcome jolt. Without explanation, and before the panel even issued a decision, the Virginia Court of Appeals had decided to rehear the case en banc, meaning that every judge would participate in the oral argument. En banc arguments are very rare, reserved for cases of extreme complexity, importance, or without clear precedent. Haynesworth's case seemed to fit all three categories. But though the rehearing was not itself bad news, the judges posed a new question beforehand that seemed to signal grave doubts:

> What, if any, non-biological evidence in the record conclusively establishes that the person who sexually assaulted the other victims, based on the newly discovered DNA, is the same person who sexually assaulted the victims that are the subject of the petitions for writ of actual innocence before this court?[16]

It was the phrase "conclusively establishes" that worried Cuccinelli and Armstrong the most. It appeared that the court was demanding a higher level of proof than the statute itself required—a level of proof that they could not supply. Conclusive evidence was DNA; nonforensic evidence, by its nature, never could be. And while DNA had once existed in Mary and Tracy's cases, that evidence had been destroyed by the state. The attorney general's brief made this point explicitly, responding, "It seems paradoxical to demand 'conclusive' evidence from Haynesworth when the commonwealth has deprived him of the opportunity to present such evidence."[17]

Haynesworth's advocates were also concerned. Armbrust said, "It was a tough legal standard as written, and the question really emphasized that in a scary way." She tried to manage Haynesworth's expectations, telling him that no matter how strong the facts or how righteous the case, the odds were against him. After some deliberating, it was decided that Armbrust would argue the case this time around. As Haynesworth's main attorney, she knew the facts of his five cases and Leon Davis's subsequent string of convictions better than anyone else. And, unlike Neufeld, Armbrust had the ability to put everything else aside for four weeks and do nothing but prepare.

Armbrust, then thirty-four years old, with only six years of experience as a lawyer, had never done an oral argument. She was also ten weeks pregnant and suffering from morning sickness. Still, she plunged into the preparations, with professors at Georgetown University standing in for the appellate judges and grilling her at practice sessions multiple times per week. On the day of the argument, September 27, 2011, Armbrust was terrified but ready. The court was formal; she had been told to wear a skirt suit, but at that point, nothing fit anymore, so she put on a loose dress and a blazer. As she approached the lectern, Armbrust said, "My hope was not to throw up." Afterward, she felt a surge of exhilaration and also hope. The judges, she felt, had not been too hard on Haynesworth.

The Attorney General's Office had also decided to switch players, with Cuccinelli taking Armstrong's place. Before yet another packed audience, he withstood a hailstorm of questions, some pointed sharply at him. Cuccinelli's position as the state's top prosecutor and the traditional responsibilities that went with it were not lost on the justices. They wanted to know how the attorney general could sanction undoing the verdicts of two separate juries, both of which had found Haynesworth guilty beyond a reasonable doubt.

Cuccinelli had a ready answer. "My job," he explained, "is not to defend convictions, it's to defend justice." Demanding that two wrongful convictions remain affixed to an innocent man was a perversion of his role in the legal system. Cuccinelli's view echoed back to a US Supreme Court case from 1935, where Justice Sutherland famously declared that a prosecutor is "a sovereignty whose obligation to govern impartially is as compelling as its obligation to govern at all; and whose interest, therefore, in a criminal prosecution is not that it shall win a case, but that justice shall be done. As such, he is in a peculiar and very definite sense the servant of the law, the twofold aim of which is that guilty shall not escape or innocence suffer."[18]

Haynesworth did not want to attend the second argument. It was, he said, simply too intense, both the stakes and the scrutiny: "Ten judges with your life in their hands, looking at you and you have no idea what they are thinking." Afterward, there was nothing to do but wait. Haynesworth remained optimistic: "I got this far, and when I had so much evidence pointing in my favor, I kept thinking that they must believe I was telling the truth."

The ruling came down five weeks later, on December 6, 2011. Haynesworth was standing in the lobby of the Attorney General's Office when his cell phone rang. It was Armbrust. "We won!" she told him. Haynesworth said that when he announced the news to the room, which was crowded with prosecutors and staff headed out to lunch, "Everyone busted out clapping."

When Haynesworth's former trial attorney, Ramon Chalkley III, read about Haynesworth's exoneration in the paper, he vomited. In a bizarre coincidence, Chalkley had also prosecuted Marvin Anderson, Haynesworth's friend and fellow exoneree, when Chalkley was the head of the Commonwealth Attorney's Office in Hanover County, Virginia. Knowing that he had been directly involved in two wrongful conviction cases, Chalkley said, was simply too much to bear in that moment.

In fact, Haynesworth had prevailed by the barest of margins. In a terse order, six of the ten judges stated that, after consideration of the full record, "this Court hereby grants the petitions, issues writs of actual innocence, and vacates the convictions." The two-sentence decision offered nothing by way of explanation.[19]

The four dissenters were as explicit in their reasoning as the majority was opaque. Three of them issued separate opinions that detailed their fierce opposition. Judge Beales wrote, "Just because two other women apparently misidentified Haynesworth as the man who sexually assaulted them, when later DNA tests suggested that the attacker was instead Davis, does not somehow mean that [Mary] and [Tracy] *also* mistakenly identified Haynesworth as their attacker." Judges Elder and Petty went further: "The facts in these cases could not be more compelling. The victims have not recanted, no one has confessed, and there is no direct evidence that

Haynesworth did not commit these crimes." They continued: "Overturning a conviction simply because the attorney general believes the defendant is innocent judicially empowers him to pardon a convicted criminal, a power he does not have."[20]

Cuccinelli did not dwell on these details. Haynesworth's exoneration, he said, personified the Constitution's guarantee of liberty, which "is big and grand writ large, but here it is for one person and for our system, which in some ways feels more important." The ruling could not give Haynesworth back the decades he had lost, but it could restore his reputation and validate what he had been saying all along by providing an official decree of innocence. "It is," Cuccinelli said, "the professional accomplishment I am the most proud of."

Burke's feelings were much more complicated. The victory was what she had hoped and prayed for, but it came with a crush of media attention and potential consequences that frightened her. She feared that her name would be leaked to the press, piercing the shield that her anonymity had provided. She feared for her children—the invasion of their privacy, the endless questions and unwanted attention. And she feared what Haynesworth and his family might do: "For so long, I believed that he really should be angry with me, that his family should be angry with me, because even though the system had failed, I was part of that system." Dark thoughts swirled, intensifying her stress until "I was suffocating from the pressure of everything between the guilt and the anxiety and the unknown."

Burke and her family packed up and left the state, spending a few days at her brother's house on the outer banks of North Carolina. It was winter and the place was deserted. Burke welcomed the beauty and isolation of her surroundings, and the chance to take deep breaths of cold ocean air. Being far away with her husband and children on this isolated stretch of beach gave her time to collect her thoughts. Like Haynesworth, she wanted to feel completely free, but was unsure if that was even possible or, if it was, whether she deserved to be.

For Haynesworth, it took a while to absorb the magnitude of what had happened. His feelings were deeply personal and difficult for him to share with anyone. He did not want a big celebration with cheering and back-slapping and bear hugs. That night, he went home, had dinner with his mother, and watched Netflix. "I wanted to sit back," he said, "and feel whole again. The joy I experienced, I experienced by myself." For the next few days, Haynesworth did not take the bus to work. Instead, he walked the four miles, taking detours to go through parks and watching children play in the schoolyard. He made it a mission to visit every place he had not been permitted to go. For months, he said, "I had not been part of life, and to get all these things restored to me was to have my life back."

CHAPTER SEVEN

The Myth of Happily Ever After

ONCE UPON A TIME. Happily ever after. The narrative connecting these two lines is powerful and uplifting. Though the darkness can appear impenetrable—the hero of the story is subjected to senseless abuse and often left for dead—after many twists and turns, seemingly impossible odds are overcome with bravery, fortitude, and a bit of serendipity. Youth, beauty, and hope are restored. Soul and spirit intact, the protagonist rides off into the sunset. There is no lingering trauma.

The fairy tale narrative is deeply embedded in our culture. We cheer fervently for the underdog, turn out in droves to watch our superheroes do battle at the multiplex, root for the star-crossed lovers, and privately cherish the idea that our own lives will follow a similar, if less dramatic trajectory. This aspiration is rooted firmly in our collective belief in the power of second chances and the cauterizing effect of retribution.

Justice is done. Villains receive their due. Good triumphs over evil.

The narrative arc of an exoneration story seems to fit neatly within the fairy tale framework. What the public sees is a snapshot in time: the bang of the gavel, the embrace between client and attorney, the press conference at which the exoneree gives thanks—to his tireless advocates, to his family, to God. There are tears, but they are joyful. We come to the end and think, "Thank goodness the horror is over! Now comes the happily ever after."

But an exoneration is not a happy ending. An exoneration is an earthquake. Loud and terrifyingly disruptive, it leaves upheaval and ruin in its wake. After the euphoria comes the rude realization that getting out of prison was a small step in a much longer journey with no clear path forward. Yes, the physical shackles are gone, but invisible ones remain firmly in place.

Many exonerees suffered horribly in prison. Separated from their families, they were assaulted, raped, and terrorized, and spent years in solitary confinement. Some are full of anger and fear while lacking the tools to express themselves because they had learned to stifle their emotions in order to survive. They have no ready access to services that can help them reacclimate to society: no parole officer or other legally guaranteed support system is in place to help them find work and a place to live. The road to obtaining compensation from the state, if that is even possible, can be long and arduous.

Many exonerees have been imprisoned for so long that their parents are dead, their families have scattered, and their close friends are now mere acquaintances. Even putting aside the immediate need for food and shelter—and the fact that many exonerees have serious physical health conditions—there is the daunting psychological task of finding the will to move forward after losing trust in the basic decency of other people. Some exonerees die within a few years of their release, from health problems that went untreated in prison, substance abuse, or suicide.

Nor is the damage limited to the exonerated. Now-grown children face the challenge of forging a relationship with a parent they knew only from limited interactions in the prison visiting room; spouses must make radical adjustments to share physical and emotional space with a partner who has been absent for years, sometimes decades. Not surprisingly, many of these relationships collapse under the strain.

The original crime victims are forced to relive the worst experience of their lives with the knowledge that the actual perpetrator was never caught, or caught far too late, after victimizing more people. For survivors like Burke, who unwittingly played a role in the wrongful conviction because they mistakenly identified the innocent person as the attacker, the trauma is compounded by confusion and overwhelming guilt.

The victim's family members, whose lives were forever altered by the rape, assault, or murder of a loved one, are left to watch as stricken bystanders. For many, the news comes as a shock because law enforcement did not alert them beforehand. They too relive the trauma, this time in isolation, because the exoneration process is not concerned with their suffering. Many feel ignored, cast aside, and, like the exonerees, without the resources to cope with overwhelming and wildly conflicting emotions. Often reduced to statistics or receiving a brief surge of media attention before falling back into obscurity, they are human beings, and their pain is real.

Thomas Webb III

In 1996, Thomas Webb III became Oklahoma's first DNA exoneree. Webb, who is African American, served fourteen years in prison for the 1982 rape and sodomy of a white female college student named Sarah.[1] The state's case rested on Sarah's eyewitness identification and an expert who testified that hairs recovered at the crime scene were consistent with Webb's.

Ironically, had it not been for O. J. Simpson, Webb might still be in prison. Webb's wife, Gail Snow, learned about DNA testing for the first time in 1995, watching on TV as Barry Scheck, one of the members of Simpson's Dream Team, used it to cast doubt on the reliability of the prosecution's evidence. If DNA could help OJ, Snow reasoned, why not her husband? Snow cashed in her pension to pay a private laboratory to test the semen found on Sarah's bathrobe. The DNA evidence excluded Webb; six months later, after the state performed its own confirmatory test, he was released.[2]

In 1996, DNA exonerations were rare in the United States; in Oklahoma, they were unheard of. The state offered nothing by way of compensation, much less support services. It had no Innocence Project of its own, and Scheck and Neufeld's Innocence Project in New York was not involved in Webb's case. Still, for the first few years, Webb thought he was doing fairly well. He was still in his midthirties, tall and good looking, with a friendly, open demeanor that won people over. And he had Snow, who loved him unconditionally, provided a place to live, and helped him find a good job. "Externally," he says, "I felt like I had moved on. Internally, I still had issues."

In fact, the trauma Webb experienced during his imprisonment and after his release was profound and pervasive. Left untreated, even unspoken of, it spread like a cancer. Other than his wife, Webb had no connection to Oklahoma. He had come there several months before his indictment in Sarah's case for a job opportunity that never panned out. Twenty-one years old, carefree and reckless, he spent his time partying with friends. He also committed several burglaries, selling stolen stereo equipment and using the money to buy alcohol. One led to his arrest and a short stint in the county jail, which is how his mug shot ended up in several photo arrays presented to Sarah.

Webb met Snow, who is white, when her church choir came to sing at his prison. But Snow's family rejected him and disowned her for marrying a black convict. A devout Christian, Snow had developed a churchgoing community of supportive friends, but Webb felt isolated, even freakish, an alien who had arrived from another planet. Webb's own family, who lived in St. Louis, Missouri, stopped speaking to him after he was accused of raping Sarah. They did not attend his trials—the first ended in a hung jury. His mother and sisters never called, wrote, or visited him in prison. His father came once, then not again. None of them got in touch after his release. Webb was never able to understand why his family continued to shun him even after the DNA evidence had proved his innocence. Their rejection, he said, contributed to a feeling that "even though I had gotten out of prison, I was still guilty."

After a few years, Webb became disillusioned, then depressed, ultimately turning to drugs and alcohol to blunt feelings that were too overwhelming to acknowledge, much less directly address. "Once that newness of being released and that gratitude for having my freedom back wore off and life appeared in all of its complexities, I was lost," Webb explained. "I felt like after all the hoopla in the media and the press died down that really, no one cared anymore. 'You're old news now.'"

Webb knew his wife loved him and her intentions were good, but "when I got out, she took over the role of warden. I had to report in, I had to be at a certain place at a certain time, I had to eat a certain thing." Snow's attempts to impose boundaries and structure, he said, felt like house arrest. He knew she was just trying to protect and help him, but "it had the opposite effect, it made me run away." He began staying out all night, then for days at a time. He had one affair, then another.

Despite the strain on their marriage, Snow and Webb worked together to lobby Oklahoma legislators to pass a wrongful conviction compensation statute. In 2003, after several failed attempts, Democratic governor Brad Henry signed a bill that allowed exonerees to receive a total of $175,000.[3] But despite the fact that Webb was, literally, the poster child for the bill—he and Snow were at the state capital when it passed, receiving plaudits from members of the assembly—Webb's application was denied. In a short letter, then attorney general Drew Edmondson informed him that the law was not retroactive.[4]

At that point, Webb lost all hope. The attorney general's letter was the final sucker punch in a fight that had been rigged from the outset. The message was clear, Webb said: "'We don't have any intention of trying to make amends. You are on your own.' And that was how I felt during that whole fourteen years; that I was on my own, that everyone gave up on me. That I was not worthy to be considered for justice." The state's refusal to pay him a dime, much less offer an apology, reinforced that feeling to a soul-deadening degree. Webb's addiction to alcohol and methamphetamines spiraled out of control. He lost his job and became homeless. He spent the next ten years alternating between living out of his car, crashing with friends, and occasionally convincing Snow to take him back in before she finally divorced him in 2010.

Sarah

One of three girls from a striving family, Sarah was excited to be a college student at the University of Oklahoma in Norman, living on her own in a small ground-floor apartment and working part-time at a shoe store. "I wanted to make something of myself," she said. Small and slight with long hair and large brown eyes, Sarah had always loved children, and she hoped to go on to get her teacher's certificate. The rape destroyed that ambition and, more essentially, her belief that she could accomplish anything at all.

Sarah was attacked during her third year in school. On March 20, 1982, someone removed the screen from one of her windows and broke in a little before 1 a.m. Sarah heard a noise, got up to investigate, and saw a black man in her living room. He came toward her quickly, covering her nose and mouth with his hand. Holding a knife to her throat, he forced her back into the bedroom. Pushing her down on the bed, he shoved his penis into her mouth. "Don't even think about biting down," he told her. Afterward, Sarah said, "He raped me and I just left my body as he was raping me. I was just thinking, this is the easy part, because then he was going to kill me." Sarah's dog, barking frantically, jumped out of the window.

The man stayed in Sarah's apartment for some time. For a while, he lay on the foot of her bed, just talking to her. Sarah, pressed up against her headboard, grabbed a pillow to cover herself, and he ripped it away. Eventually, he pulled her up from the bed and forced her back into the living room, demanding to know if she had any guns or items of value. He ordered her to open the front door to let him out, as if he were an invited guest. As she stood, naked and shaking in the doorway, calling for her dog, he turned back to look at her. "If you call the police," he said, "I will come back and kill you."

In hysterics, Sarah called her boyfriend, who summoned the police. A female officer drove her to the hospital, where a rape kit was done. The next day, Sarah went to the police station, where she looked at photo arrays. When she saw Thomas Webb's picture, Sarah said, "I remember thinking, he looked like the man who raped me. I was alone in this little room. I turned the picture over, and the physical description of Thomas was just identical to everything I had given the police—height, weight. It all added up in my head that this was the man, and I thought that I had identified him, you know, the correct person."

Webb's conviction and sixty-year prison sentence brought little relief. Crippled by anxiety and depression, Sarah dropped out of school. She became suicidal and had to be hospitalized several times in a psychiatric ward where she was heavily medicated. During one of those hospitalizations, a male doctor performed a pelvic examination for no apparent reason. Afterward, he told her she was "dirty" from the rape and that she would never have children. "I just remember lying there staring out the window at the darkness, wondering why there was no nurse with him," Sarah said.

Sarah's father paid for her medical and psychological treatment, but Sarah did not feel that she could turn to him or to her mother for emotional support: "I didn't have the type of parents that kids have today where they can just talk, and the parent is your friend and you can express your feelings and emotions. I didn't grow up like that. You mind. You say, 'Yes, sir,' and 'Yes, ma'am.' You got in big trouble if you did something wrong. It just wasn't the type of situation where I felt really comfortable discussing much of anything."

Several years after the rape, Sarah followed a boyfriend to Baton Rouge, Louisiana, but she returned to Oklahoma City when the relationship ended. In 1985, she met John, a quiet man eleven years her senior. After fifteen years of living together, they got married in 2000. She described John as "my everything," a gentle person who provided for her, protected her, and took care of her. Still, she said, the feeling of imminent danger "doesn't stop, doesn't go away. I am the kind of person who wakes up in the middle of the night and walks around. I am never comfortable at night, never still." The couple lived an extremely private life, rarely going out or socializing. Over the years, Sarah has worked sporadically, holding down a few temporary office jobs and also caring for a neighbor's baby. She and John have never been able to have children.

In 2004, at the age of forty-two, Sarah began to have problems with her heart, and doctors inserted a stent. Several years later, she went into cardiac arrest and spent weeks in the hospital. Heart problems run in the family—Sarah's father had triple-bypass surgery and died of a heart attack in 2003—and Sarah has smoked cigarettes. But she believes that the years of accumulated fear and stress is what is really killing her: "I don't expect to live a long life."

When Sarah found out that Webb had been released because DNA evidence had exonerated him, she went into a state of denial, at first continuing to insist that he was guilty. Then came acceptance and, with it, unbearable guilt and self-blame. After learning that Webb and Snow were trying to get money from the state, Sarah looked up their number in the phone book and called their house. Snow answered, and the two women talked for hours; Sarah did not ask to talk to Webb and Snow did not offer. A second conversation followed, after Snow and Webb had split up. At one point, Snow said in a tone of frustration, "What do you want from me?" It caught Sarah off guard. "I don't want anything," she said. "I just called to say hello." She never called again.

During one of my first conversations with Sarah, in July 2015, she told me, "I wish now that I had never called the police. If I could go back in time; I wish I had never told a soul, because it has been a hellacious life and even worse for Thomas. If I had been right, I would feel differently.

But because I was wrong, I wish I had told no one and lived with it. If I had, I wonder what life would have been like for both me and Thomas."

Christy Sheppard

Christy Lucas Sheppard was eight years old in 1982 when her cousin, Debbie Sue Carter, twenty-one, was brutally raped and murdered in her apartment in Ada, a small town in Oklahoma. The Carters and the Lucases were very close: Sheppard's mother, Glenna, and Debbie's mother, Peggy, were sisters. Sheppard, whose parents were divorced, was deeply attached to Peggy, and "in awe" of Debbie. She used to sit on the edge of Debbie's bed, watching with fascination as her pretty, dark-haired, older cousin applied mascara before going out at night, impossibly glamorous and self-assured. Debbie's violent, horrible death struck with the unexpected ferocity of lightning.

Peggy began drinking heavily within months of the funeral. "She led a double life," Sheppard said. "She would work all day and then go home, drive around and drink and cry." Once, late at night, Peggy came to her sister's house, falling down drunk. There were leaves in her hair, dirt on her clothes. She told Glenna that she had been out to the cemetery to visit her daughter's grave. "I know she's not there," Peggy said, "but that was the body that was in my body. I bathed that body. I brushed that hair. It's my only connection."

Over the years, the case became a monstrosity, deforming the lives of Debbie's family members like an extra body part. The murder remained unsolved for five years, until a woman arrested for fraud implicated Ron Williamson, who also happened to be in the jail. The state also charged Dennis Fritz as Williamson's accomplice, using the same so-called hair science evidence that had been used against Thomas Webb, as well as the testimony of a jailhouse informant. It was a high-profile case: the murder of a pretty white girl was sensational enough in and of itself, and Williamson—who like Fritz, was Caucasian—had been a baseball star with real prospects for a major league career before drug use and mental illness engulfed him. The nonstop media coverage was yet another source of stress for Debbie's family, all of whom felt increasingly sidelined and powerless as the case moved from investigation to prosecution. Sheppard explained, "From the victim's standpoint, it's no longer your case. It's the state's case.

For a rape victim, her body isn't even her body anymore; it's a piece of evidence. Even the name of the case belongs to the perpetrator. Debbie was literally erased."

Before the case went to trial, the state determined that Debbie's body had to be exhumed for further testing. Asked to sign the consent form, Peggy "lost her mind," Sheppard says, believing that she would get to hold and touch her daughter again. Sheppard's mother had Peggy committed to an institution. Afterward, Glenna told Peggy, "I can't do this anymore. I can't relive this with you every day. I love you, but I can't do this. I have a child to raise."

In 1988, the jurors returned guilty verdicts against the defendants. Williamson was given the death penalty; Fritz, life in prison without the possibility of parole. What Sheppard felt for them, she said, was "true hatred. We were all disappointed that Dennis didn't get the death penalty, too." She went to bed at night praying that they would suffer as much as possible.

Sheppard remained in Ada as an adult. She married her high school boyfriend, Dustin, and became a licensed professional counselor who specialized in helping broken families. Sheppard stuck close to her own family, particularly Peggy. Now the mother of three, blonde and still cheerleader pretty, Sheppard exudes warmth. She stands only four feet ten, but she is tough and implacably determined to steamroll over any obstacle in her path. She is also blunt about the impact of the case on her own choices: "What happened to Debbie—to say that it did not shape me personally and professionally? Come on, it's obvious."

In 1999, when Sheppard was twenty-five and pregnant with her first child, her mother called to say that the newspapers planned to print a story that Williamson and Fritz were about to be exonerated by DNA evidence. Sheppard was shocked and then outraged: no one from the prosecutor's office had told any member of the family.

As it turned out, the judge had placed all of the parties under a gag order, so Sheppard learned the details for the first time sitting in the courtroom as the judge explained that there had been a terrible mistake. DNA evidence recovered from Debbie's body matched that of one of the state's key witnesses, a man named Glen Gore.

Peggy and her surviving daughters sat with Sheppard and Glenna, staring in disbelief as Williamson and Fritz walked out of the courtroom flanked by Barry Scheck and the other Innocence Project lawyers, trailed by a horde of flashing cameras and breathless reporters. It was only then that the prosecutors took Debbie's family to a separate room to provide the details, including, "Oh, by the way, Glen Gore escaped from prison and was on the run." Head District Attorney Bill Peterson added to the family's confusion, continuing to insist that Williamson and Fritz were somehow involved and promising, "We'll figure this out." It took the family several years to accept that Williamson and Fritz were innocent.

In early 2005, the author John Grisham came to Ada to research what later became his bestselling nonfiction book, *The Innocent Man*, which focused mainly on the tragic arc of Ron Williamson's life and the dubious tactics the prosecutors had used to convict him and Fritz. Williamson, who, at one point, had been five days away from being executed, sued the state and won a settlement after his release. But he never recovered, continuing to drink and suffer from mental illness.[5]

Williamson told the *New York Times* in 2000:

> No matter what happens to you, you are constantly under this eye of distrust that you never can shake. I walked into a supermarket in town and a lady picked up her child. The little girl said, "That's the guy who was on the TV, Mommy." She rushed over and grabbed her child and said, "Don't go near him." I just left my stuff and walked out. It never, ever ends. It never ends. It never ends. It never will be ended.[6]

Sheppard agreed to be interviewed by Grisham and used the renewed attention on Debbie's case as a way of educating herself. She read everything she could find about the case, studying court documents and asking Grisham plenty of questions of her own. Learning the full extent of the injustice—that the police and prosecutors relied on junk science and lies to win the convictions of Williamson and Fritz, including the testimony of the real killer—"was so disheartening and so sad."

Williamson died of cirrhosis of the liver in 2004, before Grisham's book was published. He was only fifty-one. In the years before Williamson passed away, he reached out to Peggy, calling her at home unexpectedly one day. "Is this Peggy Carter?" he asked, and when she said yes, he said, "This is Ronnie Williamson. I want you to know I didn't kill your daughter."

"I know you didn't," Peggy replied. Sheppard said the conversation opened the door to a connection of sorts, where Williamson would call Peggy up from time to time and they would chat. Neither of them mentioned the relationship to anyone, and when Peggy called Williamson's sisters, Renee and Annette, to pay her condolences, Sheppard said, "They were just blown away. There were no words to describe how they felt."

One year earlier, in 2003, Glen Gore was convicted of Debbie's rape and murder and given a death sentence, but the Oklahoma Court of Appeals threw out the verdict, finding that Gore had been denied a fair trial.[7] Gore was convicted again in 2006 and sentenced to life without the possibility of parole. Sheppard felt none of the vitriol toward Gore that she previously directed at Williamson and Fritz. "If there is one thing I've learned," she said, "it's that I would never be stupid enough to say that I was 100 percent sure about anything." Sheppard was "fairly confident" that Gore was guilty, "but to me, it's just more sadness." She has regularly run into Gore's mother, whose grandchildren attend the same school as Sheppard's. Looking at the now-elderly woman, Sheppard sees a fellow victim: "I just feel sad for her."

Beverly and Katie Monroe

In the spring of 1992, Beverly Monroe was fifty-four years old and enjoying life to the fullest. Her three children were thriving: her daughter Katie had just graduated from the prestigious University of Virginia School of Law and her other two children, Shannon and Gavin, were in college. Beverly, an attractive, vibrant woman with a master's degree in organic chemistry, had built a satisfying and solidly upper-middle-class life in the suburbs outside of Richmond, Virginia, where she had worked for ten years in a patent office. Divorced from the father of her children, Beverly had a longtime boyfriend, Roger de la Burde, an entrepreneur and art collector who made no secret of his great wealth, living in a mansion on a 220-acre farm where he kept horses.

De la Burde was charming, but he had a dark side: paranoia caused him to lash out at those closest to him. He was narcissistic but also prone to bouts of anxiety and depression, and rumors constantly circulated that he lied about his lineage, falsely claiming an aristocratic heritage, and engaged in fraudulent business practices. He was also unfaithful, having a number of affairs during the course of his relationship with Beverly, including with a much younger woman whom he had recently impregnated.

Beverly and de la Burde's neighbor discovered de la Burde's body on the morning of March 5, 1992. De la Burde was lying on a couch, dead of a single gunshot wound to the forehead, his own gun lying beside him. The sheriff's department and the local medical examiner initially concluded de la Burde had committed suicide and did not treat the room as a crime scene. But Dave Riley, the state police officer assigned to look into the case, quickly became convinced that de la Burde had been murdered and Beverly was the obvious suspect. Under the guise of investigating the case as a suicide, he convinced her to waive her right to an attorney and, after a lengthy interrogation, tried to convince her that she had still been with de la Burde when he committed suicide and suppressed the memory of it, instead of leaving earlier when he was still alive, as she had reported. Later, after pressuring her with murder charges, Riley convinced her to sign a statement he had written to that effect: that she had been asleep on the couch in the same room as de la Burde when he shot himself, then blocked out the memory due to trauma.

Within months, Beverly was indicted and convicted of first-degree murder. The trial was big news in Virginia, as de la Burde was notorious in the community and his private life was the subject of much gossip and speculation. The prosecution argued that Beverly plotted and carried out the killing to ensure her place in his will and to exact revenge for his most recent infidelity. Beverly's lawyer put on a vigorous defense. A slew of character witnesses testified, a purchase receipt was put into evidence showing that she was miles away at a grocery store, and a witness testified to seeing her there. Gavin confirmed that she slept at home that night. But the jury was unconvinced. Instead, they credited Beverly's admission to Riley and a forensic expert who said that the placement of the gun meant that de la Burde could not have shot himself. They also relied on the testimony of a convicted felon, who claimed Beverly tried to buy an untraceable handgun months earlier.

On December 22, 1992, Beverly Monroe was sentenced to twenty-two years in prison, but four months later the family was able to secure Beverly's release on bail while her appeal was pending. In the fall, her daughter Katie began a job with the US Commission on Civil Rights in Washington, DC. At the time, Katie truly believed that her mother's conviction would be overturned, and the family, hemorrhaging money, needed the income. But Beverly lost in the Virginia Court of Appeals and again in the Virginia Supreme Court. In January 1996, she was sent back to prison.

Katie Monroe promptly quit her job and devoted the next eight years of her life to freeing her mother—digesting treatises on the law of habeas corpus as she sought to undo the conviction through what is known as a "collateral attack"—that is, a long-odds petition claiming that the prisoner must be released because her trial violated basic constitutional principles.

An effort that started with the support of a single law school friend gained momentum as friends, church members, neighbors, and other lawyers came aboard. Beverly called them her "band of warriors." Five years later, Beverly, Katie, and the warriors had uncovered evidence hidden by the prosecution, including a secret deal with the convicted felon witness, a statement by the neighbor that he had moved the gun after discovering the body, and a report from the state medical examiner's office, which, in contrast to the local medical examiner, had ruled the death a suicide.

But it was not until Beverly's case came before federal judge Richard L. Williams in 1998 that her luck began to change. Judge Williams credited some of the new information and allowed Beverly's legal team to depose witnesses, bringing even more exculpatory information to light, including Dave Riley's coercive and manipulative tactics in interrogating Beverly. In 2002, Judge Williams ruled that the hidden evidence fatally infected the conviction and overturned it. It was the first time in more than thirty years on the bench that he had ever granted a habeas petition. The state appealed, insisting that Beverly was guilty. Judge Williams released Beverly on bail, but she spent another year in limbo before the United States Court of Appeals for the Fourth Circuit affirmed the decision in 2003, holding that "it is impossible to say that Beverly Monroe got a fair trial."[8]

For Beverly, Katie, and their family, the legal resolution was an enormous relief but far from a panacea. When I interviewed Katie and Beverly in November 2016, we met at the comfortable, sun-filled northern Virginia home that Katie, now fifty-one, shared with her longtime boyfriend. Beverly, who had remarried, drove over from her house, which is nearby. Katie, who was dressed casually in cargo pants and a long-sleeved T-shirt, has long dark hair, heavy bangs, and a heart-shaped face. Beverly, now

seventy-eight, was wearing dark slacks and a dark shirt, her haircut styl-
ishly short. Both women look younger than their ages, though Beverly is
painfully thin. Katie speaks in full, fluid paragraphs; Beverly, more slowly
and with painstaking care over her choice of words.

The bond between mother and daughter was a palpable force in the
room. But so, too, was the wrongful conviction and its lingering effects.
It had redrawn the map of their lives. "Financially," Beverly said, "it was a
disaster." After her release from prison, she could not find a job. Though
Beverly was no longer a convicted murderer, for many, she was forever
tainted, both by lingering doubts about her culpability and by the notoriety of her case. And she was released at the age of sixty-six, when most people are retired. But Beverly needed a job: she had used up her savings and
sold her house to pay her legal bills. And she had health problems. As the
result of stress and bad nutrition, Beverly had developed high cholesterol
and osteoporosis. She had no money left: not for rent, health insurance,
or dental care. For the first year, she lived off and on with Katie and her
younger daughter, Shannon, moving constantly and never feeling at home.

Beverly remained haunted by what she had seen and experienced
during her six years in prison. Early one Saturday morning in the spring
of 1996, she watched as a forty-year-old inmate, Tina, collapsed and
died on a concrete floor. The prison had no hospital or medical personnel on site. When another inmate, who was a trained nurse, tried
to give Tina CPR, she was forcibly restrained. An hour passed before
an ambulance was called. Beverly later learned the cause of death was
a brain aneurysm. Beverly tried to tell herself that nothing could have
been done to change the outcome, but the inescapable fact was that the
woman "had been left to die."

Beverly herself became seriously ill, contracting hepatitis A from fecal
matter in the food prepared by infected inmates who worked in the prison
kitchen. It was months before she was diagnosed. She became debilitated,
feverish, nauseous, wracked by joint pain but unable to lie down on her
bunk during the day because of prison rules. It was weeks before she saw
a doctor, which required being shackled and loaded into a van at dawn to
go to a hospital at a men's prison miles away.

Contamination was not the only problem. Katie says, "Mom was starv-
ing in prison. There was not enough food, and the food that was there was
inedible." More than anything, Beverly craved vegetables, looking forward

to the days where she got two slivers of raw carrot with her meal. With a smile, Beverly said that on her fifty-ninth birthday, "Mrs. Hawkins, who ran the cafeteria, gave me a double paper plate with aluminum over it, and I get to my place at the table and I took off the foil and it was a whole plate of fresh asparagus." Beverly described the thin green spears as akin to a small miracle: "It was like something had fallen out of the sky." These and other similar moments of kindness gave her strength, as did what she called the "resilience by the women" who refused to let prison make them ugly or indistinguishable: "They would wake up and iron pleats into their blouses, and there was always lots of hair styling."

Almost all of the inmates were poorly educated. Because Beverly was older and kind, she became something of a role model and gained the trust of the prison staff. The prison had no library, but Beverly was allowed to teach classes in science and basic math, which she said gave her days structure and purpose. As much as she could, Beverly emotionally divested from her case by viewing it objectively, analyzing it in the same way she had when she was a chemist confronting a particularly daunting data assessment assignment at her old job. She tried to make up for the loss of the daily pleasures that gave meaning to her life—playing her piano, listening to music, reading poetry, and dancing—by using her memory to relive those experiences. She listened to the music in her head and trained herself to memorize poems, which she quietly recited in the brief moments when she was alone.

Some horrors, though, proved impossible to wall off. In addition to physical problems, many of the inmates had serious mental health issues, which some of the guards exploited. Enforcement of the rules varied wildly depending on who was in charge, and periodically, the guards would confiscate the inmate's property for no apparent reason. She recounted:

> There was one woman who was fairly young and attractive and they took boxes of maxi pads out of her cell and just confiscated them. They told her, "You have too many." This young woman, she refused to come out of her room; it was over the maxi pads. She literally went crazy on the spot and ended up in what we called the Dungeon, officially Cottage 3. It was just cells with bars and we would hear the electric door click. They put a lot of women in there who had mental issues and they screamed and screamed and screamed.

As she told me this story, Beverly's eyes filled with tears and her body shook. We stopped the interview while she went into another room.

Another profound loss was Beverly's faith in the criminal justice system. "If anyone involved had been honest and straight and interested in the truth, this never would have happened," she said. "I thought, well, once we show them everything we had found, they would change their minds." But the state fought to preserve the conviction to the bitter end, in a legal war that dragged on for eleven years. She said, "To realize that, in fact, they were actively resisting the truth, it was frightening. That is when I knew that evidence and logic and truth do not matter."

Katie handled the stress by treating the fight for her mother's exoneration like a regular job. Unless there was a pending deadline, she would be at her desk in her home office at 9 a.m., breaking for lunch and clocking off at 6 p.m. But she put the rest of her life on pause. Katie fell in love with a man named Andy, but they did not get married: "I couldn't imagine doing it with his parents there and my mother not present." When Katie became pregnant and gave birth to a son, Asher, in 1998, it was a source of joy. At the same time, Asher's existence brought the daily humiliations and long-term consequences of her mother's incarceration into sharp relief.

Katie visited her mother every week at the prison, and Asher went with her. She said, "I had to breastfeed him in that awful visitor's bathroom that had a toilet with no rim and roaches on the wall." Katie thought she had become inured to the strip searches, but watching as the same guards removed the diaper from her naked baby, Katie felt utterly wretched. The visits with her mother and son took on a kind of rhythm after a while, with Beverly reading him stories and Asher watching in fascination as popcorn Katie bought from the prison vending machines popped in the microwave. But the rhythm itself was unnerving, particularly as Asher got older and more aware of his surroundings. "Once we pulled into the prison, and Asher said, 'Mimi's house,'" Katie said. "That made me really angry."

Once Judge Williams granted the petition in 2002 and ordered Beverly released on bond, Katie and her siblings were anxious to put everything behind them and catch up on what they had missed: time together. There was the initial excitement and buzz of activity, but also anxiety followed by grief. "In some ways, that was the worst year," Katie explained, "because Mom was finally home but then the state appealed and it was like 'Why can't you leave our family alone. We had all the proof in the world and she had been in prison for seven years?'" Then Beverly's beloved mother died of a sudden illness just a few months after Beverly was released.

When the case finally ended with the Court of Appeals decision in 2003, the Monroes "came out of combat mode and into triage mode," focused on finding Beverly health benefits, a job, and a place to live. It took years. "You try to live as presently as possible but something catches up with you after a while," Katie says, "which is all the pain and suffering you didn't deal with. There was a desperation to get your old life back and live as normally as possible. It takes a while to set in, that you are not going to get your old life back."

Both Beverly and Katie say they feel "very lucky." Without Judge Williams and the band of warriors, Beverly would likely have died in custody. Compared with many exonerees, the time Beverly spent in prison was relatively short, and there was no physical violence. But in the years since her release, Beverly has found that many of the things she used to enjoy make her feel empty. "I can't read fiction anymore because it seems trivial," she says. "I have tried to watch a little of the World Series, and I can't watch it anymore. I go to the football game at William & Mary and I think, 'This just doesn't matter.' There's this huge stadium. I want to build a stadium full of people who care about justice and science."

Beverly doesn't play the piano anymore. She is retired now, from a part-time, low-wage job she held for seven years with a land conservation nonprofit, yet she feels as if there is not enough time. She spends hours reading about wrongful conviction cases and worrying about the people who are still in prison. "I am driven by a need to fix things and respond to things and I don't have the measure of order and peace necessary to sit down and play," she said, pointing to her head. "I don't have the same access. Before the case, my life had a cadence to it that allowed me to do those things, and I never got that cadence back."

The loss of order and peace that Beverly describes is one of the abiding wounds inflicted by a wrongful conviction. Beverly grew up believing that the American system of justice—and the police, lawyers, judges, and jurors who work within it—was fundamentally decent and rational, only to learn in the most visceral way imaginable that it was arbitrary and cruel.

Beverly's expressions of isolation, bewilderment, and anguish are shared by Webb, Sarah, Sheppard, Williamson, Katie, and so many others like them who are struggling to recover from this profound trauma. While the crimes that shattered their lives happened thousands of miles apart and in different decades, the repercussions have a familiar rhythm. There is the life-upending violation—be it the victimization or false arrest. There is the result—conviction, removal from civilized society, and the leaden certainty of an ending. When the truth erupts with all of its outsized consequences, exposing a system that is rife with venality, bias, and cruelty, the revelations are not freeing. A wrongful conviction is a psychological prison for everyone snagged in its net. The question is how to get out.

CHAPTER EIGHT

Reframing Harm and Accountability

RESTORATIVE JUSTICE IS a centuries-old approach that seeks to empower people to address the harms, needs, and obligations that arise when a crime has been committed by bringing together victims, offenders, and members of their respective communities. The face-to-face open-dialogue process is focused on personal accountability and reparations; it is achieved when victims and offenders share deeply personal and painful life experiences with the least likely person in the world—each other. Restorative justice requires its participants to lay bare feelings of self-loathing, suffering, rage, loneliness, and rejection that they have hidden from the world and often from themselves. They must face reckonings they have long resisted.

Victims may ask offenders questions and gather information about the crime; they describe the particulars of their suffering, how they have come to this point and place in their lives, and what they need to move forward. Offenders answer questions and, in facing up to what they have done, delve deeply into their own pasts, which are often rife with deprivation and abuse. Together, the parties agree upon a series of remedial measures designed to bring about peace and progress rather than meting out punishment.

The Anglo-American legal system, which is fundamentally adversarial, asks three basic questions: what law was broken, who broke it, and what punishment is deserved? Restorative justice, which focuses on rebuilding lives and communities, asks three similar questions in a radically different way: who was harmed, what are their needs, and whose obligation is it to meet those needs?

Howard Zehr has done more than anyone to bring the principles and practices of restorative justice into mainstream American thinking about crime through his teaching, writing, and advocacy. In his book *Changing Lenses: Restorative Justice for Our Times*, Zehr explains that restorative justice is in many respects the polar opposite of the "state justice" to which Americans are accustomed, where, "legally, the question of guilt is an either-or question. Degrees of severity of the offense may vary, but in the end there are no degrees of guilt. One is guilty or not guilty. Someone must win, and someone must lose."[1]

"Guilt," Zehr writes, "adheres to a person more or less permanently, with few known solvents." It reduces the offender to his worst act. Offense and identity merge: he is a fraudster, a robber, a murderer. Even prisoners who have served out their sentences cannot escape the label—they are ex-cons. At the same time, the mechanics of the adversarial system create a process in which "the victim of the crime was redefined, with the state becoming the legal victim. Victims were abstracted, and individuals become peripheral to the problem or the solution."[2]

Much has been said about the failures of the American criminal justice system: the mass incarceration, particularly of young men of color; the lasting legal stigma upon release; the decimation of families by crime and by the loss of their young men to prison; high recidivism rates; the sidelining and alienation of victims. Restorative justice recognizes the failures of that system and aims to correct them through the active involvement and empowerment of those harmed most directly, a group broadly defined as victims, offenders, their family members, and others in the community.

Zehr said, "I think about restorative justice as a philosophy and do not assume I will use a particular model from the start." There are many different ways to practice the philosophy, tailored to the particular circumstances of the case and the individuals involved. An offender and victim may come face-to-face in a meeting with a trained facilitator or third party. Rather than jail an offender, judges can order facilitators to preside over family conferences where mothers, fathers, and siblings address the offending family member with the goal of reintegrating the person into the fold. There are healing circles in schools, workplaces, retreats, and community centers. In these settings, a broad range of participants come together to engage in activities and exercises that explore the causes of harmful behavior and its effects. The group as a whole determines what the reparations will be.

Often, restorative justice is an adjunct to the criminal process or occurs years after that process has concluded. But, in some cases, it is an alternative to the criminal process. There are few predetermined expectations other than open-minded and full-throated participation by all sides and a commitment to accountability by the offender. Zehr is emphatic that "we don't impose a goal of forgiveness. People feel that pressure anyway—victims get it all the time—pressure to forgive." He told me, "There are so many misunderstandings about what forgiveness is: that if you forgive, that means you are not holding people accountable or forgetting about the harm that was done to you." But the victims who do forgive, he said, talk about it as a kind of personal liberation, a gift as much to themselves as to the offenders. Although most restorative justice programs are not overtly religious, for some, it is a profoundly spiritual experience. They describe participating in a restorative justice process as one of the most intense and life-altering experiences of their lives.

These concepts are foreign to most Americans, who are accustomed to a justice system modeled on retribution and just deserts, usually in the form of lengthy prison sentences and permanent social ostracism. Yet, restorative justice was practiced for centuries on our soil by Native Americans, and it is popular in other countries. Beginning in the 1970s, it was rediscovered by activists such as Zehr who were searching for ways to reform the system in the United States. Over the years, restorative justice has slowly gained a certain level of acceptance in pockets of the country. Today, it is used in a small number of jurisdictions across the US, and pilot programs have launched in others, with the hope that a show of successful results will allow it to gain a permanent foothold.

South Africa's Truth and Reconciliation Commission

Usually, restorative justice happens in a private or semiprivate space that recognizes the abject vulnerability of the participants, but it can also occur in a public forum. The most famous example is South Africa's Truth and Reconciliation Commission, which brought survivors of apartheid face-to-face with their oppressors.[3]

Apartheid—the forcible separation of the black and white races under the iron rule of the white supremacist National Party—began in South Africa in 1948 and did not end until 1990. During that time, tens of thousands of black South Africans were robbed of basic civil rights and human dignity: barred from voting, education, and all but the most menial jobs, and forced to live in overcrowded, squalid camps. Those who resisted the apartheid system were routinely abducted, imprisoned, tortured, and killed. The Truth and Reconciliation Commission, or TRC, was the result of negotiations between the National Party and the African National Congress as a condition of a peaceful transfer of power.

The TRC began its work in 1995, after the famous political prisoner Nelson Mandela was elected president and black people assumed control over their country through a parliamentary majority. Under a law called the Promotion of National Unity and Reconciliation Act, the TRC was established to investigate human rights abuses that had transpired under apartheid from 1960 to 1994. The preamble of the act stated that "the pursuit of national unity, the well-being of all South African citizens and peace require reconciliation." Before that could happen, however, "it is deemed necessary to establish the truth in relation to past events as well as the motives for and circumstances in which gross violations of human rights have occurred, and to make the findings known."[4]

The TRC's purpose was threefold: to hold formal public hearings where any victim of apartheid and any perpetrator could testify, to grant amnesty to those who qualified by telling the complete truth about their crimes, and to make reparations to the victims. Archbishop Desmond Tutu, who had won the Nobel Peace Prize and was a powerful and outspoken critic of the old regime, was selected to chair the commission. Of the most controversial aspect of the TRC's mandate, the granting of amnesty, Tutu said,

> Certainly, amnesty cannot be viewed as justice if we think of justice only as retributive and punitive in nature. We believe, however, that there is another kind of justice—a restorative justice which is concerned not so much with punishment as with correcting imbalances, restoring broken relationships—with healing, harmony, and reconciliation.[5]

In the end, approximately twenty-two thousand victims, witnesses, and perpetrators submitted written statements. Two thousand people appeared in person before the commission in Cape Town to give searing testimony about the devastating impact of the apartheid regime on their lives. The testimony of the victims—and some of the thousands of offenders seeking amnesty—was broadcast on the radio and on national television.

The TRC hearings riveted the nation and captured the attention of many leaders around the world. Campaigning in her unsuccessful bid for the presidency in 2016, Hillary Clinton praised the TRC as:

> just an astonishing leap of faith, to bring together those who had been oppressed by Apartheid, often physically abused, imprisoned, members of families whose loved ones had been murdered, with their oppressors, their abusers, their murderers, in a process that truly was a national effort to try to forgive enough that the country could be held together, that the nation could be born, that the work could begin. It was to me a stunning example of what is possible.[6]

The TRC was not without its detractors. Many were dismayed by the grants of amnesty to some of the worst offenders, the government's rather meager monetary awards to the victims, and the delay in giving out those awards. But the work of the TRC—both the recorded testimony and the evidence gathered in a comprehensive report prepared by the commission—is widely regarded as groundbreaking in its scope and ambition. It was a turning point in South African's history, essential to the ability of a divided nation to heal and to move forward without massive and destabilizing outbreaks of racially and politically motivated violence.

Juvenile Justice in New Zealand

In New Zealand, restorative justice has become an integral part of the juvenile justice system. If the youth denies the charges, he is entitled to an attorney and a hearing. But if he admits to wrongdoing—which is nearly always the case—the default option is a family conference presided over by trained state employees called youth justice coordinators. The youth participates in the conference with his family members; more often than not, the victim, the victim's family, and community members also participate.

Former New Zealand District Court judge Fred W. M. McElrea helped implement restorative justice practices when they became law under the Children, Young Persons, and Their Families Act of 1989.[7] He has since become a de facto ambassador for this method. In a 2012 article in *Tikkun* magazine, McElrea wrote that in the twenty-five years since the law was enacted, more than a hundred thousand conferences have been held with a "massive reduction in custodial outcomes," leading to significant fiscal savings for the country as well as better outcomes for the involved parties, who "pursue consensus about outcomes among those affected" rather than being told what the end result will be.[8]

New Zealand has also taken steps to implement restorative justice practices in the adult criminal justice system in several pilot programs, but only at the sentencing phase of court proceedings. McElrea's *Tikkun* article notes that while there is institutionalized resistance by many in law enforcement toward dispensing with a more retributive model, preliminary studies of the use of restorative justice in adult cases are encouraging, indicating that victims are more satisfied with the adjudicatory process and that recidivism rates are lower. Perhaps in recognition of these studies, the New Zealand government has continued to fund these programs.

An Antidote to the School-to-Prison Pipeline

The United States, with its emphasis on retribution and punishment, has been slow to embrace restorative justice, although it has a foothold in isolated parts of the country. Across the Bay from San Francisco, the Oakland Unified School District (OUSD) has instituted restorative justice programs in nearly half of its eighty-six schools in collaboration with the nonprofit Restorative Justice Oakland Youth (RJOY). In reaction to an alarmingly high suspension rate among its black and Latino students, and concerns that harsh discipline was sending them down the school-to-prison pipeline, the OUSD-RJOY collaboration began to use healing circles in middle and high schools in 2007 and 2008. Students who committed offenses had to face the students they harmed, their parents, and other community members.

In 2013, Cedric, an African American sixteen-year-old, was required to participate in a restorative justice circle as a condition of his acceptance into Oakland's Ralph J. Bunche Academy. He had just spent ten months in a juvenile justice camp for bringing a loaded gun to his previous school, which went off in the middle of class. Cedric's receptivity to the restorative justice circle weighed heavily in deciding whether to admit him to Bunche.

Cedric freely admitted that he was unhappy about having to sit in a circle with his parents, the school's principal, a psychologist, teachers, and peer mentors and talk about the pain he had caused to other people or the deprivation and harm he had experienced himself. The prospect, Cedric said, "made me feel like walking out the damn room." But he did it.[9]

As with most circles, a "talking piece" was passed around the room; only the person holding it could speak. As Cedric, his mother, and his stepfather spoke, it became clear that Cedric felt driven to commit crimes to provide his mother, who could not find a job, with money to pay the rent. "I probably wouldn't be into this if she wasn't struggling," Cedric said. "I just did it because my family needed it." In talking about her own struggles, Cedric's mother broke down in tears. Cedric swiped clumsily and repeatedly at his own eyes.

Over and over, when it was their turn, the adults in the room told Cedric they loved him and supported him, urging him to accept their help and tell them what he needed to do better. Eric Butler, who facilitated the circle and worked as RJOY's school coordinator at Bunche, addressed Cedric directly, saying, "I will be your brother, I will be your uncle, I got your back. I got stuff for you. Come and get it. And I say this in front of everybody because if I don't, I need all these people to hold me accountable." In the closing round of the circle, Butler led the group in writing out a life plan for Cedric on a whiteboard, and the group agreed to reconvene in thirty days. Butler said, "Next time we meet, we gonna celebrate."[10] When I spoke to Butler about Cedric four years later, Butler told me that Cedric had been admitted to Bunche, had graduated, and was now working in the construction industry.

The use of restorative justice as an alternative to traditional discipline in disadvantaged public high schools has its critics. In Los Angeles and Fresno, California; Des Moines, Iowa; and New York City, teachers have publicly protested, stating that the programs were not well designed or consistently applied, leaving the worst-behaved students to believe that they could physically and verbally abuse their peers and teachers without suffering any real consequence. In such an unsafe and disruptive environment, they said, real learning was more difficult than ever.[11]

Fania E. Davis, the cofounder and executive director of RJOY, says, "There must be a mindful, rigorous approach to implementation. We have seen cases where a school district will decide to stop suspending students and use restorative justice, but they haven't created an infrastructure or trained the right people to come in and oversee the work." It cannot be, she says, a "cookie-cutter approach" but rather a process that grows organically from the ground up. "In Oakland," she said, "we started at just one school" putting together general practices and tailoring them to meet the particular needs of other schools in the district.

In January 2015, the OUSD announced that it would incorporate restorative justice practices into all of its schools by 2020, based on results of the participating schools, which showed sharp drops in truancy and suspensions, while test scores and graduation rates rose as much as 60 percent. Davis says that RJOY "worked ourselves out of a job." Her nonprofit is now focused on implementing a strategic plan approved years earlier by judges, prosecutors, public defenders, court personnel, and probation officers to convert the juvenile justice system entirely to a restorative system, similar to the one that exists in New Zealand. A less ambitious model exists in other parts of the country, such as Boulder, Colorado, and North Bend, Oregon, where police and prosecutors are using restorative justice practices as an alternative to juvenile court in specific cases.

Black Lives Matter

It is rare to see restorative justice used as an alternative to criminal prosecution for adult offenders, but it occasionally happens. One notable example, in Oakland, California, came about in the wake of a Black Lives Matter protest on November 28, 2014. It was Black Friday, one of the busiest shopping days of the year. The protestors, who became known as the Black Friday 14, chained themselves to two opposite-facing Bay Area Rapid Transit trains, known by the acronym BART. They locked themselves to each other, starting from one platform and continuing through both trains to the far platform. Service ground to a halt, and tens of thousands of shoppers and commuters were stranded for more than four hours, some deep underground in the tube linking Oakland to San Francisco through the Bay.[12]

This particular Black Lives Matter protest was set off by a decision made days earlier across the country in Ferguson, Missouri. There, a grand jury declined to indict a white police officer named Darren Wilson for his fatal shooting of Michael Brown, an unarmed, eighteen-year-old African American man. Brown's killing, which occurred in the middle of the day and in the middle of the street, further convulsed and divided the country along racial lines. Many people—often white—believed it was reasonable for Wilson, who was driving a patrol car when he stopped Brown for suspicion of stealing cigars, to feel an immediate and deadly threat. Others—mostly African American—believed Wilson murdered Brown because he was unarmed and posed no threat at all.

The Michael Brown shooting became a catalyst for the Black Lives Matter movement.[13] The movement, a loose collection of local activists, had been working at the grassroots level since the shooting of another unarmed black teenager, Trayvon Martin, in Sanford, Florida, in 2012. Several years later, it had gained national attention by organizing a number of protests and demonstrations across the country.

The decision by the Black Friday 14 to hold the demonstration at an Oakland BART station carried significant symbolic meaning. On January 1, 2009, one of Oakland's residents, a twenty-two-year-old African American man, Oscar Grant, was fatally shot as he lay facedown with several friends on a subway platform by BART police officer Johannes Mehserle. Multiple people captured the shooting on their cell phones. The Alameda County District Attorney's Office charged Mehserle with second-degree murder. But the jury convicted him of a far less serious offense, involuntary manslaughter, and he served less than a month in jail. After the verdict, Oakland was awash in protests and riots, resulting in the arrests of scores of people for rioting, looting, and setting fires.

From the perspective of the Black Lives Matter protestors, the shooting deaths of Grant, Martin, Brown, and so many others added up to a stinging indictment of law enforcement. The situation was not improving;

instead it was getting worse. The Black Friday 14 were incensed and alienated when the Alameda County District Attorney's Office responded to their protest by arresting and charging them with twenty-eight misdemeanor offenses, while the BART transit system demanded that the defendants pay $70,000 in restitution.

Nancy O'Malley, the elected district attorney for Alameda County, said she reached out to the defense lawyers at the beginning of the proceedings to try to work out a settlement but "there was no movement." As to the decision to bring charges, she pointed out that their actions were illegal and, more than just an inconvenience, posed a real physical danger. Because the protestors had chained their necks to the vertical pole and to others on the platform with Kryptonite locks, they had to remain almost completely stationary. "Had the train moved forward even by three feet, their necks might have snapped," she said. The vertical poles had to be removed from the train walls before the protestors could be freed, a process that took hours.

The case dragged on for a year. The defendants filed motions to dismiss and lost. Meanwhile, community pressure on the prosecution increased, with calls and petitions from local union leaders, civil rights organizations, and members of the clergy to drop the charges. O'Malley's home was picketed. Eva Paterson, a high-profile civil rights attorney and the executive director of the Equal Justice Society, a nonprofit organization focused on racial justice advocacy, talked the situation over with Alicia Garza, one of the Black Friday 14, to discuss a possible sit-down.

In addition to her part in the protest, Garza was also a prominent national figure: a longtime Oakland-based activist, she is one of the founders of the Black Lives Matter movement. After speaking with Garza, Paterson reached out to O'Malley. Paterson said, "She was very open. I felt like we were just two gray-haired ladies who had been around the block. There was mutual respect." The two women talked for some time about Dr. Martin Luther King Jr. and the history of nonviolent protest to advance civil rights, even if it meant breaking the law.

Following that conversation, in late November 2015, O'Malley's office changed course. Together with her chief assistant, her chief of investigations, and other high-ranking members of her office, O'Malley met with the defendants, their attorneys, and other community activists, including Garza, in a conference room for several hours, engaging in a restorative justice process. Paterson facilitated. "My MO," Paterson said, "is to get people to have open minds and open hearts." O'Malley wanted to get across "who we were and what we were about, but for me it was as much to hear and understand what compelled them to do what they did."

Garza said she went into the meeting "on guard," but she praised Paterson as "masterful at creating opportunities for us to consider and acknowledge that there was a basis for how each party was feeling and how those feelings very much shaped the way we act. [The DA's] stubbornness in not dropping the charges had to do with feeling personally attacked either for harboring or perpetuating racist practices." For their part, Garza said she and her fellow protestors "did get an opportunity to expose them to [Black Lives Matter], to learn more about why people were taking the kinds of risks they were taking to change policy and, I would say, show the impact of anti-Black racism and making visible how it plays out in the various systems that organize our society."

O'Malley said that, from her perspective, "it was an extremely honest and forthright conversation." But it was volatile and difficult, awkward and strained. There was, O'Malley said, "a lot of pain in the room. I could feel it, we could all feel it." Paterson acknowledges that "there were some hard-ass people from the DA and some hard-ass people from Black Lives Matter, but in the end, we reached an agreement."

The protestors were required to acknowledge the consequences of their actions—violating the law, causing inconvenience, and posing a potential safety risk—in a public statement. But in a public statement of its own, the District Attorney's Office acknowledged that the protestors "conveyed an important message" and were given a chance "to deeply express their own experiences."[14] The transit system, for its part, dropped the restitution demand. On the website of her nonprofit, Equal Justice Society, Paterson wrote, "The #BlackLivesMatter movement has forced America and the world to acknowledge that state power is often unleashed on innocent people in deadly and dehumanizing ways. I want to thank District Attorney O'Malley and her staff for opening their hearts and taking the just course of action in this matter."[15]

Speaking about the process years later, Paterson said, "I think people were surprised by how it went down"—that they had been seen and heard by an opposing side they viewed with skepticism and mistrust. The dialogue in the room was often uneasy, angry, and sad, "but both sides were able to see the humanity of the other and that is how we were able to resolve the problem."

RISE

Judge Leo Sorokin, fifty-six, has spent his professional life working in the criminal justice system. A graduate of Yale College and Columbia Law School, Sorokin served as an assistant attorney general, a federal public defender, and a magistrate judge. In 2013, President Barack Obama nominated Sorokin to a seat on the federal district court in Boston; the Senate confirmed him the following year.

Sorokin, a soft-spoken, balding man with pale-blue eyes, has an unassuming manner that gives no hint of his ambition and tenacity. In the fall of 2015, less than eighteen months into his appointment, Sorokin launched a pilot program he had been envisioning for years, and which had no precedent in the federal system. He called it RISE—Repair, Invest, Succeed, Emerge. RISE offered a rare second chance for adult defendants convicted of serious federal crimes to avoid the likelihood of having to go to prison.

Beginning in late October 2015, a committee of judges, prosecutors, defense lawyers, and probation officers met monthly to screen possible RISE participants; the program could accommodate up to twenty at a time. To be eligible, the defendants had to have a verifiable history of addiction or a life of extreme deprivation. They also had to be out on bail, plead guilty, and agree to have their sentencing hearings postponed for twelve months, during which time they had to get clean, get jobs, go to school, and find a safe, stable place to live.[16]

But the core non-negotiable component of RISE was attendance at a two-day, sixteen-hour restorative justice workshop. Sitting in a room for eight hours a day, the RISE participants came face-to-face with people who had lost children and close family members to overdoses and shootings. Also in the room were prosecutors, defense lawyers, judges, and probation officers, but not in their traditional roles. They, too, participated in the circle exercises, sharing personal experiences, and offering support and encouragement. Mostly, they listened without judgment as the offenders haltingly described their own victimization at the hands of other people. They spoke of their addiction, mental illness, abuse, and poverty.

It had taken months of work for Sorokin to convince skeptics within the criminal justice system that RISE was worth a try. A key ally in that effort was Maria D'Addieco, a federal probation officer with a master's degree in social work and extensive training as a restorative justice facilitator. She worked with a colleague, Allyson Lorimer Crews, to develop a series of exercises to fill every minute of the two-day workshop. D'Addieco said that the participants have told her that the restorative justice workshops were harder than doing time, where they could "put their game faces on and just get through it without facing up to what they did." Most, if not all, of the participants had long told themselves that their crimes were "victimless," as they never saw the direct effects of the drugs and guns they sold.

Sorokin also reached out to Janet Connors, a well-known local activist and sought-after public speaker. Connors, who grew up in Dorchester, a working-class neighborhood in Boston, had spent more than forty years as a community organizer, mainly working on behalf of children and families. Now in her early sixties, her short hair gone white, Connors became deeply involved in restorative justice after she experienced every mother's worst nightmare—the death of her son, Joel. In the early evening of January 31, 2001, four masked men came to Joel's apartment and kicked down the door. They were there to steal money, stereo equipment, and marijuana. They ordered Joel to lay down. When he refused to do so, one of the men stabbed Joel through the heart with an eighteen-inch knife, killing him.

The four men were arrested—all were between the ages of seventeen and twenty-two. One, Ryan Conway, pleaded guilty to second-degree murder and received a sentence of twenty-five years to life. Two others, Michael Buckley and John George, had their sentences reduced to manslaughter after agreeing to testify against the fourth, David O'Donnell, who was responsible for the fatal stabbing. For that cooperation, Buckley and George received sentences of between eight and twelve years.

Watching the legal process play out over a period of nearly three years left Connors with little consolation. O'Donnell went to trial and was acquitted; the others were seemingly lost to the system. "I had to make my own justice," she said. Connors wanted answers and accountability. She knew that Buckley and George would be released back into her community within a matter of years because of their relatively short sentences, and she did not want another family to suffer at their hands. Connors decided she wanted to meet them face-to-face, and after some bureaucratic wrangling, prison officials agreed.

In 2006, Buckley agreed to sit down with Connors in the presence of a trained facilitator. Several years later, Connors drove back to the supermax prison to meet with Buckley a second time—with his mother, Helen, present—shortly before he was due to be released. As it turned out, Connors and Helen had come from the same community, both struggling to raise their sons as single mothers. Connors knew what it was like to work hard and yet be eligible for food stamps, to be the best mother possible and still not know what to do when your kids get in trouble.

In between her first and second meetings with Buckley, Connors also met with George. Both Buckley and George stumbled over what to say, knowing that an offer of apology was meager compensation for what they had taken. Connors told them she was less interested in "I'm sorry" than in "I'll never do this again." She wanted a commitment from her son's killers to live decent, law-abiding lives. They promised.

When they were released, at Connors's request, Buckley and George went with Connors to Joel's grave. Buckley broke down and sobbed. "The finality of what he had done really hit him at the grave," Connors said. In 2012, the three of them sat next to each other in a panel discussion sponsored by the Suffolk County District Attorney's Office to talk about the impact of the restorative justice process on their lives. Buckley and George were fathers, with regular jobs. Both said that without restorative justice, they would be dead or back in prison.

In February 2016, D'Addieco and Connors cofacilitated the first restorative justice workshop for the first RISE class of eight offenders. They were a diverse group: men and women, black, white, and Latino; one young man was nineteen years old; others were in their early fifties. Their offenses included trafficking in heroin, cocaine, and marijuana; selling illegal firearms; and assaulting a federal officer. Judge Sorokin and Magistrate Judge Page M. Kelley, who had been holding monthly meetings with the program participants to monitor their progress, came to observe at the end of the second day. Assistant US attorney James Herbert participated, as well as several activists from the community.

Connors said it was obvious that none of the RISE participants wanted to be there: "You could see when people came in, by their body language, they were like, 'What the fuck is this?'" One of the eight offenders, Bobby Fitzpatrick, agreed with Connors's assessment: "At first, I thought it was bullshit. When you deal with the feds, you know they rig everything."

But Fitzpatrick was in the worst trouble of his life, and he knew the program was his only way out. In late September 2014, he had been indicted for conspiring with three other men to bring more than fifty kilograms of marijuana into Massachusetts from California. He did it on behalf of the New England branch of a Mafia crime family, which claimed him as "an associate." A thirty-nine-year-old cocaine addict and alcoholic, Fitzpatrick had been using his position as a driver for UPS and other delivery companies to facilitate the safe delivery of drugs for the Mafia, off and on, for more than fifteen years. He used the money to feed his drug addiction.

At the urging of his lawyer, Fitzpatrick signed up for the RISE program shortly after his arrest. First, he agreed to get clean, spending seventy days in a residential drug-treatment facility and emerging in June 2015. Since then, he had followed every RISE directive: his twice weekly drug tests were all clean, he had steered clear of his codefendants, and he was working seventy hours a week for a different delivery company, which was aware of his ongoing case but agreed to give him a second chance.

Late in 2015, Fitzpatrick reinitiated contact with his fifteen-year-old son, Brendan. They had not seen each other in two and a half years. Brendan was struggling, smoking marijuana daily, and failing out of school, and his mother could not control him. Fitzpatrick was trying to regain Brendan's trust and be a real father for the first time in the boy's life.

But despite his progress in RISE, Fitzpatrick viewed the restorative justice workshop skeptically. Introspection and self-reflection—never mind sharing his feelings with a roomful of strangers—seemed like a lot of touchy-feely fluff. "Rainbows and lollipops," he called it. A bald, trim guy with a broad Boston accent, Fitzpatrick came from a working-class background in Quincy, near Boston. His father was a truck driver; his mother stayed at home and later worked at a day-care center owned by a friend. He described his upbringing as "very normal, very middle class. Or at least it seemed that way," he added after a moment. In fact, Fitzpatrick's father was a drug addict who was gone for long periods of time, because of both his work and his own addiction.

Fitzpatrick's paternal grandfather was an active member of the Winter Hill Gang, an affiliation of Irish and Italian American gangsters whose members included the notorious crime boss Whitey Bulger. Growing up, Fitzpatrick was very close to his grandfather and impressed by his power, his associates, and the gangster persona he perpetuated. It all seemed glamorous and high stakes, he said: "The money, the women, the booze."

Fitzpatrick was drawn to drug dealing to support his cocaine habit and to have the money to live the lifestyle that his grandfather had enjoyed. A brief attempt to "clean up my act" in 2005 by getting married and going straight ended when his wife divorced him two years later. By 2012, he had moved back to Quincy and "got heavily into the whole criminal enterprise thing again." He never believed he would get caught, having gotten away with it for so long. When he did, he said, "I was once again in the throes of addiction."

The exercises Fitzpatrick did in the restorative justice workshop forced him to acknowledge that beneath the image that he cultivated—of a man who took what he wanted and did what he wanted—"I hated myself so much." On the second day, when it was his turn to hold the talking piece, Fitzpatrick was asked to list the people he had harmed over the years. At the top of the list was his son, Brendan. As Fitzpatrick spoke, he realized he was perpetuating a family cycle of ruinous relationships between fathers and sons. Fitzpatrick's grandfather, an alcoholic, hated Fitzpatrick's great-grandfather. Fitzpatrick's father, a drug addict, hated Fitzpatrick's grandfather, whom he viewed as an unrepentant criminal. Fitzpatrick grew up alienated from his own father, whose addiction made him seem weak and neglectful. Fitzpatrick's son, in turn, felt abandoned by Fitzpatrick, an alcoholic and drug addict who had played little or no role in the first fifteen years of the boy's life. The revelations were painful, but also motivating. There was a larger purpose to his sobriety beyond getting off drugs and staying out of prison. He could reclaim his son.

Two months later, in April, with the consent of Brendan's mother, Fitzpatrick took physical custody of Brendan. The probation department was supportive, albeit concerned about Fitzpatrick's ability to handle the additional challenge: he had been sober less than a year and his criminal case was hanging over his head. Judge Kelley was concerned, too, telling him, "Bringing home a sixteen-year-old boy that you haven't had a relationship with is pretty much a life-changing experience."

At first, the transition was difficult. Brendan had to change schools and make new friends. He was angry, fell in with the wrong crowd, and failed two classes. "His level of trust with me," Fitzpatrick said, "was low." A breakthrough came when Fitzpatrick sat Brendan down on the couch one day in the late spring of 2016. "I started off the conversation by telling him about me and my father, and how I live every day with a huge hole in my heart knowing that we could never be honest with each other," Fitzpatrick said. "I talked to him about my addiction and my father's addiction and how we never really connected, and that I saw it happening all over again with him and me."

The turnaround did not happen overnight; it was more like a large bus navigating a narrow turn. But the dynamic between father and son changed. Brendan made a decision to play football, trained all summer, went to summer school, and got a job mowing lawns. In the fall, his grades went up and he made the football team. "Now we have normal parent-kid problems," Fitzpatrick said. "I told him, 'I ain't going nowhere,' and he trusts me now." Fitzpatrick focuses on maintaining what he calls "a good clean healthy environment so we can have this life that we should have had a long time ago."

Fitzpatrick attended another restorative justice workshop on December 11, 2016, as a peer mentor, and a third in February 2017, even though he has long since graduated from the RISE program. Participating remained raw and difficult, but worthwhile. He called Janet Connors "literally, a saint," and her willingness to talk about her son's death and how drug dealing led directly to that death was impossible not to respond to on a personal level. Fitzpatrick never spent time thinking about the downstream effects of the large amounts of drugs he sold. Now he had no choice. He was impressed by Connors's openness and humbled by her ability to forgive. "I really believe if Ted Bundy could listen to her, he would have changed," he said.

Fitzpatrick, who pleaded guilty to using a cell phone to distribute marijuana, was sentenced on March 16, 2017. More than two years had passed since his arrest, and his life was in some ways unrecognizable.

Referring to his sobriety, Fitzpatrick said, "I don't even count the days anymore. It's just my life." He was a single parent working seventy hours per week whose idea of cutting loose was spending Sunday mornings running football drills with his son and going for long swims at the YMCA.

Because of the seriousness of Fitzpatrick's offense, he was facing eighteen to twenty-four months under the guidelines, which calculate a range that judges often follow. In the weeks leading up to the court date, Fitzpatrick became increasingly anxious, especially fearful of the impact on Brendan if he was sent to prison.

But four days before the hearing, Timothy Moran, the assistant US attorney assigned to the case, filed a short memorandum requesting no prison time at all. Moran wrote that Fitzpatrick's "excellent" results in RISE "has served as an example to others and ought to be rewarded." Fitzpatrick's lawyer agreed, writing, that his client's turnaround was "extraordinary." He continued, "More importantly, Mr. Fitzpatrick has recognized the importance of not just acting, but being a real role model for his son."[17]

Appearing in front of Judge Patti Saris in the early morning of March 17, 2017, Fitzpatrick, dapper in a gray suit and blue tie, felt fearful and overwhelmed. His apprehension grew when Judge Saris noted that she had given his codefendants prison sentences; she wanted to hear from Fitzpatrick directly about why he deserved greater leniency. "I didn't write anything or prepare anything. No poems, no cards, no quips," he said. Instead, Fitzpatrick talked about RISE and its impact on his relationship with his son: "I keep going back to the values, and that's really what's changed in me. The things I value today are my son, my family. And I love those things. And I wish to God I woke up earlier."

When Saris imposed a sentence of probation, it was, Fitzpatrick said, "one of the best feelings of my life.[18] I was so ecstatic and thankful." D'Addieco and Lorimer Crews, who had come to watch the proceedings, embraced him afterward. "They told me I earned it," he said.

One of Fitzpatrick's classmates in the RISE program was Laura Santana, twenty-seven, a petite woman with shoulder-length dark hair. Born in the Dominican Republic in 1987, she came to the United States with her mother, Yvonne, and twin brother, Gus, when they were infants. They followed Santana's father, who lived in New York, but she rarely saw him.

Her primary relationship was always with her mother, whom she described as "the love of my life. She was my everything."

But Yvonne struggled financially to support Laura and Gus. An alcoholic prone to severe depression, she also struggled psychologically, at one point slashing her wrists and having to be hospitalized. The family moved constantly, and not always for rational reasons. Santana said, "If she didn't like the vibe, it was like, 'We're leaving.'" In 1999, Santana's mother settled the family in Boston, where they remained for six years—the longest they had ever been in one place. Like her mother, Santana was also plagued by depression, but the newfound stability helped her. Santana put down roots, developed friendships, and committed to her studies.

But in the fall of 2005, when Santana was eighteen, Yvonne announced that she was moving to New Jersey. Caught off guard, Santana became overwhelmed by anxiety; her mother had made it clear that she had no intention of staying in Boston for the duration of the school year. In February 2006, Santana tried to commit suicide. In April, Yvonne carried out her plan to move to New Jersey. Without a place to live, Santana dropped out of high school six weeks before graduation and never went back. She decided not to follow her mother and instead took a friend up on his offer to spend time at his house in a small town in Vermont "to try to get my life together."

Santana decided to return to Boston later that year. In 2007, she found a job at Virgin Atlantic airline as a cargo agent. The fast-paced work was consuming and cathartic: Santana excelled and was promoted, first to cargo supervisor, then station manager. In 2009, at the age of twenty-one, she got married.

In 2012, at the age of twenty-four, Santana took a job with Embassy Freight, a London-based company where she worked as an export agent. Santana lived by the work-hard/play-hard ethic: "I partied a lot. I traveled a lot. I was always working. Pretty much I was just enjoying life. I clubbed a lot and went out drinking. Living very carefree." Her marriage grew troubled.

Yvonne continued to be Santana's primary source of support and love. Though the relationship was long distance, mother and daughter spoke on the phone every day. When her mother's heart disease got worse, Santana took every opportunity to visit her.

One day in 2013, Yvonne called to say she was very sick. Frightened, Santana immediately starting driving from Boston to New Jersey. Her mother died before she got there. Though Yvonne's health had been poor, there had been no hint that she was nearing the end of her life. After the shock, Santana felt crushing despair. Her marriage collapsed, and suicidal thoughts returned.

For the next eighteen months, Santana had trouble eating and sleeping, going off and on medication because she was unable to find a combination that didn't make her feel like a zombie or a robot. She tried different coping mechanisms: partying, taking days off to isolate herself in her room, and putting on her game face when she went back to her job. Nothing worked.

In February 2014, Santana was out partying at a club in the Dominican Republic when she met a charming older man who called himself Choco: "He kind of, like, complimented me, and I got the attention I needed. Usually, I don't go for that, but I wanted to be irresponsible and I was on a very self-destructive path, and I didn't care." They flirted, went out to dinner, and stayed in touch by phone when Santana went back to Boston. Santana flew back to see Choco in June. When he asked her to bring back a package into the United States and deliver it to his friend at the airport after clearing customs, she agreed. In exchange, he promised to pay her $5,000.

Santana's flight left at 4 a.m. on June 16. She boarded the plane drunk, having been up all night dancing and drinking with friends. When she headed to the customs checkpoint, a border patrol agent pulled her aside for secondary inspection; he and his partner then searched her carry-on bag and her suitcase. Inside, agents found two purses, which appeared to be empty yet were bulging at the sides. When they cut into the lining, the agents found just under a pound of cocaine. Stricken with fear and sick from the alcohol, Santana immediately threw up. She then confessed and was charged with importing drugs into the United States.

Santana's assigned federal public defender, Jennifer Pucci, was on the RISE committee. She thought Santana fit the program's criteria— Santana had already pleaded guilty to the offense, was out on bond, and still working at Embassy, which knew about her criminal case and continued to support her. Pucci encouraged her to apply.

On October 28, 2015, Santana entered the RISE program. She was given a list of tasks that included finding a mental health provider and pursuing an education, while continuing to work. Santana immediately began studying. Two weeks later, she got her GED. In January 2016, she enrolled in a community college.

The following month, Santana attended RISE's first restorative justice workshop. Like Fitzpatrick, she was skeptical, though for different reasons. Santana expected to be judged harshly for her crime, the way she felt when she went to court and "the prosecution was kicking me down so much." And, in fact, some in the prosecutor's office had been opposed to Santana joining RISE, believing she had no insight into her conduct. They felt strongly that she needed to go to prison. But to her surprise, the members of the restorative justice circle offered her acceptance and hope. "They told me, this crime does not define who I am, and I gained confidence," Santana said.

Talking about her mental illness and her suicide attempt, always a source of shame, was much harder. D'Addieco asked Santana to describe her state of mind when she committed the offense. Santana described her unbearable grief after losing her mother and her growing sense—given her intense identification with her mother and their psychological similarities—that she was destined to the same fate. Heartsickness, depression, and an extreme sense of isolation made her good-girl choices seem pointless. In a perverse way, it felt good to tear her life down by taking crazy chances, because it made her feel, however briefly, more alive. Describing the events of the past several years and what her life had become, Santana broke down in sobs.

The process marked the beginning of facing her pain, anger, and fear. The following month, Santana began seeing a therapist every week: "At the beginning, it felt forced, because I had to go." But after a while, Santana began looking forward to the sessions. At the same time, Santana threw herself into school. She took classes in business and writing on Saturdays at Bunker Hill Community College, earning As and Bs in the first year. "I love school and consider it a form of therapy," she said. A relationship she had with an on-again, off-again boyfriend became steadier shortly after her arrest; in May 2016, they bought a house together.

On October 26, 2016, Santana graduated from the RISE program. Appearing in court before Judge Kelley, Santana spoke at length about her accomplishments and her determination to get her associate's degree and then a bachelor's degree. While there was no changing the fact that she was a convicted felon, Santana planned to "emerge on the other side triumphantly." When she finished speaking, Santana was wiping away tears. Clearly moved, Judge Kelley said, "You are just a great person."

Exactly one month later, on November 28, 2016, Santana appeared for sentencing before Judge Patti B. Saris. Under the federal guidelines, Santana faced three years in prison. Santana said she walked into court prepared "to accept whatever happened." But she was still terrified.

Jennifer Pucci pushed hard for probation, listing Santana's accomplishments and writing of her client: "In every way, she has proven to be a star."[19] Even the prosecutor, convinced by Santana's progress in the program, agreed that Santana did not deserve to go to prison. Judge Saris sentenced Santana to three years of probation instead.[20] Looking back, Santana feels relief that "everything turned out okay" and is determined to continue moving forward.

As of this writing, the RISE program has fifteen graduates and eleven current participants. Four people have been terminated from the program for failing to complete it. Shortly before Fitzpatrick was sentenced, Judge Sorokin traveled to Washington, DC, to testify about RISE before the United States Sentencing Commission, hoping to encourage other federal trial courts to adopt it as a model.[21] Judge Saris said that "it is too soon to tell" if RISE will be a successful program in the long term because there is not enough data to make an empirical assessment. But, she says, "the initial signs are excellent."

Some dismiss restorative justice as a lot of Kumbaya hooey. But if you ask the men and women who have engaged in it, they will tell you emphatically that it is not. At the same time, restorative justice is not a magical antidote for everything that is wrong with the criminal justice system. It is hard—programmatically, logistically, and emotionally. To work, the participants must approach it with an open mind, willing to engage with each other and with the darkest parts of themselves. For many people, that is not possible. Of the four people who left RISE, Judge Kelley said that three were taken into custody before sentencing for failing to comply with their bail conditions and the fourth was terminated "because he was simply not motivated to fulfill the requirements."

But for those who are willing and able to do the hard work—victims, perpetrators, prosecutors, defense attorneys, judges, family members, teachers, community activists, and other leaders—the results are well worth the effort. It is not an understatement to say that restorative justice has the power to heal and give hope to those who had long ago resigned themselves to lives of brokenness and despair.

CHAPTER NINE

"Restorative Justice in Its Purest Form"

AT FIRST PASS, it might seem counterintuitive to use restorative justice practices in wrongful conviction cases: crime victims and exonerees are not typical "victims" and "offenders." All are essentially blameless, as are their families, many of the witnesses who testified at trial, the jurors, and the officials who followed the standard legal procedures in good faith to secure—unwittingly—a false conviction. But blameworthy or not, many people directly affected by a wrongful conviction experience the vortex of emotions that comes with trauma and a loss of faith—in institutions, in other people, in God. Anger, bewilderment, shame, guilt, and fear are common feelings. For some, engaging in restorative justice practices with others both like them and unlike them in background and perspective has been surprisingly effective in bringing about individual healing and enduring social change. Consider the story of Jennifer Thompson and Ronald Cotton.

Like Burke, Thompson had been raped at knifepoint by an African American man in 1984. The assault occurred at 3 a.m., in Burlington, North Carolina, after the rapist broke into Thompson's college apartment while she slept. She barely managed to escape with her life.

Determined to identify her attacker, Thompson paid careful attention to the rapist's face during a terrifying assault that went on for more than half an hour. Like Burke, she was able to provide a detailed description to the police. Like Burke, Thompson identified a man who fit that description. And like Burke, Thompson identified the wrong man: Ronald

Cotton. As a result, Cotton had spent more than a decade in prison before DNA evidence exonerated him, showing without a doubt that the real rapist was a man named Bobby Poole. As with Thomas Haynesworth and Leon Davis, the resemblance between Ronald Cotton and Bobby Poole was striking. Thompson took little comfort from that fact.

Captain Mike Gauldin—the detective who had conducted the pretrial photo array and live lineup thirteen years earlier—delivered the awful news to Thompson in person in June 1995. Thompson trusted and respected Gauldin, who had always been steadfast in his support of her. But when Gauldin told her, "We all made this mistake," his words were lost on her. Thompson felt that she alone was to blame: "I was almost paralyzed, debilitated emotionally. I could function as a mother and do day-to-day things like going to the store, making the kids' beds, cooking dinner and walking the dog, but my spirit was just dead." The persona Thompson had so carefully reconstructed—as a blonde, vivacious woman who still turned heads in the grocery store, the devoted wife and adoring mother of triplets—had collapsed completely.

Thompson, then thirty-five years old, was forced to confront the fact that she had not moved on, as she had told herself for so long. "I realized that I was still in the same broken place that I had been thirteen years ago. I was really struggling," she explained. "The exoneration had taken place, Ronald was free and some people would say, that's good, the end. For me, I was left hanging and hurting and not understanding what I was supposed to do with this new life that I had entered into."

After two years of living in a kind of fugue state, Thompson made a decision: "I knew if I was going to move forward, I was going to have to readjust my memories and replace the image of this man in my head, the monster I had created, with the real person." Thompson contacted Gauldin to see if he could arrange a meeting with Cotton. Gauldin readily agreed. He told Thompson that he, too, was deeply disturbed by the case, poring over the file to try to figure out what had gone so wrong and determined to make sure it never happened again.

When Thompson entered the First Baptist Church of Elon in North Carolina on April 4, 1997, and came face-to-face with Cotton, she was desperate for his forgiveness, although she knew he was unlikely to give it. So when Cotton did forgive her, wholeheartedly and without any hesitation, Thompson said, "That's the first moment that I had begun healing in thirteen years. It's when we shared our mutual hurt and our mutual trau-mas. It was when I started, slowly, to find my way back." What was sup-posed to be a onetime meeting became a series of deliberate encounters and, ultimately, a friendship that profoundly altered both of their lives.

Looking back, Thompson said, "What Ron and I did that day in the church was restorative justice in its purest form. And it was so simple. It doesn't take someone with a PhD, it doesn't take wealth; it takes two people who are harmed to come together and share their experiences of being victimized and being made to feel like a perpetrator. I thought, why can't we implement that at a deeper and wider level?"

More than a decade passed, however, before Thompson circled back to the concept of restorative justice. For years, her focus was intensely practical: working with Cotton to change the way that eyewitness identi-fication procedures were conducted in North Carolina. Thompson, as it turned out, was ideally suited for activist work: a natural public speaker, she radiated charisma. When Thompson and Cotton told their story—to police organizations, Innocence Projects, and lawmakers—their audi-ences sat spellbound. The more they spoke, the more people wanted to hear from them.

By the early 2000s, Thompson and Cotton had become famous. After they were interviewed separately for the PBS *Frontline* documentary *What Jennifer Saw*, Thompson later appeared on *The Oprah Winfrey Show* and wrote an op-ed that was published in the *New York Times*. She and Cotton were featured in *People* magazine and gave their first joint interview to *20/20*. More media requests and speaking engagements followed.

Skeptics became believers. Thompson recalled a conversation with a North Carolina state legislator who told her, "I have listened to the exonerees tell their stories and it's sad, but it is hearing the two of you talk together that changed it for me. It was only then that I saw the com-plete picture." Using their name recognition and compelling narrative, Thompson and Cotton, along with a few other exonerees whose cases had attracted public attention in the state, successfully advocated for im-portant reforms.[1]

In 2000, Gauldin was promoted to chief of police of Burlington County. Working with Thompson and Cotton, he instituted best prac-tices that included the sequential showing of photographs to witnesses rather than grouping them together, requiring that the officer conducting the identification procedure have no knowledge of who the actual suspect was, and obtaining a confidence statement from the witness, stating, in her own words, her degree of certainty in the identification. Eight years later, the state of North Carolina passed the Eyewitness Identification Reform Act, which mandated the same procedures for every law enforcement agency in the state.[2]

Darryl Hunt

Ronald Cotton was the first North Carolinian to be exonerated by DNA evidence, but he was not the last. And as badly as the state's justice system had failed Cotton, the breakdown was far more disastrous when it came to another young black man, Darryl Hunt. On August 10, 1984, Deborah Sykes, a young white woman, was found dead in Winston-Salem. She had been raped and stabbed sixteen times. The race of the victim, the fact that she worked at a local newspaper, and the heinous nature of the offense kept the case in the headlines for weeks. Hunt, nineteen years old at the time, was charged with the crime.[3]

Hunt's girlfriend initially provided him with an alibi, but when the police subsequently arrested her on outstanding theft charges, she changed her story and implicated him. So did three other men, including a convicted criminal and a member of the Ku Klux Klan, who said they saw Hunt with Sykes before the crime and leaving bloody towels in a hotel bathroom afterward. But their identifications were shaky and so, it seemed, was the case: the jury deliberated for three days. In the end, though, the jurors returned guilty verdicts and voted 11–1 to give him the death penalty. Because of the lone holdout juror, Hunt was sentenced to life in prison.[4]

Several years later, however, the state's highest court threw out Hunt's convictions, finding that his girlfriend's testimony was inadmissible. Released on bail in 1989, Hunt was offered a deal: plead guilty to the rape and murder of Deborah Sykes in exchange for immediate release from prison. Hunt, who had been incarcerated for five years, said no. Because of the extensive publicity generated by the case, the 1990 retrial took place in a different location: rural Catawba County. Hunt was retried before an all-white jury. This time, in addition to the three male witnesses from the first trial, the prosecution introduced the testimony of another black man, who identified Hunt only after the police threatened to charge him with Sykes's murder. Hunt was convicted again, and again sentenced to life in prison.

But one of Hunt's original trial attorneys, Mark Rabil, was convinced of his client's innocence and refused to give up. He pressed for DNA testing, and the judge, overruling the state's objections, ordered it. In 1994, the results came back: the semen retrieved from the victim excluded Hunt. Rather than concede that Hunt had been wrongfully convicted, the prosecutors fought back, arguing successfully for the next ten years in state and federal court that Hunt was still a participant in the crime, which they claimed included more than one attacker.

In 2003, Rabil obtained a court order to have the semen from the rapist's DNA run through the state's offender data bank. It matched that of another man, Willard Brown, who had been tentatively identified years earlier by another victim, Regina K. Lane. She had been kidnapped, raped, and stabbed repeatedly six months after Sykes was assaulted and killed, while Hunt was in jail. But when Lane tried to point out the similarities between her case and Sykes's, she said, the police got angry and shut her down. Her case was never prosecuted.[5]

On December 22, 2003, confronted with the DNA evidence, Willard Brown confessed to raping and murdering Deborah Sykes, stating that he acted alone. Hunt was released on Christmas Eve and fully exonerated on February 6, 2004. He was thirty-eight years old and had spent half his life in prison. After suing the city of Winston-Salem and the state of North Carolina, Hunt settled for approximately $2 million. His case attracted national attention: he was the subject of two books; an eight-part, prize-winning series in the *Winston-Salem Journal*; and a 2006 documentary called *The Trials of Darryl Hunt*, which was screened at the Sundance Film Festival.[6]

Hunt used part of his settlement money to form a nonprofit, the Darryl Hunt Project for Freedom and Justice, which helped former prisoners reacclimate to society. Hunt did not discriminate between the innocent and guilty.[7] He called everybody "Homecomers." Working with a small staff and longtime supporter, the Reverend John Mendez, Hunt provided free services, ranging from help getting a GED and driver's license to writing résumés and preparing for job interviews. Hunt and Mendez also held group therapy sessions where exonerees talked about their darkest moments in prison, which for some included rape or prostitution for favors or protection.

Darryl Hunt's case was the inspiration for the nation's first and only independent state agency devoted to the investigation of wrongful conviction cases, established in 2006. The former chief justice of the North Carolina Supreme Court, I. Beverly Lake, teamed up with prominent activists like Chris Mumma, the executive director of the North Carolina Center on Actual Innocence, to create the North Carolina Innocence Inquiry Commission. "Darryl's case was the poster child," Rabil said. "I think the chief was surprised that we had twelve postconviction motions before we were able to get relief."

Composed of a prosecutor, a defense attorney, a judge, a sheriff, a victim's rights advocate, a community member, and "two discretionary appointments," the eight-member commission has restrictive criteria—it will not review claims that had already been litigated in court. But it does solid, if slow, work, exonerating ten people to date.[8] Jennifer Thompson has served as a commissioner since 2013.

Working to reform the criminal justice system in North Carolina made Thompson acutely aware that many exonerees would never have the kind of reconciliation that she and Cotton had achieved. Deborah Sykes's mother, Evelyn, and her husband, Doug, continued to insist that Hunt was guilty. On the day of his release, Evelyn told the judge, through tears, "What you are about to do today is set free a guilty man, who's guilty of my daughter's death."[9]

Thompson heard similar stories when she spoke at various events organized by the Innocence Project: "I started to meet all these exonerees, and what stood out to me was that so many had never received an apology. No one had validated their harm, and they almost began to see me, by proxy, as the victim of their case. My work and my relationship with Ron—they wished they had it. I stood in the victim's place, apologizing and saying, 'I am witnessing and hearing your stories, and I am sorry for what happened to you.' Exonerees would tell me how meaningful that was, never having heard it from the actual victim or the victim's family."

In 2008, Thompson and Cotton, working with writer Erin Torneo, received a Justice Media Fellowship from billionaire George Soros's Open Society Institute to write *Picking Cotton*, a firsthand account of their story from their alternating perspectives. The book, published in March 2009, became a best seller.[10] Thompson said, "We were on a different platform—it wasn't just lawyers and lawmakers and Innocence Projects who wanted to hear from me. The book put us in Sweden, in Madrid, in Mexico." More press followed, including a *60 Minutes* interview on mistaken eyewitness identification, which is now required viewing in many law schools around the country.

But not all of the press was good. Some people put the blame for Cotton's conviction squarely on Thompson, attributing her misidentification to racism. Thompson, for her part, felt she had to accept the condemnation that came her way "because it was part of my penance." In forum after forum, she found herself apologizing, convulsed with guilt and shame.

Before the book came out, Thompson had met only a few crime victims with similar stories. Many in the victim's rights community saw her as "having gone to the dark side" by supporting the exonerees. But after *Picking Cotton* was published, she met many more, including Janet Burke and Sarah, who were reeling just as Thompson had been, unsure of what or who to believe. They had read *Picking Cotton* and seen their own lives described. Thompson stayed in touch with many of them, listening to their stories and counseling them through the same denial, depression, anger, and fear that she had been through.

Thompson decided that she needed to stop apologizing, for her sake and for the sake of others who had survived the same double victimization: the trauma of the original crime compounded by the wrongful conviction with all of its cruel revelations—that they had been unwitting participants, that the true perpetrator had gone unpunished after victimizing more people, and that the system, which had promised them justice and finality, had delivered neither.

Thompson began to fight back against the premise that what happened to Cotton was her fault. She said, "Hold up a second, I didn't do anything wrong. And that means that Sarah and Janet hadn't done anything wrong, either. We were raped and nearly killed and then given the wrong information. Why would any victim not want to get this right?" For years, Thompson had been focused almost entirely on her own guilt, never questioning that she was to blame, and trying to make up for it by using her story as a siren call for reform in North Carolina. "Psychologically," Thompson said, "I had stopped at that point." Thompson started to think about what she calls "the aftermath"—a healing that remained elusive to her and to so many of the people she had met through her work.

Beginning in 2013, Thompson circled back to restorative justice. Reading about it and talking to practitioners, she saw the power of restorative justice practices to mend broken lives. Rather than leading people away from the crash site, restorative justice practitioners took them back to the wreckage to sort through the pieces together. What if she could draw on restorative justice practices to add depth and nuance to her own story and find a way to replicate what she and Cotton had been able to achieve? For so long, Thompson had believed that their experience was uniquely and horribly their own. Now she knew that there were many more like them.

Thompson's vision was ambitious: she was determined to try to reach people within the concentric circles of harm that rippled beyond the exonerees and the victims. The families. The juror who sentenced an innocent person to death. The district attorney who believed in his heart that he had gotten the right guy. Detectives like Mike Gauldin who remained haunted by what had happened. "We need to bring these folks together that got hurt in a room to have a safe open dialogue about these mutual traumas, and if we can, we can really effect change," she said. "But we can't come together as a community unless we are healed."

As an activist, Thompson also saw the possibility of achieving systemic changes in other states through a broader coalition of advocates. "You can publish papers all day long about wrongful convictions," Thompson said, "but it is the stories that cause the change. And it is much more powerful when it is collective voices—when all of the harmed people can come together and share their stories, the totality of the harm becomes clear."

What Harm Was Done to You?

Jennifer Thompson and Katie Monroe met in the spring of 2005, when Thompson and Cotton did a joint presentation on eyewitness identification at an event cosponsored by Shawn Armbrust's Mid-Atlantic Innocence Project. They collaborated for the first time in 2007, for a similar presentation at the Rocky Mountain Innocence Project in Utah, where Monroe had moved to take on the position of executive director. The two women bonded right away and kept in touch, continuing to collaborate on training programs and going on long hikes together when they were in the same place.

By 2013, Monroe had left Utah for New York to be the senior advocate for national partnerships with the Innocence Project. She decided to design a program focused on the impact of exonerations on original victims and survivors for the annual Innocence Network conference. She said, "We are always asking survivors to be involved in our policy work without being sufficiently respectful to them. We had never honored what their experience had been beyond what we needed them for and never recognized that the work that they do for us came at an emotional cost. It has to be a reciprocal relationship."

Monroe explained that she would be serving as the moderator and asked Thompson and Christy Lucas Sheppard, the cousin of murder victim Debbie Sue Carter, if they would be panelists together. Monroe also asked Yolanda Thomas, whose sister Jacquetta had been murdered in 1991 in Raleigh, North Carolina. Gregory Taylor, who was convicted of killing Jacquetta, spent nearly twenty years in prison before DNA evidence exonerated him in 2009.[11]

The room was packed with exonerees. "It was standing room only," Sheppard said. Thompson, seated next to Thomas, with Sheppard on the other side, was not particularly nervous though. She had participated in hundreds of such forums. She expected the usual questions about the specifics of her story: what she believed was her rock-solid memory of the event and subsequent mistaken identification.

Instead, Monroe posed a different question: "What harm was done to you as a victim in the way that the exoneration process unfolded?"

"No one had ever asked me that before," Thompson said, "I almost couldn't talk because I was crying."

Listening to Thompson speak in a choked voice about how she often felt blamed, shamed, used, and left out, even by the Innocence Project, Sheppard said, "I was doing the ugly cry." It was the first time that Sheppard had spent any significant amount of time with Thompson, and, she said, "I saw her pain in a different way than just hearing about it at a conference. That she was speaking to the revictimization and not being included. I felt that, too."

Sheppard thought back to the first time she had met Monroe, at a different conference organized by the Innocence Project in New York in

Kash Delano Register and his lawyer, Lara Bazelon, in court on November 7, 2013, after a judge threw out his murder conviction. Register spent thirty-four years in prison for a murder he did not commit.

Wilma Register, Kash's mother, and Keith Chandler, his longtime friend and advocate, after the judge exonerated Kash on November 7, 2013.

Janet Burke in 1982. Two years later, she was raped at knifepoint by Leon Davis while opening the day-care center where she worked. In court, she mistakenly identified Thomas Haynesworth as her assailant. "I was positive," she said. "I never second-guessed myself one bit."

Thomas Haynesworth during a prison visit with his family in 1986. From left to right: cousin Douglas McGee; sisters Sandra and Janet Haynesworth; mother, Dolores Haynesworth; niece Keyshawn Henry; and cousin Donnie Webb.

Thomas Haynesworth embracing his mother after he was released on parole March 21, 2011, his forty-sixth birthday, after serving twenty-seven years in prison. "I am glad my mother is alive, that she can see this," Haynesworth said.

Thomas Haynesworth and Janet Burke in July 2014, shortly after Burke decided to go public with her story.

Christy Sheppard, Debbie Sue Carter, and their grandfather Oldie Williams in the summer of 1981. Debbie was murdered one year later.

Dennis Fritz in an undated photograph.

Photos courtesy of the Innocence Project of New York

Ron Williamson in 1999, two weeks after his release from death row in Oklahoma.

Photos courtesy of Christy Sheppard

Christy Sheppard; her mother, Glenna Jones; her aunt, Peggy Carter (Debbie's mother); and Christy's daughter, Addison, in April 2016.

Christy Sheppard's daughter, Addison, at the Oklahoma City National Memorial, holding the Survivor Tree sapling, April 19, 2017.

Thomas Webb and Sarah in 2017. Thirty-five years earlier, Sarah mistakenly identified Webb as her attacker.

Ronald Cotton and Jennifer Thompson, restorative justice advocates and coauthors of *Picking Cotton*, in 2009.

Darryl Hunt with his attorney, Mark Rabil, at Hunt's retrial in 1990.

The Healing Justice memorial to Darryl Hunt, his initials spelled in wildflowers and branches.

Jerome Morgan, Easter, March 13, 1991. Four years later, Morgan was wrongfully convicted of murder and sentenced to life in prison without parole.

Jerome Morgan presenting at PitchNOLA 2015: Education, on November 4, 2015.

Jerome Morgan and his legal team, from left to right: Rob McDuff, Kristin Wenstrom, Morgan, and Emily Maw, on May 27, 2016, the day Morgan was exonerated.

Anthony Wright holding his granddaughter, Romera Wright, in August 2016.

In 1993, Anthony Wright was accused and convicted of the rape and murder of an elderly black woman named Louise Talley in Philadelphia. Decades later, Talley's niece Shannon Coleman (right) and grand-niece Lauryn Coleman (left) threw their whole support behind the effort to free Wright from prison, after discovering the extent of the misconduct in his case.

Kash Register and Lara Bazelon in July 2017.

2006. Sheppard, who was pregnant with her youngest daughter, had come with her parents to speak about Debbie's case to a small group of policy makers seated around a table. It was the first time she had spoken about the case in any kind of public setting, and she had no idea what to expect. As she began to explain what it was like to grow up in the shadow of her cousin's murder, it occurred to Sheppard that she was describing the end of her childhood. There were no more Christmases, no more casual family get-togethers, no more walking to school. Her mother got a pit bull; her aunt went to an institution. The world was dangerous in a way that was undeniable and unspeakable at the same time. Sheppard never felt safe again.

And there was no moving on from it. Year after year, there were new developments: the investigation, the trials, the death penalty sentence for Williamson, the shocking news that the wrong men had been convicted, the arrest, prosecution, overturned conviction, and reprosecution of Glen Gore. What had happened to Debbie Sue Carter happened to her family over and over again in the public square: the town was small, the case was notorious, and the glare of the media was unrelenting. No one, it seemed, could ever stop talking about the case, and yet no one had any interest in hearing about the suffering of the victims who were still alive.

When Sheppard finished speaking, she was crying and so were her parents. Monroe came over and knelt before Sheppard. Taking her hands, Monroe said how sorry she was, not only for what had happened to Debbie, but for the suffering inflicted on her aunt, Peggy; her mother, Glenna; and their entire family. Sheppard's voice caught as she described Monroe's offering—that this woman, whom she barely knew, would acknowledge and receive her pain. Seven years later, Monroe was giving Sheppard a public platform to speak from her heart in the same way, not about the facts of the case, or the awfulness of the injustice experienced by the men who had been wrongfully convicted, but about what it had done to her family.

Afterward, there was a long line of people who wanted to talk to Thompson, Sheppard, and Thomas. Some were exonerees who wanted to express how deeply their words had resonated. Until then, they had never considered that they shared so much in common with the same people who once had accused and condemned them.

Thompson left the conference feeling that she had come to a turning point in her activism. Her personal life had recently changed, substantially for the better. After a messy and protracted divorce from her first husband in 2009, she had met and married Frank Baumgartner in 2011. In 2012, she had moved from Winston-Salem to Chapel Hill, where Baumgartner was a political science professor at the University of North Carolina. Thompson, however, had held on to what she called her "divorce house," uncertain what to do with it.

In 2014, Thompson sold the house with a very specific purpose in mind. "The divorce was hateful and mean and angry and the money from the house made me feel crappy," she said. "I wanted to use the money for something positive and life affirming. In my head, the way I conceived it was to provide support services to folks who had been harmed and figure out how we can heal together. People want their story to bring about change. They want it to mean something. I wanted to give them the opportunity to find their voices again."

Thompson asked her husband, "What would you think if I just took the money and used it to start 'Healing Justice'?" In her mind, she had already named her organization. "He told me to go for it."

Shortly afterward, Thompson called Monroe, told her about her idea, and asked if she would be willing to come on board. Monroe said it did not take much convincing, and she became the organization's executive director in June 2015. Shortly after, Thompson reached out to Ronald Cotton and Darryl Hunt to gauge their level of support. They told her they were in. The goal of Healing Justice was simple and grand at the same time: to use restorative justice practices to connect isolated individuals who might otherwise shy away from one another out of fear or resentment.

Both Thompson and Monroe knew from lived experience that the kind of suffering experienced by those involved in a wrongful conviction case varies greatly in degree, but arises from a shared trauma. They had come to believe that this shared suffering could unite very differently situated people—Burke, Haynesworth, Sarah, Webb, Sheppard, Hunt, and so many others—in a common cause. In voices too powerful to ignore, they could help each other heal and advocate for reforms to the system that broke their lives. When Sheppard heard about Healing Justice, she was all for it: "It was clear to me that no one else was going to do anything unless we did it ourselves."

CHAPTER TEN

Bittersweet Reunions

Burke and Haynesworth

When Thomas Haynesworth was released from prison in 2011, the world around him bore little resemblance to the one he had left as a teenager. He experienced the frequent humiliation of feeling like a child again, only this time, he was a middle-aged man. Figuring out how to operate a gas pump took a full twenty minutes. He tried taking the bus to work, but the routes had changed and he ended up lost and on the wrong side of town, forced to walk a long distance in his suit. For the next few days, Haynesworth took the same wrong route because it was easier than learning a new one. "You get stuck in that zone," he said. "You think things are the same as when you last seen them. When I left, my niece was six years old. When I got out, she was married with kids, but in my mind, she was still six years old."

Over time, though, Haynesworth found his footing. He excelled in Cuccinelli's office and was promoted twice, the second time to deputy of operations. He got a $1 million settlement from the state, which meant that he could retire comfortably from the Attorney General's Office once his pension vested. He built himself a house and bought four new cars, which he washed daily and detailed himself. Haynesworth kept the cars looking as if he had just driven them off the lot; the interiors, too, were pristine. "It makes me feel good," he said, "like I accomplished something." He got a dog.

Haynesworth's daily life slipped into a comfortable routine. Every morning on the way to work, he would stop by his mother's house to see if she needed anything. He became a devoted uncle to his nieces and nephews. But Haynesworth did not consider having a family of his own. Seeing the joy on a coworker's face over the approaching birth of his first baby, he felt wistful. But he says, "If it was meant to be, it would have happened."

Haynesworth made a point of not forgetting his friends who were still incarcerated. One of the first things that he did after his court victory was visit the Buckingham Correctional Center to see his friend Thomas Perkins, who was serving a life sentence. When he arrived, a guard approached him, saying, "Leon Davis is here. If he comes into the visiting room, is there going to be a problem?" Since that day in the Richmond city jail twenty-seven years earlier, their paths had never crossed. For Haynesworth, the possibility of seeing Davis again meant strangely little. The truth had come out, extinguishing Davis's power over his life. Haynesworth looked back steadily at the guard. "I am here to visit Thomas Perkins," he repeated.

Haynesworth also stayed close with Marvin Anderson and another friend, Julius "Earl" Ruffin, who served twenty-one years for raping a woman in Norfolk, Virginia, before he was exonerated by DNA evidence in 2003. Once again, it was the unusual practices of Mary Jane Burton, the same serologist who had saved evidence samples in Haynesworth's and Anderson's cases, who held the key to Ruffin's freedom. In total, the slivers of evidence she had kept in her files resulted in the exoneration of eleven men.

Haynesworth, Anderson, and Ruffin shared a unique bond. And because Ruffin and Anderson had been released years earlier, Haynesworth could rely on them for advice and support, particularly in the beginning when he often felt unmoored. But Haynesworth also kept up his prison visits, returning regularly to see friends in Southampton, where he had spent the bulk of his life. He wanted to convey that there was someone in the outside world who was invested in their survival and who would be there if, one day, they were ever able to make it out. When he first starting visiting, none of the inmates could believe it. He said, "I had grown men crying."

When various police departments asked Haynesworth to tell his story—to at-risk youth, ex-offenders, or as a cautionary tale to young police officers—he readily agreed. He spoke to standing-room-only crowds in churches, high schools, detention centers, and prisons. He talked about his faith and his strong feeling that what happened to him was part of a larger plan. "I try to set an example," he explained, "tell people how I walked my path." Amazingly, Haynesworth still wanted to be a police officer, "a beat cop," he said. "That is my dream. People can't understand it. I tell them, you are in a position to be helping people. I know what to look for. What they get wrong, I will get right." But Armbrust advised against it, reminding him that he would lose his pension and benefits if he left the Attorney General's Office.

Haynesworth's exoneration received significant media attention, and two of the jurors from his trials reached out to him. One told Haynesworth of the guilt she carried; in hindsight, she had been unwilling to give the evidence a hard look and fixed on the victim's story, ignoring the contradictions in the identification by allowing her emotions to get the better of her. Even though Haynesworth had once felt only rage toward his jurors, he told the woman that he forgave her. And he meant it. Listening to her stumble over her explanation, he felt an emotion close to sympathy. Haynesworth said he could never serve as a juror: "It's too much responsibility. I couldn't live with either result." His thirty years in prison were the result of three separate jury verdicts. He wanted no part of the machine that put them into motion.

Haynesworth and Armbrust remained close. Every year, the Mid-Atlantic Innocence Project held an annual luncheon fund-raiser at the up-scale Washington, DC, Mandarin Oriental hotel, where attorneys at the white-shoe law firms who provided pro bono assistance rubbed shoulders with celebrities and activists in the criminal justice world. It was MAIP's biggest fund-raiser of the year.

In 2014, Armbrust decided to give MAIP's Champion of Justice Award to Jennifer Thompson at the luncheon and considered the possibility of having Haynesworth and Burke present the award together. They seemed like the perfect fit, given the striking similarities between the cases and the personal connection between the two women—Burke called Thompson her "life raft." But Armbrust had no idea if either of them would be open to it. In the three years since Haynesworth's release, they had never spoken.

Armbrust was familiar with restorative justice practices, although she was quick to say she was no expert. But clearly, a joint public appearance would be impossible without a private meeting first—a meeting that was certain to bring in a tide of raw emotion.

"For something like this to work," Armbrust said, "you have to have the right victim and the right exoneree at the right point in their lives." In the years right after Haynesworth's release, neither he nor Burke was ready. Armbrust had no insight into how Burke might be feeling, but she was hopeful about Haynesworth, who was emotionally and financially autonomous in a way that had seemed impossible three years earlier. Still, Armbrust was nervous, broaching the topic gingerly and bracing herself for a poor reception. "Thomas likes to play jokes on me," she said, "so when I asked him, he pretended to be all outraged." Armbrust backed off quickly, apologizing. "Then he started laughing, saying, 'Oh, yes, it's totally fine. When do I get to meet her?'"

For Burke, the decision was more difficult. She was terrified of what Haynesworth would say and more terrified still about presenting the award. For years, Burke had advocated for Haynesworth's release, but she had always done so anonymously. Now she would be exposed, telling her rape story on a brightly lit stage with five hundred strangers in the audience. The press would be there, with their microphones and cameras. She thought of the strain on her children. She had told them about the rape in 2009, when the DNA came back, but then it had been a private matter, not something that could explode on social media. And she knew, from her conversations with Thompson, that many people would blame her.

At the same time, there was a part of Burke that was desperate to meet Haynesworth. Several months after Haynesworth's release, Burke wrote a letter that she gave to Armbrust to forward to Haynesworth. She wrote, "I have spent my life trying to forget what happened to me when I was twenty and now I have spent the last six months trying to remember every detail to see what I could have done differently. People say that things happen for a reason. I am still trying to figure out the reason."

Burke did not receive a response to her letter, but Haynesworth was never far from her thoughts. On occasion, he burst unexpectedly into view, leaving her shaken for days afterward. Once, shortly after Haynesworth was released, Burke drove by him as he sat waiting for the bus: "I kept thinking, should I have stopped to pick him up? Should I have told him who I am? That seemed crazy. But what happened seemed so wrong, here I am in my car zooming off to work and he has to wait for the bus. This isn't the way it should be." Ashen-faced, Burke told her coworker, "I saw Mr. Haynesworth today." It seemed presumptuous to use his first name.

The day after Thanksgiving in 2013, Burke saw Haynesworth again while out shopping at the local Target. Burke was with her daughter and her mother. She said, "I didn't want to make a big deal of it so I positioned myself in the store so that he wouldn't see me. I had to pretend nothing was wrong, but I felt sick."

Burke also wanted to come out of the shadows. "For my whole life," she said, "the rape had been this thing I could never bring up. It was not a story for a dinner party or a family picnic." Burke came from an old-fashioned family. No one talked about getting their period, never mind physical intimacy. As for the sexual violation she had experienced, "you definitely did not talk about it." Now, thirty years later, she could tell the story in her own words and "make it mean something bigger." After several days of mulling Armbrust's request, Burke finally said yes.

In June 2014, Burke and Haynesworth met at an office in downtown Richmond. Armbrust introduced them to each other, but said little after that. Burke was trembling. She started to cry, then sob. At first, it was hard to find the words, and then they poured out of her. She apologized over and over, and told Haynesworth she had spent years searching through the bits and pieces, trying to figure out how she could have made such a terrible mistake. But Burke had made a promise to herself and she kept it: she would not ask Haynesworth to forgive her. How could she expect him to when she could not forgive herself?

Armbrust looked over at Haynesworth. His face was expressionless, and she wondered how much he could absorb and respond to in the moment. When it was his turn to speak, he told Burke the truth. Yes, it was deeply frustrating and painful to know that he was locked away for almost three decades while she went on with her life. But, he said, "It was an honest mistake that was made." He had long ago come to see Burke as a victim twice over, first because Leon Davis had raped her and then because she had identified someone else for his crime.

Haynesworth explained his philosophy, which was deeply infused by his religious faith. He assured Burke that he harbored no ill will or a desire for vengeance: "I had to let go to really be free. You can sit here and be mad all you want, bitter all day long, but it's not gonna change the situation. The damage has been done." Being a devout Christian meant that while "I cannot forgive with my love, I can forgive with God's love. My love is not perfect, but God's love is perfect. I can give that." Haynesworth also told Burke that prison had given him skills that allowed him not only to survive, but to live every day of his free life with gratitude and purpose.

As they were saying goodbye, Burke tentatively reached out to shake Haynesworth's hand. Haynesworth shook his head. "Oh, we are long past that," he said. He opened his arms and put them around Burke, pulling her close.

One month later, Burke and Haynesworth stood on stage together and presented Thompson with her award before a packed ballroom. Each told their story. Thompson, who had never met Burke in person and had no idea she and Haynesworth would be appearing together, was overcome with emotion. Watching Burke and Haynesworth felt as if she were looking through a time machine and seeing herself and Ronald Cotton reflected there. She said, "Everything that I had been through and everything I had been trying to do for fifteen years came together in a perfect circle that made sense. This work was so much bigger than me."

Burke continued to mine the past, looking for answers. In retrospect, she wished she had understood how the test "match" that gave her so much confidence in 1984 was just blood typing, or how inaccurate cross-racial identifications can be. She said, "But I didn't know any of that then. I am not a racist, but race has a place in this, in the respect of, you don't just pick out certain details about people that you would with your own race. You don't know how to look for certain things." Yes, she had gotten Haynesworth's skin tone and approximate build correct, but there were thousands of men with those same physical characteristics, including Leon Davis. Add to that, Burke said, "the fact that you are put in a situation where you think you might die; you think you are paying attention to certain things but really you are paying attention to the knife against your throat."

Haynesworth told Burke that her mistake was a common one: Davis and he had been confused before, by people in their own neighborhood. But on some level, Burke doubted that she would ever be able to forgive herself. She also wondered if it would be possible to stay connected to Haynesworth. She found herself thinking about him all the time, wondering what he was doing and if he was happy. She pictured sitting down together for lunch or coffee, maybe even having dinner. And then she would stop and think: "Every time we've been together, we've had other people with us to spearhead the conversation. So there's this question: what would we talk about?"

Webb and Sarah

In December 2012, Thomas Webb was walking down the street in downtown Oklahoma carrying a duffle bag with everything he owned inside of it. He said, "I was fifty-three years old, and it occurred to me, my life is over. I had no job, no home, no money, no wife, nothing." A friend of Webb's had gotten clean the year before and recommended that he try Narcotics Anonymous. Webb attended his first meeting on January 24, 2013. He kept going, working the twelve steps, his mind focused on getting through a single day without using. A day turned into a week, a week into a month, a month into a year.

"Every addict has to get to this point where they surrender, where they realize that they are powerless over their addiction. I was ready to surrender," he said. "I had reached the bottom and I was in a state of desperation." In the daily Narcotics Anonymous meetings, Webb found fellowship with the other addicts who could relate to lies he had told himself for so long. He recalled: "You are dealing with a mental and emotional condition called insanity where you don't accept reality. You want to control it and distort it to fit your frame. Drugs do exactly that: create a reality that makes the addict feel comfortable and less fearful and less distressed until it is time for the drugs to wear off. Strangely enough, the way that I am recovering is the same way I got through the fourteen years in prison, with a daily routine and trusting in God to get me through this experience."

It was a struggle. Webb had used drugs to anesthetize himself. Now he felt everything. There were "physical, emotional and mental consequences I had to come to grips with. Instead of getting high, I prayed to give me courage to do the next right thing," he said.

As Webb approached the second year of his sobriety, his life had stabilized. A diagnosis of PTSD had provided for $720 a month in disability payments, and he moved into subsidized housing. His case—unfairly handled and incompletely resolved—was finished, and Webb had to accept it and move on.

But it wasn't. In 2014, an Oklahoma online journalism site called *Investigative Watch* began looking into whether the DNA that had exonerated Webb had ever been uploaded into the national database called CODIS, which contains the profiles of hundreds of thousands of offenders. It had, in 2006, and there had been a hit: to fifty-eight-year-old Gilbert Duane Harris, a former sanitation worker from Norman, the city where Sarah was living when her rape occurred. Despite knowing this fact for eight years, the Oklahoma authorities had never followed up. Shaun Hittle, the reporter whose story led to the public release of this information and led the police to get a warrant for Harris's arrest in July 2014, said the cause appeared to be bureaucratic ineptitude.[1]

In the fall of 2014, Corey Lambrecht, a detective from Norman, went to Sarah's home. No one was there, so he left his card. When Sarah called, he asked her to come to the police station in Norman. Sarah, whom Hittle had visited, was expecting to be told of the DNA match, but she was wholly unprepared for the rest of the story. Somberly, the Norman detective informed her that Harris raped a fourteen-year-old girl less than a year after he attacked Sarah. He had taken a plea deal and served only seven years. The police had located him in Biloxi, Mississippi, and extradited him to Oklahoma, where he was in jail awaiting trial on charges of raping and sodomizing Sarah, thirty-two years after the fact.[2]

Sarah stared at a recent color photograph of a black man wearing a blue watchman's cap. His hollowed-out cheeks were covered with gray stubble, and there was a vacant expression on his face. He looked ten years older than his stated age. Sarah pressed her hands over her chest. It felt as if a wound had been reopened, the knife cleaved more deeply into her body.

As long as the perpetrator remained unidentified, Sarah had clung to the faint hope that maybe Webb was guilty after all: "I did it maybe for my own sanity. Saying, no, I couldn't have been wrong, even though I knew I had been wrong." That tissue-thin self-deception had shredded, replaced by the nauseating realization that her mistaken identification had claimed an additional victim. It was, she believed, all her fault. Christy Sheppard, who has become friends with Sarah, says that listening to her tell the story "is like watching somebody be physically tortured. The amount of responsibility that she carries that she did not get him off the streets and that he did that to a fourteen-year-old child, it was like she was standing right there and let it happen."

Sarah retreated further. Her chest pains worsened, and she spent days without leaving the house. Then, one winter morning in 2015, Sarah was scrolling through her Facebook page when she came across a flyer posted by Heritage Hall, where she had gone to high school, about an event planned for February 23. In cooperation with the Oklahoma Innocence Project, Heritage was putting together a panel to talk about wrongful convictions. When Sarah clicked on the details, she caught her breath. One of the speakers was Thomas Webb.

It seemed like fate had intervened. "I just knew, this was it," she said. But on the day of the event, it took every ounce of courage she had to go. "It was icy and snowy, and I was scared to death," she said. Sarah showed up early, walking into the empty auditorium clutching a copy of *Picking Cotton*. When Webb came in and took a seat in the front, she approached timidly, tapping his shoulder and asking if they could talk outside.

Standing face-to-face in the narrow hallway, Webb saw a middle-aged white woman, pale and slight, her brown hair threaded with gray. He saw a stranger.

"I'm Sarah," she said and held out Jennifer Thompson's book, inside of which she had placed a note with her phone number. "This is my story." Her shoulders collapsed inward as she started to cry, telling him that she was sorry, so very sorry. For a moment, Webb stood completely still, unable to move or speak. Then he stepped forward, wrapping his arms around Sarah and folding her into his body. "I forgive you," he said. "I forgave you a long time ago."

But Webb's forgiveness was difficult for Sarah to accept. Sitting in her old high school auditorium afterward and listening to Webb tell his story, the pain in Sarah's chest got so bad that she had to get up and leave as soon as the event was finished. For Webb, the experience was surreal, "almost like I was speaking directly to her." Webb called her the next day; they talked on the phone for hours and made a plan to meet for lunch. When the chest pains continued, Sarah decided to go to the doctor because, she said, "I finally felt like I had something to live for." The cardiologist told her that the stents and other attempts to clear the blockages around her heart had failed. In late March 2015, Sarah underwent quadruple bypass surgery.

Webb's appearance at Heritage Hall brought another unexpected surprise. Seated in the audience was Eric Roth, an executive with Love's

Travel Stops and Country Stores, a family-owned chain of truck stops with more than four hundred locations. Roth was so impressed with Webb that he set up a lunch. On March 25, 2015, the day that Webb turned fifty-six, Roth called to ask if he would come on board as a coordinator helping to manage operations at its new stores. The money and benefits were good. Elated, Webb said yes.

Gilbert Harris, meanwhile, was scheduled to have a court hearing in May. Sarah was still recovering from the surgery, but she and Webb made plans to go to court together. Sarah said, "We wanted to tell everyone there, listen, we are the real victims of this man." Then came the terrible blow. Checking the case docket online a few days before the hearing, Sarah saw that the charges against Harris had been dismissed on May 8, 2015, after the judge concluded that the statute of limitation had run out.[3] Neither the police nor the district attorney's office had called to let her know.

Terrified, Sarah called Detective Lambrecht to find out where Harris was. She was so afraid Harris would come back and find her that she offered to pay for his bus ticket back to Mississippi. Lambrecht promised to look into the matter. Later, he sent Sarah an email confirming that Harris was back in Biloxi. The police had spotted him on the beach collecting cans.

In 2016, Webb renewed his fight for compensation from the state. It was not only the money he wanted; it was the official acknowledgment by the state that he was innocent. Larry Helman, a law professor and the former director of the Oklahoma Innocence Project, enlisted the help of Rand Eddy, an attorney in private practice. Eddy, looking at the case anew, realized that the trial court had never issued Webb an order formally undoing his conviction based on a finding of innocence, a prerequisite for obtaining compensation. On June 30, 2016, a judge signed the order, and Eddy submitted the application for compensation to Attorney General Scott Pruitt the following month.

Pruitt, a rock-ribbed conservative, did not respond to the petition for ninety days, which amounted to a denial under the statute. Webb took the news hard, breaking into tears as he described his anger and frustration. The state's steadfast refusal to admit any wrongdoing was incomprehensible and infuriating. The criminal justice system was failing again, deepening the injury of Harris's release with a refusal to acknowledge that it owed Webb any kind of reparation. It was another blow to Sarah, who had been praying for at least this small measure of justice. "They are denying us both from moving forward," Webb said.

In a fairy tale, the reunions between Haynesworth, Burke, Webb, and Sarah would bring about a perfect happy ending. But their face-to-face reckonings—poignant and at times emotionally overwhelming, particularly for Burke and Sarah—forced deeply buried shards to the surface. Closure, a word favored by some therapists and many in the media, proved a poor fit. There would be no neat mending of the tear in their lives. After the initial catharsis and relief came the questions. What would be different now? Would they stay connected? And if they did, was there a way to heal together?

CHAPTER ELEVEN

The Retreats

JENNIFER THOMPSON AND KATIE MONROE had lived their lives determined to turn personal tragedy into something bigger. Healing Justice presented an opportunity to do that work systemically on a much larger canvas by building a nationwide community for survivors of wrongful convictions. They envisioned their new organization providing the crucial foundation for that community by holding retreats where crime victims, exonerees, and family members could come together to engage in restorative justice practices. The retreats would be the integral first step in forging improbable alliances that would help the participants heal and even choose to become advocates, as they had.

Thompson had already tested the idea. In late 2014, before she created Healing Justice, Thompson had organized a two-day restorative justice retreat at a conference center north of San Francisco. Working with a prominent restorative justice practitioner, Sujatha Baliga, and partnering with the Northern California Innocence Project, Thompson had brought together four exonerees, two crime victims, and a victim's family member—Christy Sheppard. There were no lawyers, cameras, or intrusions from the outside world. Instead, there were group projects to complete and pointed individual questions to answer. The participants were asked to make themselves emotionally vulnerable, but at the same time, they felt safe, with their own people.

Thompson chose the Aqueduct Conference Center in Chapel Hill, North Carolina, for the first Healing Justice retreat. On a map, the Aqueduct seemed like a remote cluster of dots on a wash of unbroken green. Set on twenty-three acres of farmland, it had a lodge with a wide front porch looking out into a broad meadow surrounded by tall trees. Inside was an open dining hall and a light-filled meeting space. Two smaller buildings accommodated more guests. The furnishings were cozy, the food simple and distinctly Southern: fried chicken and macaroni for dinner, eggs and grits for breakfast. Instead of soda or alcohol, there was lemonade and sweet tea. And it was convenient, only a few minutes' drive from downtown Chapel Hill, making it relatively easy to access for the people who were coming from the airport.

The retreat was scheduled in mid-March 2016, when the weather would be warm but not unpleasant. In preparation, Thompson and Monroe trained to become restorative justice facilitators and partnered with Kim Cook, a sociology professor at the University of North Carolina in Wilmington. Cook, a sexual assault survivor herself, was the coauthor of the book *Life After Death Row: Exonerees Search for Community and Identity*. She, too, had gone through the restorative justice certification process.

Thompson sounded out exonerees with whom she has a close relationship, including Darryl Hunt. She saw him in late February, when she and Monroe had organized several listening sessions for federal officials at the DOJ's Office for Victims of Crime in Washington, DC. Hunt had been one of the featured speakers. Afterward, Thompson and he spent several hours together catching up.

At that point, Thompson and Hunt had been friends for more than a decade. But Thompson had known of Hunt for far longer. They both grew up in Winston-Salem. Deborah Sykes, the victim in Hunt's case, was sexually assaulted and killed just days after Thompson was raped. Thompson followed Hunt's case in the newspapers, positive he was guilty. "I went through years of hating Darryl, just detesting him," she said.

Winston-Salem is a small town in many ways. Thompson had gone to high school with members of Mark Rabil's family, and she knew that Rabil was Hunt's lawyer. Sometime in the early 2000s, Rabil approached Thompson at the YMCA where they were both members. He asked Thompson if she would be willing to use her platform to be an advocate for Hunt.

Thompson felt uneasy. Memories of the Sykes case and her feelings toward Hunt came flooding back. But she also felt a sense of responsibility. If there was another Ronald Cotton languishing in a North Carolina prison, Thompson felt a duty to use whatever influence she had to get him out. After reviewing the transcripts and case files, she came to the conclusion that Hunt was innocent and became an outspoken advocate for his release. Later, at Hunt's request, she served as the chair of the Darryl Hunt Project for Freedom and Justice.

But in 2007, Thompson left Hunt's organization. After *The Trials of Darryl Hunt* premiered at the Sundance Film Festival in 2006, it aired on HBO and was shown at film festivals around the world. Hunt went from being a well-known local figure to an international sensation, constantly traveling and speaking. As Hunt's celebrity grew, so did the demands of those around him, and it made Thompson uncomfortable to watch. It was all too familiar: like Thompson, "Darryl was being pulled in every direction and used up."

Thompson warned Hunt against putting too much pressure on himself to accommodate the desires of other people. She also knew, from her own experience, that "being famous and having notoriety is addictive." The limelight provided welcome adulation and attention after so many years of being cast aside. It also provided a level of noise and distraction that drowned out feelings of detachment, isolation, anger, sorrow, and loneliness. But at the end of the day, Thompson said, "there will always be a new exoneree with a compelling story. That place in the sun is fleeting. Your place will be taken, and you will have to go home to an empty space."

In recent years, it had been harder for Thompson to keep in touch with Hunt: "He would fall off the radar." When Thompson told Hunt about the retreat during their time together in Washington, DC, she emphasized that he would not be expected to perform or mentor anyone. Instead, he could take time for himself in a quiet, beautiful place to reflect and heal. Hunt seemed excited and enthusiastic. He assured Thompson he would be there.

Rabil was relieved to see Hunt so energized. Recent years had been difficult. In 2012, Hunt closed the Project for Freedom and Justice. During its five years of existence, the foundation had helped more than five thousand Homecomers reacclimate to society, but the recession had made raising money difficult. More trouble followed. In the spring of 2014, Hunt and his wife, April, separated after fourteen years of marriage. They later divorced, and Hunt had moved to Georgia to live with his sister. In 2015, Hunt told friends that he had been diagnosed with stage IV prostate cancer. Rabil said, "I was all worried about it. I went down to Atlanta and tried to go to the doctors' appointments with him, and he didn't want me to go." Rabil let the matter drop, wanting to respect Hunt's independence.

Meanwhile, Hunt was rapidly running out of money. Rabil, cognizant that people would likely be approaching Hunt with their hands out, had carefully structured his $2 million settlement to provide for several lump-sum payments, followed by a set amount every month for life. Several times, Hunt enlisted Rabil's help going to court to get judicial approval to sell off the monthly payments to private companies that took a cut in exchange for providing large and immediate infusions of cash. Rabil obliged, believing that Hunt needed the money to help April financially and to afford his cancer treatments.

On February 26, 2016, the day after Hunt's fifty-first birthday, Hunt and Rabil began a long drive from North Carolina to the University of Virginia, Frank Batten School of Leadership and Public Policy, where they had been invited to speak. During two days together in the car, they talked about Hunt's recent decision to move back to North Carolina and his renewed commitment to criminal justice advocacy, including Healing Justice. On stage, Hunt was his usual public self: a gifted and charismatic speaker with an innate ability to size up his audience—in this case, mainly white, well-educated graduate students and professors—delivering a message of personal redemption and ending with a call to action. And although Hunt seemed distracted at times when Rabil and he were alone, excusing himself to go up to his hotel room to take his medicine, Rabil figured that was to be expected under the circumstances. Before saying goodbye, Hunt and Rabil made plans to go to the annual Innocence Network conference, which was taking place a month later in San Antonio. Rabil purchased two tickets.

Then, on March 5, Hunt went missing after borrowing a truck from his friend Larry Little, an attorney and civil rights activist. Hunt had been staying with Little at his home in Winston-Salem off and on, and when he did not return, Little found a suicide note among his possessions. Ultimately, Little filed a missing person's report with the Winston-Salem police. By March 11, the first day of the Healing Justice retreat, Hunt had been missing for nearly a week, but Thompson did not know it. When her calls and texts went unreturned, she was hurt, baffled by Hunt's decision not to show up.

Sarah did not attend the retreat either. "I didn't feel strong enough," she said. "I thought I could, I thought I would, I had every intention, but in the end, I just could not do it." Sarah wanted to be there to show her support for Webb, but she feared the unknown. "I decided to wait until I felt physically and mentally stronger."

But the other participants, including Christy Sheppard, Janet Burke, Thomas Webb, and Thomas Haynesworth's friend and fellow exoneree Marvin Anderson, made the trip. Webb described the retreat as a life-changing experience. On the plane, he said, he was "dreading it, like something I had to get through and get it behind me." But when he arrived, he found a fellowship. He continued, "People were saying, 'I am no better no worse, I have been through the same thing that you have been through and I can receive what your experience was.' That was the first time I was in a group with other people who understood my exoneration experience from the inside out."

Webb had gone to several annual Innocence Network conferences, but he felt resentful and out of place there. Unlike most of the other exonerees, he had never been represented by an Innocence Project. That disconnect, and the fact that some exonerees had received hundreds of thousands if not millions of dollars in compensation, made the gathering seem like another elite club that was denying him membership. Webb spent the majority of the time in his hotel room, barely interacting with anyone.

After he got clean, Webb said, "I did not want to get hurt again; I did not want to get pulled into this thing again and feel like I was exposing myself again for nothing. Even though I had the opportunity to connect to these exonerees and this wonderful organization, emotionally I could not get there. With the retreat, I was on a different plane. I broke through a lot of those issues that I had. I was able to see that there's a lot of innocent people that are hurting and needed to hear my story."

The participants were asked to bring an object that was important to them. Webb brought a photograph of himself as a young boy with his family. He broke down as he told the group how worthless and abandoned he felt when his parents and siblings gave up on him. When it was his turn to listen, Webb gained a new understanding of the victims' perspective. "Listening to the experience of someone that has thought that you were guilty when you were really innocent, just to be able to hear how that works," he paused. "I can't tell you how many times I wracked my brain to understand how someone I did not know could point to me and say I was guilty. So it was important to see how that happens and to see how they were victimized by a system that was supposed to support them."

Sheppard said, "Exonerees are kind of taken aback at the victim's perspective. They never considered it because it was always like the victim belonged to the prosecution." She mentioned a conversation she had at the retreat with a death-row exoneree. When he told Sheppard that crime victims and exonerees lacked a shared experience, she said, "But we were lied to just like you were." His resistance came from the same place as Webb's: because a mistake of that magnitude was unfathomable, on some level, it had to be fault-based. Sheppard challenged him: "I said, 'There is no one who wants to get the right guy more than the victims. Think of the pressure that is mounted on them. Are rape victims any more responsible for picking the wrong one than someone who is coerced into confessing?' And he was receptive to that."

For Burke, learning of her mistake brought a loss of identity: "I was a rape survivor, but what am I now? What do you call that person who messed it up with the identification? People have told me I am the offender and I should be the one in prison." At first, Burke was inclined to accept the blame that was heaped on her. At the retreat, her view became more nuanced. The word "offender" suggested a criminal mind-set. And yet, however unintentional her mistake, it had been catastrophic and caused deep and irreparable harm.

Burke was also struggling to explain to her family why she needed to reengage with what had happened to her and participate in the retreat. Some of the retreat participants brought family members. Burke was given the option of bringing her husband, Paul. She didn't. In the nearly twenty years they had been together, the rape rarely came up; when it did, the references were terse and oblique. Burke had never told Paul what had happened to her in any detail—not the crime, testifying at trial, her role in the exoneration, or her relationship with Haynesworth.

Burke was protective of her family, careful to control her emotions whenever possible when it came to her case. She knew the retreat would force a relinquishment of that control, erasing the boundaries she had carefully established, and if Paul saw her crying, it would frighten him. He would want to stop her anguish, and it was hard to explain that she was crying tears of relief and release.

And she did cry. A lot. Burke explained that she had spent decades perfecting the skill of pushing aside feelings of guilt, shame, and anger to go about her daily life as a wife and mother with a demanding, full-time job. Flashbacks and dark thoughts broke through the smooth surface of her life only in isolated moments, usually when she was alone in the car. "But at the retreat there was no denying any of it," she said. "It is all laid out there." Listening to the exonerees describe the barriers and challenges they faced made Burke feel responsible all over again. Haynesworth had not been able to attend, but his friend Marvin Anderson was there, and Burke spent time talking with him. When Anderson told Burke that Haynesworth wanted and needed Burke to absolve herself, she knew he was right.

Burke started thinking about how she could use her professional skills to improve the system. Surely police officers could be better trained to prepare victims for the shattering news that the wrong person had been in prison all along. She wanted to use her years of experience with trauma victims at Childsavers, a nonprofit that focuses on child victims, to educate law enforcement officers and help connect survivors with one another so that they would not feel so alone. Burke mulled how to explain to her family the desire she felt to do this work and whether they could accept this new part of her.

Two days into the retreat, Thompson and Monroe were feeling almost giddy. Their group had cohered. But the final morning, Sunday, March 13, brought devastating news. Checking Facebook, one of the retreat participants told Thompson and Monroe that the police had recovered Hunt's body seventy-five miles away in Winston-Salem. Hunt was inside Larry Little's pickup truck with a gun between his knees, dead from a bullet wound to the stomach.[1]

The car had been parked in a strip mall for days, Hunt's slumped body unnoticed by the steady stream of shoppers going about their daily business. Thompson, who had learned that a missing person's report had been issued Friday night, said she had a growing sense of foreboding, but the lonely, violent way that Hunt had taken his life shocked her. When Rabil learned that the official cause of death was suicide, he refused to believe it. The Winston-Salem officers, after all, were part of the same police force that had targeted and railroaded Hunt. For a while, Rabil considered the possibility that Hunt had been murdered: "I put on my lawyer hat, questioning the medical examiner and threatening the police." But the physical evidence and Hunt's note left little room for doubt.

For Monroe, Hunt's death was yet another indictment of how the system continued to fail the wrongfully convicted. She said, "Shooting yourself in a borrowed truck in a mini mall—there is something so wrong with that. From beginning to end, he was not getting the support he needed. Whether it was medical or emotional. Because if he was, his death would not have happened in that way."

More than a decade after his release, Hunt had succumbed to depression, PTSD, and the unending struggle to feel free. Monroe saw his despair reflected in the experiences of the participants at the retreat and, more viscerally, her own family. Just when Monroe was starting to believe they had rebuilt their lives, her mother, Beverly, had told her she was feeling worse than ever. Running in an endless feedback loop in Katie Monroe's brain were questions she could not answer: "Where am I still broken? How am I going to fix it? Do I really want to look at it?"

Initially, what Rabil felt most was anger. He recalled how people in Winston-Salem liked to say that the best thing that ever happened to Hunt was getting charged with Sykes's murder. The exoneration had brought him money and fame—wasn't that better than the likely alternatives? Hunt had grown up in poverty, without a father. His mother died when he was nine, and his grandparents died when he was nineteen. When Hunt was arrested, he was homeless. Maybe prison had even saved his life.

Now Rabil wanted to scream in all of their faces: "Darryl Hunt never had any great desire to be a hero." Before he was arrested, Hunt went to the city employment office every week looking for a job. Rabil continued, "He wanted to work for the city and retire, have a little house, have a dog, have some kids. He was a strong person but being in prison just fucked him up. It is a crazy thing to be ripped out of the world and turned into a slave and tortured for twenty years."

The attention, adulation, and the demands that followed "imposed this great pressure on him to be *that* Darryl Hunt." Always on. Always doing for others. For Hunt, Healing Justice had come too late. Rabil said, "What we have ignored, and what we need to pay more attention to, is to bring this healing into the process from the get-go, but we are all afraid of it." Ironically, what Hunt needed was the same care and attention he gave to his Homecomers. What he got instead were expectations—some self-imposed, others coming from family members, friends, exonerees, and his own lawyers. Rabil believed that trying to fulfill those expectations exacerbated Hunt's trauma and PTSD.

But even confronting this harsh truth left Rabil unprepared for the autopsy results and the brutal revelations that followed. Hunt's body showed no signs of cancer; apparently, he had never had it. According to his ex-wife April, Hunt was addicted to cocaine and had been for more than a decade. The treatments and doctors' visits Hunt described were not real, only the drugs, which April said Hunt took to get "numb."[2]

For years, Hunt had lived in prisons where skinheads conspired to kill him while guards looked the other way, where his best hope of survival was to spend years in solitary confinement. He had talked to Rabil about his panic attacks but less about his depression, which worsened over time. Intellectually, Rabil understood that "a traumatized brain has a propensity toward addiction." He also knew that Hunt had suffered more severe trauma than most people could begin to fathom, which was different in kind and in duration from the trauma of rape or combat. Rabil said, "It is a whole different story when the entire criminal justice system screws with you."

Three weeks after the funeral, Rabil went alone to the Innocence Network conference, which, he said, "had a nice tribute for Darryl." Asked how he is feeling a year later, Rabil paused. "This was very, very hard on me. It is only in the last few months that I am coming out of it." What Rabil was forced to confront was that Hunt—a man he loved deeply and who had shaped his life's work—was in many ways a mystery to him. "In retrospect, I see now that there was always going to be this barrier, because the respect we had for each other prevented him from opening up to me. I don't think he wanted to disappoint me or anybody that he worked with." In the end, Rabil said, he was left with a bitter truth: "Darryl did get the death penalty, and it was imposed by the system."

At the retreat, Thompson and Monroe did what they could. With the help of Thompson's daughter, Britt Stone, who had known and loved Hunt for years, they organized an impromptu memorial. Stone spelled out Hunt's initials in wildflowers and broken branches. The retreat participants gathered in a circle, singing and praying. A few shared memories. Fernando Bermudez, wrongfully convicted of murder and incarcerated for eighteen years, told the group that when he arrived at his first Innocence Network conference, feeling awkward and alone, Hunt was a welcoming presence. He bought Bermudez lunch and sat outside with him and other new exonerees, smoking cigarettes and shooting the breeze.

But many of the participants, like Webb and Burke, had never met Hunt, and it was impossible to convey the depth of the loss or try to understand what had happened: the information was too raw and incomplete. For Thompson and Monroe, Hunt's death was the materialization of their darkest fears: for themselves as much as for the people they were trying to help. But it also renewed their sense of commitment and the urgent need for their work. Exonerees, victims, and others deeply harmed by wrongful convictions needed to be able to safely name their feelings and express them. And they had to understand that what happened could not be fixed, only accepted and put in a place where it would not cannibalize the rest of their lives. Posting photos and forming Google groups and private Facebook groups after the retreat was over, Monroe was determined to maintain the fragile connections formed among members of the group and to find the people outside her circle of contacts who belonged in that community. "The challenge," she said, "is making sure there are no more Darryls."

Eight months later, Healing Justice held its second retreat at the Aqueduct. Some participants from the first retreat returned. For others, like Jerome Morgan, the experience was new. For Morgan, freedom itself was new. His case had come to an end only six months earlier when Leon Cannizzaro, the Orleans Parish district attorney who had fought Morgan's exoneration for more than a decade, finally dismissed the charges on May 27, 2016.[3]

A trial judge had thrown out Morgan's conviction in January 2014. Though Morgan had been released on bond the following month, his movements were heavily restricted while Cannizzaro's office appealed all the way to the Louisiana Supreme Court and prepared to retry him. For fourteen months, Morgan was confined to his home, permitted to leave only to work and go to court, where he underwent weekly drug tests he was forced to pay for himself. Throughout, the threat of going back to prison loomed.[4]

Now forty-four, Morgan speaks less in prose than in a kind of loose poetry. His features are fine-boned, almost delicate, but he is strong, his arms and neck corded with muscle, the faint indigo of old tattoos visible on his exposed skin. His clothing choices reflect an artist's sensibility and playfulness, mixing brilliant colors and textures: scarlet vests and matching socks, densely patterned pants, stylish trench coats and hats, oversized sunglasses. He has a quiet magnetism that draws others to him.

Morgan's nightmare started two decades earlier, when, at the age of seventeen, he was arrested for the shooting death of another seventeen-year-old, Clarence Landry III, and for wounding two other teenagers. The crime occurred at a sweet-sixteen party in a hotel ballroom in east New Orleans. The lights were low in the ballroom, and the shooting, which followed a group scuffle, lit up the darkness in a lightning-quick burst. No one fully understood what was happening until it was over and Landry's body was lying on the floor, a mass confusion made worse by the screaming and chaos that followed. Kevin Johnson, a friend of Landry's, chased unsuccessfully after the shooter, who ran out of the hotel and into an alley, disappearing over a fence.[5]

Rumors began to circulate that the killer was Morgan, and Johnson was brought down to the police station to make an identification from a photo array. Although Johnson twice told the police the shooter was not Morgan, they insisted that he pick him anyway. Under pressure by law enforcement and Landry's mother, Sandra, he ultimately did. So did one of the surviving victims, Hakim Shabazz. He, too, initially told the police it was not Morgan, only to be told repeatedly that he should pick Morgan's picture.[6]

All along, the prosecution was in possession of a 911 dispatch log establishing that the police arrived within six minutes of the shooting and ordered the ballroom sealed. Detectives compiled a list of names, and Morgan's was on it. Morgan's documented physical location meant that it was physically impossible for him to have been the fleeing suspect chased by Johnson. But none of this evidence was turned over to Morgan's lawyer, who did little to investigate the case.[7]

Instead, Morgan was tried and convicted in a single day of the murder of Landry based on the testimony of Shabazz and Johnson. On September 14, 1994, the judge sentenced Morgan "to serve his natural life at hard labor in the Department of Corrections."[8] No parole. Morgan was sent to the Louisiana State Penitentiary, known as Angola, the largest maximum-security prison in the United States. He was eighteen years old.

Angola bore the hallmarks of the Southern plantation it had once been.[9] For the first three months, Morgan was assigned to a "working cellblock." Every day, he was lined up and marched off to the fields with scores of other inmates—overwhelmingly African American—to spend eight hours picking cotton, digging ditches, and cutting grass with a garden hoe. They were paid four cents an hour, their labor overseen by armed corrections officers—overwhelmingly white—who patrolled the fields on horseback, Morgan said, "spitting tobacco and talking crazy." Common disciplinary citations included picking cotton too slowly. Asked whether "Angola was like a slave plantation," Morgan replied, "There is no 'like.' That's exactly what it is."

Inmates who were well behaved eventually found other permanent placements that Morgan calls more "subtly horrible," even serving in the governor's mansion. Morgan was not one of them. He spoke up and talked back, leading to regular stints in Camp J, where he was placed in solitary confinement or sent back out into the fields. When he was not being disciplined, though, Morgan took every opportunity to learn. He got his GED, taught himself to cut hair, and took classes in graphic design. His artistic ability was obvious and quickly became well known throughout the prison.

Morgan credits his upbringing, regular exercise, and spiritual practice with giving him the skills and perspective he needed to save his mind: "My childhood being in disarray helped me to overcome obstacles of enormous magnitude." Though he grew up in foster care, he never viewed himself as deprived, saying, "The neighborhood raised me." And it made him street smart. "As a young child trying to find my way in the world," he said, "I had to avoid people who are three or four times older than me and experienced and targeting me for their benefit."

A strong sense of identity and inner determination insulated Morgan from physical attacks and from turning to drugs and alcohol, which, though banned, were readily available. He said, "I had respect for everybody and I learned that growing up in my neighborhood. I respected everybody else's experience because I wanted to be respected." To Morgan, the other inmates were "in some way, my family. They were there wrongfully much in the same way that I was. I was not so prideful as to turn my experience into self-pity and make myself even more special than the circumstances may be. Because everyone in there had a similar experience, even if they were not innocent."

Morgan could even identify with Shabazz and Johnson, whose testimony sent him to prison. In 2013, sitting in the courtroom with his attorneys from the Innocence Project of New Orleans, Morgan felt an emotion approaching empathy as they recanted their false identifications. Now grown men, both described the pressure they felt as teenagers when New Orleans police detectives pushed them relentlessly to choose Morgan's picture, even after they had eliminated him as a suspect.

On the witness stand, Shabazz recounted the conversation with the police detective this way: "It was like, 'Man, do you know who shot you?' And I was like, 'No, I don't know who shot me.' And he was, like, 'Jerome shot you. Do you know Jerome Morgan?' And I was like, 'Yeah, I know him from school, went to school with him before.' He was like, 'Jerome shot you.' And I was like, 'All right.'" Shabazz continued, "It's almost like, they paint this picture for me, you know, and that it was him."[10]

Asked why he was recanting, Shabazz began to weep, saying, "I want to clear myself of some guilt, man." Over the years, he explained, he had tried unsuccessfully to justify what he had done but had known all along "it just wasn't right." At that point, Shabazz had to stop to wipe his eyes and drink a glass of water. He concluded, "I just don't think that—that he should have to spend another day in jail on my account, for what I said then."[11] Morgan said, "Him showing that kind of conscience and having the integrity to open up about what he suffers in his own situation, knowing that he contributed to my wrongful conviction and being manipulated into being a part of it, it takes an honorable individual to be able to do that. And he had no reason to put himself out there except to do right, especially given the gravity."

The consequences were grave. In 2015, Cannizzaro's office indicted Shabazz and Johnson for perjury using alternative legal theories. The prosecutor told the judge, "They either put an innocent man in jail for 20 years or they lied to get him out."[12] Morgan was outraged, not only by the charges, but by the state's cavalier attitude toward the truth, particularly when it came to Shabazz: "It opened my mind to think he is a victim twice over. First, he gets shot, then coerced, and he carries around the burden of the victim's family not getting justice, knowing what they had been told the whole time was a lie. When he admits he was wrong, he gets charged and turned into a criminal."

In April 2015, with the appeal still pending, the judge relaxed Morgan's bond conditions. Morgan had a strict curfew, but he was allowed to work and be out of the house during the daytime. At that point, Morgan and his friend Daniel Rideau started talking about opening a barbershop together. They shared similar histories: like Morgan, Rideau, who is African American, had been convicted of murder as a teenager and sent to Angola. He was released eight-and-a-half years later, after a judge found that prosecutors withheld crucial evidence at his trial and he agreed to accept a plea to manslaughter.[13] Rideau, who keeps his head shaved and wears a full beard, had become a licensed barber after his release, and Morgan was an unpaid apprentice, in training to become one. They leased space from a local organization called Resurrection After Exoneration founded by John Thompson, another Louisiana exoneree, also black, who had spent eighteen years in prison, fourteen of them on death row. But Morgan was not able to be at their makeshift barbershop much. He had to make a living.

The only steady, salaried job that Morgan had been able to find since leaving Angola was working for a company that put up advertising in the city's bus shelters. The job sounded better than it was. Before he could put up the ads, Morgan had to clean out the shelters themselves. It was filthy work. On New Orleans's famed Canal Street, homeless people lived in the shelters and used them as open-air toilets. In the early morning hours, it was Morgan's job to have them evicted by the police, then pour chemical disinfectant over the vacated area to remove any trace of their existence. At night, the homeless would return, and at dawn, the miserable circus would start up all over again.

All the while Morgan's fury grew. As long as Cannizzaro's office continued to appeal, first to the state's intermediate court of appeals and then to its supreme court, it was impossible to be physically or psychologically free. In November 2015, frustrated and fed up, Morgan appeared before the New Orleans City Council. He told the council members that Cannizzaro's crusade was nothing more than a desperate attempt to save face. The goal of the protracted litigation, Morgan explained, was to wear him down until he agreed to plead guilty in exchange for a time-served sentence. Morgan told the council members, "But I won't bow." Vowing to fight "this barbaric system" to the bitter end, he finished, "I can only hope and pray that I can finally get this process done so I can finally be able to salvage the rest of my life."[14]

When Morgan described Louisiana's criminal justice system as barbaric, he meant it. Morgan had spent a lot of time in the courtroom, not only for his own case but for the cases of friends and relatives. He watched again and again as white prosecutors convicted young black men and white judges ordered their incarceration. Whether it was the school-to-prison pipeline or the War on Drugs, the casualties on the battlefield were always drawn from the same population. In Morgan's view, the criminal courts existed to perpetuate white supremacy, handing over the convicted to the state's prisons, where they were turned into slaves.

When Cannizzaro finally dropped the case in May 2016, Morgan felt equal measures of relief and insult. Cannizzaro announced that the Louisiana Supreme Court had tied his hands by barring the reuse of Shabazz's and Johnson's twenty-year-old recanted identifications. Morgan was guilty, Cannizzaro insisted, and he spared no drama in describing the anguish of the victim's family at the injustice of the outcome: "What is most disappointing to me about this entire incident is that, as Mrs. Landry lays in bed dying of cancer, the justice for which she worked so hard to obtain is ripped from her fingers and she is helpless to stop it."[15]

Morgan said of Cannizzaro, "He is a green-eyed devil for real. You see the same evil spirit in his words: how do you have the audacity to do that to another human being? This woman never got justice, is dying of cancer, and he is trying to use her." Emily Maw, one of Morgan's attorneys, said that Cannizzaro's dishonesty was jaw-dropping, noting that the Innocence Project of New Orleans had stayed in close touch with Landry's parents throughout the case and had their full support.

When he was finally free, Morgan seized on the opportunity that Healing Justice offered: "I needed a place where I did not have to worry about the demands on my life, to get my wits back, to get my appreciation back for myself. I believe in healing, and I have never been one to ignore the fact that there was damage to me from the years I have done." Morgan was determined to reclaim his voice. Being in prison had silenced him; in court, he spoke only through his attorneys: "I wanted to be my own advocate. It is not about me, 'look at me look, at me,' but it was about using my experience." Morgan especially wanted to reach out to impoverished youth in his community before they were sucked into the void of a racialized criminal justice system he believed had been engineered to steal black lives.

After his three days at the Healing Justice retreat, Morgan decided that his life in New Orleans was untenable. For months, he had given short shrift to his true ambition, which was to open his own barbershop, figuring that it was too risky. Instead, he had gritted his teeth and continued to clean bus shelters for the security of a regular paycheck and establishing a work history: "I had very deliberately been trying to work within the system, to show an actual track record to get myself to a point where I had some foundation." The job was draining, and not only of his time and energy. It was draining his soul.

Several days after Morgan came home from the retreat, he quit his job. He explained, "Our government is committing crimes against the public, the wrongfully convicted, the victim's families, the real perpetrators and not putting them in a place where they can't commit these crimes anymore." As far as Morgan was concerned, he was being paid to run off homeless people and conceal the evidence of the ordeals brought on by their poverty and brokenness. "I felt like I was part of a system that I detested," he said. "I could not do that job anymore that was pitting me against these victims who were being robbed of opportunities, while the real perpetrators are protected by the law. So, I decided that I can't spend no more time wasted on someone else's agenda, because no one was on the agenda for real justice for whatever reason—misrepresentation, lack of understanding."

Instead, Morgan decided, he would create his own agenda.

· · ·

Sarah made it to the second Healing Justice retreat, but barely. She had not slept for two full nights before, in the iron-fisted grip of anxiety. Still, she said, "I had to go. I didn't want to let Thomas [Webb] down and I didn't want to let myself down. I was going." In the circle, Sarah was seated between Jennifer Thompson and Dustin Sheppard, Christy Sheppard's husband. Thompson and Katie Monroe passed out several sheets of paper with a list of the participants. For the exonerees, there was a description of the wrongful conviction and the years spent in prison. The list was long and, Sarah said, "hard to look at." As each person spoke, Sarah would refer back to the sheet and see a description of what had happened in that case.

When it was Sarah's turn with the talking piece, she did not say much. She felt intimidated and a little star-struck. Reading Thompson's book had changed Sarah's life by leading her to realize that she was not alone. The book's hopeful message of healing and redemption through reconciliation was what had led Sarah to seek out Webb. But Thompson was not quite real to Sarah; she was a glamorous heroine who had given a TED talk, received a shelf-full of prestigious awards, and had been on every major television news program in the country. Sarah said, "I never thought I would actually meet her."

And hearing so many stories at once was overwhelming. Sarah tried to give each speaker her full attention, but it was draining to sit in the circle, hour after hour, with only short breaks to stretch her legs and try to release some of the tension before going back for more. Sarah's focus was not really to make connections with other exonerees or crime victims and or to delve into her own experience. She was there for Webb: to show her support in what felt like a unilateral relationship, with Webb always in a caretaking role. It was no different at the retreat: he was always looking out for her, saving her a seat at every meal and signaling to everyone there that she was a special person in his life.

On the second day, Sarah fell apart. Talking piece in hand, Webb was speaking to the circle about the series of harms that flowed from his wrongful conviction: most pointedly, his lack of ability to trust people and form long-term relationships. When he felt let down by a friend or prospective girlfriend, his immediate reaction was to cut off all contact to avoid further hurt and disappointment. An emotional person, Webb wept openly as he spoke to the group. Sarah was shaking from head to toe. She said, "I just did not know whether I could take it, and I was making these sounds, trying not to sob. At that moment, I felt responsible for all that he was saying and it broke my heart. I could not talk after that. I just passed on that round. I could not even speak."

As the afternoon wore on, Sarah found herself unable to recover. Each time it was her turn, she passed the talking piece without a word: "I just wanted to get the hell out of there. I wanted to leave, to get fresh air."

That night after dinner, the group went outside into the meadow. As the sky darkened, they lit white Chinese lanterns, which were patterned with words the participants had written in black marker, describing the pain and harm they wanted to release. As the heat from the flame ignited the bit of fuel contained inside, the lanterns filled with air and floated up, high over the tops of the evergreen trees surrounding the property. One by one, they sailed away, until they were tiny orange stars that glowed for a brief moment before burning up. Sarah watched, with her arms wrapped tightly around herself. It was magical to see, but lacked the desired effect. When the last lantern was gone, Sarah felt as laden as ever.

Afterward, the group gathered around a bonfire, making s'mores, singing, and talking in small groups. Sarah hovered at the edge of the circle, away from the others. "This was my life-changing moment," she said, "because I called Thomas over to me and told him how I knew I was responsible for him feeling the way that he feels and that my heart was broken."

When Webb's expression darkened and he started shaking his head, "I realized from his tone and the way he was looking at me that my reaction was not at all what he wanted to hear."

Frustrated and angry, Webb said, "Sarah, I have told you over and over and over again that it's not your fault."

Sarah said, "Okay, Thomas, I hear you." But she didn't. What she felt in the moment was an anger of her own as he turned and walked back to the bonfire, leaving her there.

Sarah walked back to her room. She said, "I went onto the balcony. It had started to rain, and I stayed out there for a long, long time. All night, I could not sleep. Over and over in my mind, I kept asking, why am I doing this to myself? Thomas is sick of me and I am sick of me. This needs to end."

Sarah woke up the next morning physically and emotionally exhausted. Her muscles ached, her brain hurt, and she wanted to go home. But she had also come to a realization: "I had felt since knowing and loving Thomas that it would not be the right thing to do to let some of my guilt go, because I deserved it. But in that very moment of confrontation, I knew that I needed to, for both of us. I can't be responsible for this grown man who has been living his life outside of prison for twenty years. His issues are not my fault, in the same way that my issues are not his fault. I hope so many good things for him, but I also realize that Thomas is responsible for those things, not me. He has to be able to maintain that and if it doesn't work, I can't blame myself. That is what I finally learned. I finally learned that."

The retreat provided a space and a setting where Sarah could receive Webb's advice, understanding that it was not meant only for her. She had to forgive herself for his sake and spare him the impossible task of trying to fill an ever-expanding void. Webb said, "What makes me put a period behind our journey is that she forgives herself. There is nothing for me to forgive her for. Sarah has been living in her own prison, and even though the cell doors were open, she didn't want to come out." Until she did, Webb said a part of him would always be locked inside with her.

Sarah said, "I needed to see it in his face, in his eyes, in his body language. This was not some random text or a quick phone call or lunch; it was him and me. That very moment changed everything. It truly changed me. It was just this release. And I don't feel the heaviness in me, like I did. It seems simple to say it now, but it wasn't."

The trip back did not go smoothly. Coming home, Sarah and Webb's first flight, to Dallas, was delayed, and they missed their connecting flight to Oklahoma City. By the time they arrived in Dallas, everything in the airport was closed. Both had checked their bags. It had been a long day of sitting around, stressed, bored, hungry, and exhausted. Strangely though, Sarah said, "we worked. When Thomas would get upset, because we were stranded, I would step in and give him a candy bar and something to drink, and if I got pissy, he would step up." They didn't talk about the retreat, but they conversed easily and joked around. At one point, Webb lay down on his side on several plastic chairs and fell asleep. Sarah kept vigil beside him, making sure, she said, "that no one messed with him."

When it was clear that they were not going to make it back that night, Sarah called her husband, John, who drove three hours from Oklahoma City to pick them up. Webb fell asleep in the back seat on the way home. When they spoke later that week, Sarah told Webb about her revelation: "I just let him know that it hit me like a ton of bricks but that I finally got it. I didn't have to explain much. He knew exactly what I was talking about." Sarah says her new goal is simple: "Live. Just continue to live and not carry this God-awful weight around with me all the time."

CHAPTER TWELVE

The Reformers, Part I

WITH SO MANY PARTS of the criminal justice system broken and dangling, how does reform happen? Viewed as a whole, deformities create a Frankenstein monster: giant, hideous, and inhuman. The enormity of the problem can feel overwhelming: it is as if each piece has to be broken apart and reconfigured. But for some wrongful conviction survivors, the compulsion to make some sense of their suffering by taking on this work drives them past the realistic fear that their efforts will end in failure.

Oklahoma

Christy Sheppard grew up believing fervently in the death penalty as an instrument to deliver justice and retribution. When Ron Williamson was sentenced to die following his conviction for raping and murdering her cousin, Sheppard was elated. When Dennis Fritz, his codefendant, was spared by one vote, she was outraged. Death was the only appropriate punishment for two men she believed were evil. Where Williamson was concerned, Sheppard's only regret was that the medical administration of the lethal drugs meant that he was likely to suffer no more than a dog getting put to sleep.

In her fervent embrace of capital punishment, Sheppard was no different from the vast majority of Oklahomans. The state carried out its first execution by electrocution in 1915 and had put a total of eighty-two men to death by 1972, when the US Supreme Court's decision in *Furman v. Georgia* created a brief, nationwide moratorium. In 1977, after the moratorium was lifted, Oklahoma rewrote its law to comply with the Supreme

Court's new standards, becoming the first state to authorize execution by lethal injection.

Since 1990, Oklahoma has executed 109 men and 3 women, more than any other state per capita and second only to Texas in actual numbers. For two decades, Oklahoma carried out its lethal injections using a three-drug cocktail: sodium thiopental, to induce a coma-like state; a "paralytic agent" to stop respiration; and potassium chloride to stop the heart. The method was considered by the state to be safe and humane, leading to a quick and presumably painless death.[1]

But in the last decade, advocates have made inroads in their campaign to abolish the death penalty by shutting down access to the three-drug cocktail. This campaign was effective, in part because of headlines announcing the exoneration of a number of death-row inmates. In 2009, Hospira, the only manufacturer of sodium thiopental in the United States, ceased production entirely. When states sought the drug from companies in Europe, their efforts were rebuffed. Oklahoma adapted by tinkering with the cocktail recipe.[2]

In 2014, Oklahoma used Midazolam, a sedative, as the first drug in the cocktail to execute inmate Clayton Lockett, theorizing that it would be as effective as sodium thiopental in rendering him unconscious. But as the warden later described it, Lockett's execution was "a bloody mess."[3] After Lockett was given the Midazolam cocktail, he began to jerk and buck against his restraints, saying, "This shit is fucking with my mind" and "The drugs are not working."[4] Thirty-three minutes after giving Lockett the Midazolam, the state stopped the execution. Lockett had a fatal heart attack about ten minutes later. It had taken him nearly forty-five minutes to die.

The state responded by increasing the dosage of Midazolam by a factor of five and using the revised formula to execute Charles Warner on January 15, 2015. Warner's last words were, "My body is on fire."[5] It took nearly twice the amount of time the state anticipated would be necessary to kill him. Next in line was Richard Glossip, who had become a familiar name as the lead plaintiff in a federal lawsuit to stop Oklahoma from using Midazolam. Shortly after Warner was put to death, the United States Supreme Court took the case, staying Glossip's execution.

Unlike Lockett and Warner, Glossip had always insisted he was innocent, and there was reason to believe him. The state's case turned on the testimony of Justin Sneed, who admitted killing the victim with a baseball bat, saying he did so at Glossip's request. In exchange for Sneed's testimony, the prosecution agreed not to seek the death penalty. There was no physical evidence against Glossip, and Sneed's account of the crime had evolved over the years, spawning eight different variations, according to Glossip's attorneys. The list of Glossip's supporters was long and star-studded, with advocates like Oklahoma senator Tom Coburn, actress Susan Sarandon, Barry Scheck, and Sister Helen Prejean.

On June 29, 2015, the Supreme Court ruled against Glossip. By a vote of 5–4, the justices rejected Glossip's attack on the Midazolam cocktail because he had failed to come up with "a known and reliable alternative" designed to kill him more mercifully. The majority rejected the dissenters' argument that the state was barred from using a method that "could be seen as a devolution to a more primitive era." The death penalty had long been held to be constitutional, the majority reasoned, and could be carried out in any number of ways—old and new.[6]

After Glossip's execution was rescheduled for September 16, 2015, Steve Saloom, the former policy director at the Innocence Project, reached out to Sheppard and asked if she would be willing to write an op-ed on Glossip's behalf. The idea seemed crazy. "I am going to get my house burned down," Sheppard told him. In Oklahoma, the death penalty was a staple of the culture; loving it was a part of being a patriotic American.

In the small town of Ada where Sheppard lived, people still spoke with pride about a vigilante execution more than a century earlier. It happened in 1909, when a wealthy cattle rancher was killed. Four men were arrested, but before they could be put on trial, a mob broke into the jail, dragged them out, and hung them in a nearby barn.[7] According to the *Oklahoman*, their motivating belief was that "the ponderous machinery of justice seems to move too slowly."

A gruesome photograph of the four dead bodies—dangling from the rafters as chickens pecked at the ground below—was emblazoned on T-shirts, coffee mugs, and postcards. Sheppard saw the memorabilia around town when she was growing up, always with the same tagline: "Ada: A Great Place to Hang Out." "We have our own brand of justice here," Sheppard said.

A prominent attorney in Oklahoma City once told Sheppard that her fellow citizens wanted, at the very least, to make sure the death penalty was fairly and humanely administered. Sheppard wasted no time setting him straight, "No, they don't. When people hear it is a bloody mess, the more miserable it is, the better they like it. What a lot of Oklahomans will say after you describe a botched execution is, 'Good.'"

But Sheppard no longer felt that way herself. Williamson's and Fritz's exonerations were incontrovertible proof that the state could and did get it wrong. Had Williamson died according to the jury's determination, strapped to a gurney with state officials pushing lethal drugs into his veins, it would have been murder. Nor was Williamson an outlier; nine other people had been freed from Oklahoma's death row after it was discovered that they were innocent. And while Sheppard's beloved aunt had cried when the jury—by one vote—spared the life of Glen Gore, her daughter Debbie's real killer, Sheppard felt a small measure of relief. It was Gore's second trial, and Sheppard did not want her family to suffer through another round of endless appeals.

Sheppard felt that she had been complicit by joining in the state's efforts to kill the men convicted of her cousin's rape and murder. It was true that state officials declared complete confidence in Glossip's guilt. But so had the prosecutors in Debbie Carter's case, even after a judge had ordered the release of Williamson and Fritz. The state's assurances rang hollow. "I know these cases are not about the truth," she said. "It is politics, it is a game where people are moved around and played. It is not fair and it is not balanced." She decided it would be moral cowardice not to speak out. It was not the cause she would have chosen, but she felt it was choosing her.

On September 12, 2015, Sheppard's op-ed was published in the *Oklahoman*. She started by acknowledging the suffering of the victim and his loved ones. She went on to describe the suffering she and her family members experienced as the evidence unraveled against the condemned men in her cousin's case. "[The victim] and his family deserve justice," she wrote, "but justice won't be served if Glossip is put to death and we find out too late that he is innocent of this crime."[8]

Sheppard did not say that she was morally opposed to the death penalty; she made it clear she was not: "I still struggle with my desire for justice and what I know about wrongful convictions." But the question mark hanging over Glossip's involvement could not be reconciled with the finality of his punishment. As long as there was doubt, she wrote, "it actually threatens justice—and peace of mind—to make the leap to execute him."[9]

Two days later, Glossip's advocates held a standing-room-only televised press conference at the Oklahoma state capitol. Don Knight, Glossip's lead attorney, started off by quoting Sheppard and imploring his audience to take her message into consideration. An hour later, Knight ended this way: "I began by talking a little bit about that letter that Christy Sheppard gave and I think I would like to end there as well because it is a powerful letter. A very powerful letter." He proceeded to read most of it aloud. Sheppard, watching at home, was amazed.[10]

On September 16, hours before Glossip was scheduled to die, his lawyers convinced the state's Court of Criminal Appeals to issue a stay, but when it was lifted two weeks later, Oklahoma governor Mary Fallin announced that the execution was going forward on September 30. After Glossip had eaten his last meal, he got another reprieve—his fourth in a year. The state, as it turned out, did not have any more potassium chloride, the drug used to induce cardiac arrest. Scott Mullins, Fallin's legal counsel, argued that the execution should go forward anyway because the state had access to potassium acetate, a "medically interchangeable" substitute. But prosecutors working under Attorney General Scott Pruitt resisted. Potassium acetate was not an approved execution drug in Oklahoma, and using it would violate the state's protocols.[11]

Fallin ultimately sided with the Attorney General's Office, granting Glossip thirty-seven additional days to live. In doing so, she opened a Pandora's box. As it turned out, the state had already used potassium acetate—the unapproved drug—to execute Warner. Either no one had noticed, or no one had cared. That information, which had been buried for months, surfaced the following week, and with it, calls for a reinvestigation of Oklahoma's entire system for administering the death penalty.[12] On October 16, Pruitt announced a temporary moratorium on the death penalty. A grand jury was impaneled and spent the next eight months taking testimony and pouring over documents. Mullins resigned, following on the heels of the head of the Department of Corrections and the warden.[13]

Sheppard, meanwhile, found herself in demand. One month after her op-ed ran, she accepted an invitation from Kevin Werner, the executive director of an anti–death penalty organization, to appear before the Ohio State Senate to testify in support of a bill that would bar the execution of anyone suffering from a serious mental illness.[14] Sheppard described for the senators the scene at the trial for her cousin Debbie Carter's murder: "Ron Williamson screamed at the jury, flipped over the defense table, and was about as unruly and unsympathetic as a man could be." Then she described Williamson after his years on death row: "His hair turned snow white and he pulled out his own teeth."[15]

The bill did not pass in 2016, but a year later, Sheppard received an email from Werner letting her know of her "direct impact." The bill had a new sponsor, John Eklund, the chairman of the Senate Judiciary Committee. Sheppard remembered Eklund, a kindly older man who had personally thanked her after she spoke. Werner wrote in an email, "He was moved most by your testimony. And now he's our guy in the Senate. Thought you should know that."

On March 31, 2016, Sheppard traveled to Nebraska to give the keynote address at the annual awards dinner for Nebraskans for Alternatives to the Death Penalty. Ten months earlier, Nebraska's legislature voted to repeal the death penalty; when the governor vetoed the bill, they mustered enough votes to override it. But a referendum to reinstate capital punishment was placed on the ballot for the November election, and the organization was looking for an advocate who could appeal to red-state Republicans.

Earlier that month, Sheppard had been named to the Oklahoma Death Penalty Review Commission, an eleven-member, bipartisan, blue-ribbon panel tasked with evaluating Oklahoma's administration of the death penalty. The inquiry went far beyond the execution procedures themselves: the members would be scrutinizing the system at every juncture, from arrest and investigation through trial, conviction, and sentencing.[16] When Sheppard got the call, she said, "I was like, 'me'?" Cochaired by former Democratic governor Brad Henry and two former judges, the panel also included the president of Oklahoma State University, the dean of Oklahoma City University School of Law, and the former Republican speaker of the state assembly. Sheppard was the only commission member who was not a lawyer or a politician.

As the commission began its work, the death penalty remained in the headlines. On May 19, 2016, the Oklahoma grand jury delivered a scathing 106-page indictment of the botched Warner execution, calling it an "inexcusable failure" and faulting Oklahoma officials for their recklessness, incompetence, arrogance, and neglect.[17] But in November 2016, nearly 70 percent of Oklahomans voted to add an extraordinary provision to the state's constitution, which declared that the death penalty was legal in any form the state chose to use.[18] In Nebraska, people voted in overwhelming numbers to reinstate the death penalty that the legislature had just abolished.[19]

The Oklahoma Death Penalty Review Commission met ten times for full-day sessions throughout 2016 and in early 2017, conducting interviews, reviewing data, and listening to presentations by experts.[20] Sheppard decided to do her own presentation for her colleagues, which she modeled on her keynote speech in Nebraska. Too often, she felt, politicians and prosecutors invoked the death penalty in the victim's name. Over and over, Sheppard had been told that the death penalty was the only true justice for Debbie Carter and her family. Sheppard wanted to challenge that idea; more fundamentally, she wanted to challenge the idea of what it meant to be the victim of a crime.

On a large screen in a conference room where the commission members met during one of their daylong meetings, Sheppard presented a short slide show of photographs: Debbie as a pretty and carefree teenager, Sheppard as a four-year-old child standing beside her beloved aunt Peggy. Mug shots of Williamson and Fritz followed, then pictures taken on the day they were released. Sheppard ended with a picture of Williamson taken shortly before he died. He was fifty years old, bald, emaciated, and toothless. "This is what death row does to people who aren't supposed to be there," she said and left the image on the screen.

In March 2017, the commission released its report recommending that the moratorium remain in place.[21] Nearly three hundred pages long, it provided an exhaustive analysis not only of the flawed protocols, but of flaws in every step in the process leading up to the conviction. Most of the reform proposals mirrored those that Scheck and Neufeld's Innocence Project had long advocated for—the implementation of best practices in the administration of lineups, the use of forensic science, custodial interrogations, the preservation of evidence, funding of indigent defense, and the disclosure of evidence. The voters may have enshrined the death penalty in the state's bill of rights, but the commission members were unanimous in concluding that it was unenforceable under present conditions—or perhaps at all: "Many of the findings of the Commission's year-long investigation were disturbing and led the Commission to question whether the death penalty can be administered in a way that ensures no innocent person is put to death," the cochairs wrote in the executive summary.[22]

Maria Kolar, a professor at the University of Oklahoma College of Law and a member of the commission, said that the analysis of the death penalty was filtered through the lens of innocence: "To find out with certainty that it is definitely not the right person, I think it changes things for most people because it just washes away all the arguments for retribution and deterrence." Of Sheppard, Kolar said, "Christy is amazing. She has such a unique voice and perspective. Was she influential? Certainly."

Sheppard was disappointed that the attorney general immediately declared his opposition to the report—seemingly before he had had a chance to read its contents—but Kolar's reaction was more optimistic. She noted that the revival of the death penalty in Oklahoma turned on Joe Allbaugh, who had taken over as the head of the Department of Corrections and was responsible for writing new protocols.[23] He had appeared before the commission, said publicly that he was "anxious" to see the report, and appeared in no hurry to act.[24] Valerie Couch, the dean of Oklahoma City University School of Law, concurred, saying she had confidence that Allbaugh would take the report seriously.

The political climate, too, seemed to have shifted. The report was positively received in the media—including by the conservative editorial board of the *Oklahoman*, the state's most widely read paper.[25] And in the two years that had elapsed since the moratorium, there had been no public clamor for executions. In the November 2016 election, Oklahomans sent a clear message: they did not want to be told they could not have the death penalty as an option. But that was not the same thing as demanding that it be reflexively imposed. "It may be," Kolar said, "that the tide has turned."

A flurry of press followed the release of the commission's report, and Sheppard gave interviews on television and to local and national media outlets.[26] Initially, she worried about pushback from her family and community about her membership on the commission and her contribution to its ultimate conclusion. But she found little. Mostly what she heard was "you did great," and "you looked so pretty in your blue dress." Several weeks after the press conference, Sheppard went to pick up her youngest son at his school dance and ran into the father of one of his classmates. "I saw you on TV the other day," he told her, sounding surprised. "I didn't know you were an activist."

"Oh, well," Sheppard said. "I guess I've done a little bit of that."

Pennsylvania
Renewing the Fight in the Legislature

In 2017, state senator Stewart Greenleaf decided to focus on reviving his effort to broaden the state's DNA testing law so that innocent people who had pleaded guilty or were no longer serving out their sentences were eligible to access it. The revised measure would also require law enforcement to keep records of all physical evidence collected in the case, and to upload the DNA test results into CODIS to check for matches.[27] Unlike Greenleaf's previous attempts at passing reforms relating to the advisory committee's report on wrongful convictions, this effort looked promising: he had secured a Republican cosponsor in the assembly, Representative Tedd C. Nesbit.[28]

On April 24, 2017, Anthony Wright appeared before Greenleaf's judiciary committee to testify in support of the legislation. His beard edged with gray, he wore a pressed white shirt, dark tie, and glasses with thick black frames. It had been eight months and one day since his exoneration. Joining Wright as he took his seat at the table were Shannon Coleman and her twenty-one-year-old daughter, Lauryn. Coleman was the grand-niece of the victim, Louise Talley, whom Wright had been falsely convicted of raping and murdering twenty-five years earlier after the police threatened to "skull fuck" him. Wright introduced them to the senators as "these beautiful women." He said, "We have become very good friends through this tragic situation."[29]

The friendship that had grown between Wright, Coleman, and Lauryn had become a fulcrum in their lives, providing balance and connection after a series of dislocating events. It was Lauryn who had first alerted Coleman to Wright's likely innocence in early 2015, after reading about his case in an exhaustively researched *Rolling Stone* article.[30] At first, Coleman refused to believe that the prosecutors were still pursuing a conviction, even though DNA from Talley's rape kit matched another man's and there was good reason to believe that the police had planted evidence. Coleman's mother, who died in 2004, had been an officer in the Philadelphia Police Department when Talley was murdered. Her job provided the family with a foothold in the middle class and a sense of identity as part of a larger law enforcement community. Coleman said, "We stayed very close to the investigation and what I remember was that we were all convinced that Tony did it. There was never a question in my mind." Coleman knew that the police sometimes used excessive force—she remembers clearly one of her mother's fellow officers saying, about a different suspect, "we got him and we beat his ass"—but only because they were dealing with violent, guilty criminals. "I could understand that. I was a part of that culture because it was entrenched in me as a child," she said.

But when Coleman, a fifty-five-year-old black woman who wore her shoulder-length hair in loose curls, read the *Rolling Stone* article, she was beset by doubt. In May 2015, she and Lauryn sat down with one of Wright's attorneys, Sam Silver, and listened carefully as he went through the evidence. Then Coleman did her own research. What she found horrified her. When she learned that the prosecution was retrying Wright, Coleman wrote to the mayor, the governor, and church groups. She asked a friend she knew on the city council for help, "anything I could think of to get it stopped."

In May 2016, Coleman started a petition on Change.org, urging the Philadelphia District Attorney's Office to drop the case, calling the retrial "a travesty." On June 15, after collecting nearly forty thousand signatures from as far away as Israel, Coleman sent the petition to Seth Williams, the head of the Philadelphia District Attorney's Office.[31] He ignored her. But Wright's family was paying attention. Wright said, "My dad was going crazy. He wanted to hug this lady; he wanted to talk to her."

Earlier that same month, Coleman obtained the email address for Jennifer Selber, the head of the district attorney's homicide unit. She then composed a two-page, single-spaced email to Selber. It began, "I am asking that you please read this email. I know it is long, it took me all of yesterday to write it. I know you are a very busy person but this is extremely important." Coleman described the pain of living with the fact that her great aunt, whom she called "a sweet, gentle, and modest woman," had been raped and stabbed to death. She spoke of her relief that the police caught Wright so quickly, and then her revulsion at realizing, a quarter of a century later, that the DNA evidence conclusively proved he had been coerced and framed for another man's crime. She continued, "Anthony could have been my son or my nephew—young, scared, naïve, and trusting of police. It became apparent to me that I would not be able to live with myself if I do not do something to rectify this injustice."

Selber did not reply. On June 27, Coleman wrote again, saying it was her fourth and final attempt to reach someone at the DA's office. (Previously, she had sent two emails to a generic address on the DA's website that received no response.) "It is beyond belief that public servants whom I help pay your salary would ignore the relative of a crime victim," she told Selber, adding that if she did not hear back by July 1, she was going to the media. A short time later, Selber arranged to meet with Coleman. According to Coleman, Selber conceded that there were "puzzling" aspects of the case that raised doubts. But Selber said that while she was not convinced of Wright's guilt, the ambiguities were for a jury to sort out. Coleman was aghast, writing in a follow-up email, "as a prosecutor you have an ethical responsibility to only take to trial cases you believe beyond a reasonable doubt. You told me more than once during our conversation that you have doubt!"[32]

Wright's retrial went forward several weeks later. Coleman could not get time off from work, but she left early on several afternoons to sit in the courtroom and watch. Throughout, she said, "I was anxious because I knew that a jury had found him guilty once and I was afraid they were going to find him guilty again." On August 23, 2016, when Silver texted that Wright had been acquitted, Coleman said, "I stood up in my office and screamed." She immediately started a new petition to pay for Wright's living expenses, raising more than $5,000.[33]

But when Coleman finally met Wright face-to-face a few days after he was freed, she felt she had something to apologize for, having wished for so long that he would "burn in hell." She wondered if the case would have been pursued as aggressively had her mother not been a member of the police department. She felt culpable because she believed so readily. Now her worldview had changed. Eight months earlier, Coleman had been selected to serve on a jury in a criminal case. The evidence against the defendant—charged with drug distribution—hinged on the testimony of two Philadelphia police officers. Listening to them on the witness stand, Coleman did not believe a word. She was, she said, "prepared to do battle" with the other jurors, who seemed straitlaced and trusting, particularly an elderly white lady who spent most of her time crocheting. But when it came time to vote, they were all in agreement: the cops were lying. Not guilty.

Facing Wright in Silver's office, Coleman wondered how she could explain the evolution in her thinking. Standing there, she felt awkward, unsure what to say or do. When Wright held out his hand for her to shake, she hesitated, and then took a risk, saying, "Can I have a hug instead?" Wright, who is nearly six feet tall and weighs more than two hundred pounds, gave Coleman a big smile, then crushed her in an embrace. As far as Wright was concerned, Coleman was "a true champion of humanity. I love her to death."

After that, they texted every day and saw each other regularly. Traveling by train together to Harrisburg to fight for the DNA bill was a natural extension of their shared commitment to reforming a criminal justice system in what Wright called "one of the most corrupt places in America."

Ironically, Wright now worked within the court system, as an administrative assistant in the sky-high federal building at Sixth and Market in downtown Philadelphia. Shortly after his exoneration, two of Wright's attorneys connected him with a magistrate judge, Timothy Rice, who ran a reentry program for recently released offenders.[34] Rice made the job offer after meeting with Wright in his chambers with his clerks and staff. Wright said, "I did not have an ID, a social security card, credentials, nothing, and they got it for me overnight."

Wright has an easygoing manner and can-do attitude that won him many friends in the courthouse, where his various tasks—moving furniture, assisting with filings, shredding documents—keep him moving and constantly interacting with different people during the day. Getting the day off to talk to the state senate's judiciary committee was not a problem. Nor was the request particularly surprising. Wright was constantly fielding offers to talk to various people and advocacy groups about his case. At the same time, he was reconnecting with his twenty-nine-year-old son, and navigating the first-time process of leasing a car and renting an apartment. "My life is insane," he said. "I have to remember to breathe or I will pass out."

Facing Greenleaf and his colleagues in the hearing room, Wright described the pure terror he felt as a twenty-year-old alone in a room with two menacing officers, one pressed against his back, one against his front, threatening to mutilate and maim him until he finally put his initials on the papers they would not let him read. Wright said, "I understand the pressure on innocent people to plead guilty, because I was faced with the death penalty. When I was arrested, they said if I admit to this crime they would spare my life." He offered the senators his hard-earned, haunting knowledge: "While I didn't plead guilty, I know innocent people plead guilty to crimes they didn't commit. After spending twenty-five years in prison, I know there are other innocent people in there and I hope they can get DNA testing to prove their innocence."

Wright also pointed out that ambiguities in the current DNA law had allowed the Philadelphia District Attorney's Office to argue—wrongly— that Wright's coerced "confession" barred him from having the DNA tested. What followed was a five-year battle that went all the way up to the Pennsylvania Supreme Court. Had that battle not been waged, the real perpetrator, Ronnie Byrd, might have been caught before he died. Wright would have been spared years behind bars, particularly if Byrd had confessed, voiding any reason for a retrial even by prosecutors as stubborn and relentless as the men and women working under Philadelphia district attorney Seth Williams.

When it was Coleman's turn, she spoke in measured tones that none-theless carried a thrum of barely suppressed outrage. Hands clasped in front of her on the table, she said, "When I found out what happened to Tony, it was a devastating, harrowing feeling for me to know that we didn't put him there, we didn't put him in prison, but we believed what we were fed and this man suffered for twenty-five years. It is just an awful thing to have taken part as a family member—to have taken part in the injustice that was done to him." She went on, "It upsets me even more to know that Ronnie Byrd was walking the streets, he was committing other crimes, he hurt other families and we didn't get any justice for my aunt."[35]

Coleman and Wright see their advocacy as an ongoing project. Both are willing to commit as much time and energy as it takes. "I want to make a difference," Coleman said. "Why else be here?"

A Sea Change at the Philadelphia District Attorney's Office

Marissa Boyers Bluestine, the legal director of the Pennsylvania Innocence Project, decided that the district attorney's egregious handling of Wright's case could be harnessed in service of a larger cause. In an op-ed that was published in the *Philadelphia Inquirer* five days after the exoneration, she detailed the dysfunctionality of the conviction review unit (CRU). Describing Wright's exoneration as a "watershed moment," Bluestine called upon Seth Williams to commit to a top-to-bottom restructuring.[36] Before the op-ed ran, Bluestine sent it to Kathleen Martin, Williams's chief of staff and second-in-command.

Martin, who spent two decades as a defense attorney, was relatively new to the DA's office; Williams had hired her in November 2015 as part of what he called "a long-overdue staffing reform package." Reforming the CRU was high on her priority list, and after getting acclimated, she began her research into best practices. Half-jokingly, Martin described "secret meetings" with Bluestine on several occasions throughout the late summer and early fall of 2016, and additional meetings with experts in academia and prosecutors in conviction integrity units in Brooklyn and Dallas, both of which had overturned dozens of false convictions. By December, staff and resources were quietly being reallocated.

In early February, Martin publicly announced the CRU's overhaul. Mark Gilson, the hard-line homicide prosecutor was out, replaced by Elizabeth Graham-Rubin, a well-respected twenty-year veteran of the office, and an assistant prosecutor, Andrew Wellbrock, who had experience investigating public corruption and police misconduct.[37] Both, she said, had "an open mind." Martin also moved the CRU out of the physical office space it had shared with the appellate and habeas attorneys tasked with defending convictions, and ended the overlap between the two divisions. Now reporting directly to Martin, the CRU also gained crucial autonomy and, Martin said, faced "less red tape in order to make important decisions." She described the reforms as arising from "a gut-wrenching need to do what's right."

Seth Williams's term as head of the District Attorney's Office was up the following January, and the race for his position was making headlines. So was the district attorney himself—attention that was far from flattering. For several years, there had been media reports that Williams, who was known to be struggling financially, was under federal investigation for possible improprieties relating to the use of his campaign funds. Williams had persistently denied wrongdoing and vowed to run for reelection in the Democratic primary in May. But as the rumors reached a fever pitch, five Democratic hopefuls jumped into the race to replace him.[38]

One of them was Larry Krasner, by any reckoning a highly unusual candidate. A former federal public defender and career civil rights attorney, Krasner had never prosecuted a single case, firmly opposed the death penalty, and was best known for defending Black Lives Matter and other political protestors, who were among his most fervent supporters. Announcing his candidacy on February 8, 2017, Krasner promised to "decarcerate," saying, "We have to get people out of jail." He said, "I have heard more times than I care to count jokes [by prosecutors] around the notion that someone is actually innocent."[39] The system, he said, was set up to abuse both defendants and victims, who were too often "manipulated to press for the prosecutor's goals rather than theirs, and they have not been made whole." And he addressed head-on the racialization of the city's criminal justice system: "When you have more people of color in jail than South Africa during apartheid, that's a problem."[40]

Two days later, on February 10, Williams held a press conference in which he had admitted bringing "shame" upon his office by accepting over $160,000 in unreported gifts. He withdrew his bid for reelection.[41] Williams's admission, though, provided only the barest hint of his legal troubles. Less than six weeks later, federal prosecutors brought a twenty-three-count indictment charging him with bribery, extortion, and fraud.[42] The alleged misconduct was stunning for its breadth, coarseness, and venality: Williams was alleged to have repeatedly offered to provide favorable treatment in pending criminal cases to rich donors and their friends in exchange for money and gifts, including luxury beach vacations, a Louis Vuitton tie, and a used Jaguar convertible. Still unable to pay his bills, Williams reportedly stole more than $20,000 from his mother's Social Security account—money earmarked to pay for her nursing home care.[43]

When Wright arrived at work at the federal courthouse on March 22, 2017, one of the security officers told him, "You know your boy is coming to court today." Wright laughed and kept on walking, but inside he was churning with emotions, including disbelief at the complete reversal of their fortunes. The head of the Philadelphia District Attorney's Office, who had for years deployed the vast resources at his disposal to deny Wright his freedom, was suddenly in real danger of going to prison himself. Wright had no intention of gloating, but he wanted to bear witness.

During his lunch hour, Wright stood in the vestibule of the federal courthouse looking out at a phalanx of cameras and reporters shouting and jostling for space, their microphones stretching out to Williams. It was a cool, sunny day. Williams, wearing a camel-colored overcoat and a grim expression on his face, began the slow walk of shame to his scheduled arraignment. Wright said, "I just stood there and looked him dead in the face, and he kind of bowed his head a bit and kept walking." As Williams crossed the threshold, Wright told him, "Don't worry, I got the door," bracing his arm against the heavy steel to make sure it stayed open.

Krasner's quest to replace Williams, dismissed at first as quixotic, rapidly gained steam and visibility with a huge infusion of cash from liberal billionaire George Soros, who donated $1.45 million to the campaign. Coleman was so disillusioned that she had planned to stay home, but at the urging of her son, she read up on Krasner and decided to vote for him. On May 16, 2017, Krasner defeated his four opponents in the Democratic primary by a decisive margin, winning with 38 percent of the vote. On November 7, 2017, Krasner easily won the general election. Addressing his supporters at his acceptance speech, Krasner said, "This is what a movement looks like."[44]

If Krasner keeps to his campaign promises, there will be no more cash-for-bail, a system that jailed poor defendants simply because they lacked the means to post bond. The death penalty in Philadelphia will exist only in theory, because Krasner will never seek it. And black and brown people who had long been marginalized or ignored will have a seat at the table. Insiders who resist adaptation will be asked to give up their seats. In an interview with *The Intercept* in the months leading up to the election, Krasner said, "There's going to be a certain portion of the DA's office who can't stand the idea of change. They're going to leave. There are other people who are going to be made to leave." He added that the prosecutors shown the exit door "will be people who started in this business 30 years ago, which means they'll also tend to be white and male."[45]

Meanwhile, under the interim leadership of Kathleen Martin, the revamped CRU—infamous for exonerating no one—plowed ahead. Since January 2017, Graham-Rubin and Wellbrock had been reinvestigating the conviction of Shaurn Thomas, who was serving a life sentence for taking part in the 1990 murder of Domingo Martinez. Witnesses at the scene reported that Martinez, who was driving his car after withdrawing $25,000 from the bank, was cut off by another car, after which a man got out of the vehicle, gunned Martinez down, and took the cash.[46] Bluestine, with the pro bono help of James Figorski, a former police officer who has gone to law school and become a high-powered lawyer, had been arguing for years that Shaurn Thomas was innocent. Under the old regime, the CRU had shown no interest in Thomas's case, which Bluestine and Figorski found unfathomable.

Thomas, who was sixteen at the time Martinez was murdered, had an ironclad alibi. Two nights before the murder, he had been caught trying to steal a motorcycle and was jailed, pending a detention hearing in juvenile court. The morning Martinez was killed, Thomas's mother picked him up from the police station and drove him directly to the Youth Study Center, where children with pending criminal charges go to see whether they will be placed in detention before their adjudicatory hearing. Thomas was processed and interviewed at the same time that Martinez was killed on the other side of town. There was a subpoena with Thomas's signature to prove it, and in 2012, two handwriting experts had verified that it was indeed Thomas's handwriting.

When Figorski took the case to the Philadelphia District Attorney's Office in 2011, he felt confident: "I had credibility, I had worked with them on cases, they knew me because I had been a cop for twenty-five years. But they basically said, no, we're not going to look at this and if you want to fight it out in court, go ahead." As they left the building, Figorski told Bluestine, "These people would burn the world down before they admit a mistake."

Bluestine and Figorski did go to court. A judge dismissed their petition as untimely, and they appealed, a process that dragged on for years.[47] In 2015, after learning that Williams had created a CRU and put Mark Gilson in charge, Figorski made a second pitch. There was no need to have a meeting, Gilson told Figorski. He had talked to some of the prosecutors who had opposed Thomas's petition and were convinced of Thomas's guilt. Figorski said, "I like Mark a lot. He is a great prosecutor. But he is friends with the people who have been responsible for some of these wrongful convictions, and that's a problem."

Graham-Rubin and Wellbrock took the reinvestigation seriously. They interviewed witnesses who staffed the Youth Study Center at the time and found additional evidence to corroborate Thomas's alibi. In March, they asked the Philadelphia police for the original investigative file in the case, which Thomas's attorneys had been trying unsuccessfully to obtain for years, having been told it was lost. In early May, a dusty box was delivered to Wellbrock's office. Inside were thirty-six pages of witness statements showing that the police had an alternative suspect under consideration—information that was never disclosed to Thomas's lawyer or to the trial prosecutor. The police officers involved in the Martinez investigation were the same ones who had gone after Anthony Wright.

On May 23, 2017, Philadelphia prosecutors went to court and agreed to vacate Thomas's conviction and sentence. Hours later, wearing a black knitted skullcap and a Pennsylvania Innocence Project T-shirt, Thomas embraced his mother, Hazeline, outside state prison in rural Pennsylvania. Released when he was forty-three years old, Thomas had served twenty-four years in prison.[48] It was the CRU's first true effort to be a partner in the exoneration process and, Bluestine hoped, a sign of a real—and hopefully lasting—change in the culture at the Philadelphia District Attorney's Office.

One lasting change came quickly. On June 29, 2017, eight days into Williams's federal trial on public corruption charges, he abruptly pleaded guilty to one count of bribery and resigned as district attorney. The judge, Paul Diamond, rejected Williams's request to remain free on bond while he awaited his sentencing hearing. In October, Diamond sentenced Williams to five years in prison, lambasting him as a lowlife who "fed his face at the trough."

On January 5, 2018, a few days after he was sworn into office as Philadelphia's new district attorney, Larry Krasner fired thirty-one longtime assistant district attorneys who one internal source told *Philadelphia Weekly* were "supervisors with different vision, veteran salaried do-nothings, or younger prosecutors associated with misconduct."[49] On the list: Carlos Vega, the veteran homicide prosecutor who tried and failed to convict Anthony Wright for a second time, and Mark Gilson, who headed up the CRU during the years when it was widely seen as a sham.[50] The new head of the CRU, Patricia Cummings, headed up a similar unit in the Dallas District Attorney's Office, where she is credited with helping to overturn a number of wrongful convictions.[51]

Currently, the Philadelphia's CRU has six cases under active review, and Wellbrock said he believes there will be "significant positive changes to the CRU under the new administration likely including expansion." Several of the cases Wellbrock is reinvestigating involve the Pennsylvania

Innocence Project. Figorski said he is grateful, but added that the CRU lawyers have their work cut out for them: "It's like being in internal affairs in the police department. They are all going to be hated because they are second-guessing their colleagues."

Martin, who has since resigned from the District Attorney's Office, was asked in June 2017 about the general attitude by prosecutors toward the CRU. She replied, "We are working towards acceptance."

CHAPTER THIRTEEN

The Reformers, Part II

Louisiana

The Real Gentlemen Barbershop (RGB) opened on December 31, 2016, in a small storefront on Claiborne Avenue in New Orleans's Seventh Ward.[1] Jerome Morgan and Daniel Rideau, the friends who served years together at Angola, had executed their vision down to the last detail. Above the front door of the building, which was painted royal blue with yellow trim, was the RGB logo: three black men holding shears and electric razors, flanked by the iconic red, white, and blue striped barber poles. Morgan and Rideau had built and installed the equipment and furnishings themselves, from the air-conditioning unit to the adjustable black leather barber chairs and gilt-framed mirrors. It was official: Morgan was now the co-owner of a small business born of dreams, ambition, and community support—with an unexpected assist from a quirky music industry mogul.

One of Morgan's earliest collaborators was Kelly Orians, a fiercely committed local activist. Orians, a young white woman with a mane of unruly brown curls and a contagious creative energy, moved to New Orleans in 2008 to work for the Juvenile Justice Project of Louisiana. JJPL was campaigning to end life-without-parole sentences for juveniles through a project called Citizens for Second Chances; Morgan was one of the many prisoners Orians was trying to reach at Angola. She had learned about his case through her friend Kristen Wenstrom, one of Morgan's attorneys at Innocence Project of New Orleans.

In 2009, as a way of connecting with the lifers at Angola and keeping them engaged with her organization, Orians decided to start a logo contest. Citizens for Second Chances had been using a generic piece of clip art for its marketing materials; Orians wanted a design by one of the men or women they were trying to help. She mailed out a call for submissions with a promise to gather them and send them out. The prisoners would vote on their favorite, and the winning design would become the organization's new logo.

Morgan sent Orians several drawings of a butterfly. His work stood out, she said, not only because it was beautiful, but because it was only in pencil and in draft form. The wings were carefully delineated into fine stripes. Next to each stripe was the name of a color. Each version came with instructions. Orians was to fill in different color combinations and send the drawings back for further revisions. It took a minute for Orians to understand: Morgan had been locked down in Camp J for another disciplinary violation and denied access to any kind of colored ink or paint.

Orians dutifully followed Morgan's instructions: "I had a feeling the design would resonate and I was inspired by him because it was obvious he took incredible pride in his work." Morgan responded by mailing back more sketches with notations for new color combinations. When he settled on a final version, Orians sent out his submission along with the eleven others she had received to the juvenile lifers at Angola. Morgan's won by an overwhelming majority of the vote.

Two years later, Orians left Citizens for Second Chances and, after taking off seven months to travel, began her first year of law school at UCLA in 2012. Orians, who viewed law school as a credential to further her advocacy work, had no intention of staying in California. She was homesick, traveling back to New Orleans frequently and staying in touch with the prisoners at Angola, including Morgan. She also got regular updates about his case from Wenstrom and celebrated from afar when Morgan's conviction was overturned in 2014 and he was released on bail.

In 2012, the United States Supreme Court abolished mandatory life without parole sentences for juveniles.[2] Suddenly, it seemed possible that Louisiana's juvenile lifers might have the chance to be resentenced and released. (In fact, the Louisiana courts resisted doing so until the Supreme Court forced them to, ruling in 2016 that the decision applied retroactively.)[3] In her final year at UCLA, Orians and her friend Calvin Duncan came up with the idea of starting their own foundation to help former prisoners reenter society. Duncan, who is African American, spent nearly three decades in Angola for a murder he did not commit before his attorneys at the New Orleans Innocence Project were able to free him in 2011. Now thriving after a difficult reentry process, Duncan wanted to help others in his position.[4] Orians said, "We started thinking, what if we empower these guys coming home to be engines of economic development in their communities?" She enrolled in classes at UCLA's business school, including a course on entrepreneurship, which she described as "me and all these bro-y capitalists learning about finance."

In 2014, Orians and Duncan applied for an Echoing Green fellowship to fund Rising Foundations, the new nonprofit organization they envisioned. Shortly before Orians graduated from law school in May 2015, she found out they had been selected and would receive $80,000 in start-up funds.[5] Orians moved back to New Orleans the day after graduation and started meeting with Morgan and Rideau soon after that, trying to figure out "how to make their barbershop sustainable so that they could work there full-time and not have to rely on the money from Jerome's other job."

In October 2015, Orians found out she had failed the Louisiana state bar exam. At first, she was inconsolable, crying and unable to get up from the couch. Then she got on Facebook and posted this message: "I want to ask all my people to join me in mourning this defeat by helping two of my dear friends and colleagues get a little closer to achieving their dreams of getting their own professional licenses." Orians was referring to Duncan and Morgan, who needed money to pay for professional accreditations—Duncan for a real estate, Morgan for barbering. "Let's make this day about something other than the day I had to get back on the study wagon and try to remember what the hell usufructuary means." It worked. With the funds, Morgan enrolled in barber school. He got his apprentice license on October 15, 2015.

Shortly afterward, Orians found out that Propeller, a New Orleans business incubator, was hosting a competition for fledging entrepreneurs. Selected applicants would be invited to pitch their business plan to a panel of judges before a live audience.[6] Immediately, Orians thought of Morgan and Rideau. For months, they had been informally mentoring young men—mostly teenagers—who came into their barbershop to hang out at the space they were leasing from Resurrection After Exoneration and sometimes stayed to learn a bit about the trade. When Orians told them about the Propeller competition, Morgan and Rideau decided to make mentorship an integral part of their business model. They would use the grant funds to pay and train young black men in a vocation and in developing a values system, applying their own hard-earned experience to steer them away from jail or prison and turning out a generation of "young gentlemen barbers."

On November 5, 2015, Morgan and Rideau took the stage before a standing-room-only audience of roughly three hundred people—as a pair, they were one of ten finalists selected. As middle-aged tattooed African American men dressed in black, button-down, short-sleeve shirts and black pants, Morgan and Rideau stood in stark visual contrast with the other competitors, who skewed young, white, and formally dressed— "do-gooder, earnest millennials," Orians said. The challenge was to energize the mostly white audience while conveying the cultural and economic significance of their barbershop in the black community.

Morgan said, "I was a nervous wreck." His mother was there, as was Rideau's mother, along with a carload of other supporters. But the audience was mostly white strangers. Morgan continued, "You are the one being viewed, you have a responsibility to communicate these truths." He and Rideau, like the other competitors, were given three minutes for their pitch.

Microphones in hand, Morgan and Rideau spoke in a conversation-style format, each building on a concept put forward by the other. Rideau got right to the point: "No one can deny that the rate at which we are incarcerating young black men in New Orleans is a horrific crisis or that a lack of gainful employment is the common denominator in this tragedy." Morgan explained that the prize money would fund paid apprenticeships at the barbershop with the goal of "creat[ing] jobs that will keep young men out of prison."

Rideau said, "Barbershops not only provide services to better how a person looks and feels. They also serve as a community space where many seek counseling and advice."[7]

Briefly, they gave their track record: a life skills and barbering curriculum with forty students participating and an average net income of $800 per month since they had opened their doors at Resurrection After Exoneration.

The judges had plenty of questions about the sustainability of the program and the technical aspects of the training. After answering them and listening to the other presentations, Morgan and Rideau waited in suspense with the other finalists as the judges deliberated. The decision: a three-way tie for first place. Morgan and Rideau were among the winners, taking home $3,000 in prize money.[8] They went out and celebrated, but not for too long. Morgan, whose case was still pending at that point, had received special permission from the court official monitoring his bail conditions to attend. He had to make sure he did not violate his curfew.

Then, on July 10, 2016, Morgan and Rideau suffered a serious setback. Around 2 a.m., Resurrection After Exoneration was burglarized: the thieves broke down the door and made off with $10,000 in equipment. Morgan and Rideau's barbershop was stripped bare. "Not only did they take the stuff that we use to make our money, they took the stuff that we use to give back to our community," Rideau said.[9] Having made steady if snail-like progress, Morgan and Rideau had been rudely jerked backward. Once again, they had nothing. It was at that point that Doug DiLosa, a Louisiana exoneree who was working with Orians as a project coordinator at Rising Foundations, called in a favor.

DiLosa, wrongfully convicted of killing his wife in 1987, had spent fourteen years in prison before he was released in 2001.[10] Though he was white, middle-class, college-educated, and had a solid work history, DiLosa struggled for years to find employment; his overturned murder conviction was held as an indelible mark against him. In 2012, his life changed when he accepted an invitation to a fund-raiser at the home of Jason Flom.

The CEO of Lava Records, Flom was famous for signing a list of platinum-selling recording artists that included Katy Perry, Kid Rock, and Lorde. A millionaire many times over, Flom, a wiry white guy with tortoise-shell glasses and close-cropped graying hair who cheerfully sprays his sentences with expletives, had been involved with the Innocence Project since its early days in the early 1990s. "I can't imagine a more horrifying situation than being locked up in our gulag institutions and no one cares and no one believes you," said Flom. "Once I became aware of it, I got on the phone with the Innocence Project and said, 'I am coming to see you.' I met with Peter Neufeld, and we went from there." For more than twenty years, Flom gave generously to the Innocence Project, where he served on the board of directors.[11]

When Flom listened to DiLosa tell his story, he said, "I was struck by his intelligence and his calm demeanor. He had a burning desire to help other people." The two men became close. Flom was always on the lookout to infuse creative projects with small donations, and he relied on DiLosa to "pick wisely and find highly motivated and also talented people who need a lifeline." Flom had also developed a relationship with Rising Foundations, which he called "the premiere organization helping exonerees get a fresh start, which is so fucking difficult it's like another imprisonment." When DiLosa told Flom about Morgan and his vision of owning a barbershop, Flom was interested.

Flom described Morgan as "an introspective, interesting person. He is confident. He is stylish. He doesn't have much money, but he knows how to pick clothes and how to wear 'em. I have seen people like Jerome turn their lives around with a relatively small donation from somebody. And I know he is going to pass it on and help someone else." Flom donated $12,500, enough money for Morgan and Rideau to buy new equipment and move to their own space on Claiborne Avenue.

Morgan's decision to go all-in on the barbershop came after realizing that what he had viewed as the safer, more traditional route—a job that, however much he hated it, provided a regular salary and benefits—was not helping him move forward. At the Healing Justice retreat, he had listened to exonerees who had been out of prison for years and even decades, still struggling to find meaning and coherence in their lives. He said, "I was a newbie and I saw it was a dire situation. I don't want to end up fifteen years down the line suffering as much. People who can't use their experience in a way that makes life better, it hurts them."

Morgan wanted to reach out to a particularly vulnerable population: black men in their midteens through early twenties, whom Morgan called "disregarded youth, disregarded in a political sense, in a gender sense, in a societal sense, and what the statistics show is that it is a population that our society through its institutions has said it does not care about." He saw them struggling, as he had, to bridge the seemingly impossible divide between childhood and adulthood, where self-sufficiency was suddenly demanded. For those with economic and racial privilege, that rough transition was often smoothed by money and resources. For the young African American population in New Orleans, there was no safety net. A few poor choices could easily lead to dropping out of school, incarceration, or worse.

Morgan and Rideau developed a six-month curriculum for their mentees, who were referred by local high schools and nonprofits. Some walked in off the street. They called the first two months the Green Phase, during which, Morgan said, "we teach barbershop maintenance and male etiquette—how you conduct yourself, how to give respect to get respect." Next is the Red Phase, where the young men learn hair-cutting techniques and ways to resolve conflicts peacefully. The premise, Morgan said, is that "life is about conflict, it is a natural thing and nothing to fear or be wary of. But it is something you should do without violence." The final two months, the Black Phase, focuses on business planning, leadership skills, and critical writing. The writing exercise begins with a story circle of twelve to fifteen mentees. The youths are given prompts—to describe their first encounter with the police or with handling money, for example. In response, they tell a two-minute story with the other circle members providing feedback. Morgan and Rideau then recommend reading certain authors—James Baldwin, Malcolm X—and assign the mentees to write an essay drawing parallels between the readings and the stories they tell.

At the end of the six-month training, the hope is that the mentees will be ready for apprenticeships. They are trained to be barbers, but Morgan and Rideau see other possibilities, too, in local businesses like real estate or construction. Morgan said, "We want to be advocates for young people going into adulthood as they come to grips with their true identity. No one wants to be told who they are or that they can only go so far. And it isn't about coming in and saving them. Everyone in a humble and respect-ful sense deserves the right to earn who they are and have the fulfillment of at least being able to take care of themselves."

In May 2017, Flom traveled to New Orleans to interview Morgan and his attorney, Kristen Wenstrom, for Flom's podcast, *Wrongful Convictions*. Flom wanted to know how Morgan had persevered.

Morgan replied that he had never viewed himself as a victim: "I have never thought of myself in a prison of any kind. I had been exposed to people who believed in freedom. There was a history that I was not aware of at the time, but there was a culture and climate of being self-supportive, always thinking positive knowing that you have enough capability and capacity." Describing his life philosophy, Morgan said, "The just shall live by faith. In the sense that they have the faith that my good will harm the wrong in the world."

He told Flom, "Triumph is what I want people to remember when they speak about me."[12]

Virginia

On November 3, 2016, Healing Justice held a three-hour training session at the offices of the Virginia parole board in Richmond. The goal was to improve the way that law enforcement officers interacted with crime victims: in the immediate aftermath of the attack and throughout the legal process, including the unenviable job of conveying the news of a wrongful conviction. In addition to members of the parole board, the attendees included state and local prosecutors, state and local police officers, and victim advocates.

Jennifer Thompson and Katie Monroe asked Janet Burke to participate in the training with them. Burke knew she would have to speak publicly about the rape, but the prospect was far less daunting than it had been at the Mid-Atlantic Innocence Project awards luncheon in 2014. Back then, she said, "I was so scared, I could not think." In the two and a half years since, Burke had changed in ways she had not believed were possible. Her relationship with Thomas Haynesworth, her engagement with restorative justice practices, and a sense of belonging to a larger community of exonerees and survivors had given her a newfound confidence and drive.

Several months earlier, in September 2016, Burke had been promoted to a director position at Childsavers, the nonprofit where she had worked since 1992. The new job required that she cultivate a public persona, testifying before the Virginia legislature and speaking before large community offices and small groups of well-heeled donors. "Two or three years ago, I never would have taken the job," Burke said, "because my confidence was so low." After learning of her misidentification, Burke shied away from making decisions because she no longer trusted her judgment. A self-described introvert, her initial impulse was to retreat and focus on living as quietly and safely as possible, well out of the public fray. Her family wanted this, too. Burke's husband urged her to move on. So did her mother, who felt frustration over the renewed media coverage. Burke said, "From her perspective it was, 'Why can't they just leave Janet alone? Why do they have to keep bringing it up?' And in my mind, I am thinking, it is not a question of bringing it up. It never left."

Psychologically, the rape, the misidentification, and the aftermath could not be left behind. The most surprising thing for Burke was realizing this: "I went into 2016 feeling like a switch had been flipped. I wasn't going to sit on the sidelines anymore and just let things happen."

Burke had begun to think of herself as a reformer-in-training. That August, she took a Politics 101 class organized by the Chamber of Commerce. "I needed to improve my advocacy skills and understand how state and local government actually works: how you deliver a clear message, how your issue gets to the top of the pile, how bills are passed, and how policies are enacted," she said.

Still, going to the Virginia parole board brought back a flood of memories for Burke—some expected, some not, none of them pleasant. State prisoners were brought there for their parole hearings. Burke knew this well, having received letters inviting her to come and testify against Haynesworth every time his case came up for review. Burke never went, convinced that no one so depraved would ever get out alive.

Being reminded of Haynesworth's suffering was bad enough, but when a member of the parole board told Burke that she had recently presided over a parole hearing for Burke's actual rapist, Leon Davis, she said, "It was jarring, hearing his name in that context." Another attendee was a state trooper who reminded Burke that she had been the mother of a child in the East End Church day-care center—the place where Davis had raped her. "It's like a reunion you never want to go to," Burke said.

Burke used her time to educate her law enforcement audience about the importance of bringing a trauma-informed approach when interacting with crime victims by creating programs to anticipate common survivor responses—flight, fight, freeze—and adapting communication techniques designed to avoid re-traumatization, while at the same time providing the information that victims needed and deserved to know. She described her own experience with Richmond detectives in Haynesworth's investigation as a case study in what not to do.

Burke learned the detectives had gone to her mother's house first, having not updated Burke's address in their system since she had been attacked twenty-five years earlier. Burke panicked, assuming that, despite everything she believed, the detectives were going to inform her that he had gotten out on parole: "I had five minutes to figure out what to do with my sixteen-year-old daughter, who had no earthly idea what had happened to me." After ushering Emily into her room, Burke sat down on the sofa in her living room with the two men, one of whom began with a rambling speech about DNA. Burke tried to listen, but was growing increasingly confused—what did this have to do with her?

Finally, they told her. The awfulness kept coming in nauseating waves. She remembered, "They said, 'This is going to hit the media. You are going to have to tell your family and your close friends.'" Burke froze, unable to listen anymore. It was as if the mute button had been pressed and released only intermittently so that she heard meaningless fragments of what they were telling her. When they left, she said, "My husband had questions for me that I could not answer. Then I had to figure out when I was going to sit down with my kids and tell them I had been raped."

The series of revelations—that their mother had been brutalized and that the man she had wrongly accused might soon be getting out of prison—upset and terrified Emily and Burke's twenty-one-year-old son, Paul Jr., who went out and bought a gun. He had no doubt, Burke said, that Haynesworth would be coming to kill her. Whoever makes the notification, Burke told her audience, needed to be prepared for any number of reactions: rage and denial, blankness, confusion, guilt and terror. They needed to be prepared to come back, to follow up, to stay in touch, and to provide referrals. They needed, above all, to make sure that the conversations happened on the victim's terms to give her back some small measure of power and control. The detectives who visited Burke to tell her the DNA test results were well intentioned, but clueless. They brought a hurricane and left her alone to deal with the wreckage that had once been her life.

Burke has since participated in other trainings to discuss the trauma-informed approach, including with the DOJ's Office for Victims of Crime in Washington, DC, and before a gathering of more than fifty chiefs of police in Delaware. Each time, she said, she feels she is reclaiming a part of herself and making a space for other survivors to come forward. After these events, rape victims reached out to Burke, often women who never came forward. The shame and stigma the victims described—that it must, in some way, have been their fault—was so similar to what Burke had experienced in 1984. "When you talk about rape," Burke said, "you can see people in the room close up in a way they don't when you talk about murder or child abuse. And it just reinforces the message we all learn as women, which is that what we wear, what we say and do, gives other people the right to treat us inhumanely."

Now, after Burke speaks publicly about her rape, the misidentification, and the exoneration, she feels drained and revived. But more than anything, she says, "I feel free." Before, there was no space for her story: no one wanted to hear it or, if they did, it was in a courtroom, where she had no control over the narrative. Now she can make it mean something entirely different.

Haynesworth, too, has continued with his advocacy, which centers around speaking to police departments throughout the country about faulty identification procedures. He fits in the engagements with a hectic work schedule that now includes co-owning an auto repair shop, where he works on the weekends. "I enjoy the process of figuring out how something works, how it broke, and how to put it back together," he said. When it comes to talking about his case, Haynesworth finds himself answering the same questions, including why he harbors no ill will for Burke: "For someone to go through what she went through, and then have the courage to go to court to deal with the defense attorney and society, she has all my respect." He continued, "One of the reasons I like to speak is to advocate for the victims, too. They made an honest mistake; their whole life was turned upside down. They have been victimized enough. So no, I am not going to do that. You move on."

Still, Haynesworth conceded, "you can't shake everything." In prison, the inmates were counted twice daily, once at 5:30 a.m. and once at 5:30 p.m. "You don't stand up for count, you get an infraction," he said. "They don't play with count." Recently, driving home from work, Haynesworth glanced at the clock and saw it was 5:15 p.m. He increased his speed, anxious not to be late, then pulled over to the side of the road to calm down. "Thomas, what are you doing?" he asked himself out loud. "There is no more count." He responds similarly to whistles, which corrections officers used to signal everything from an ongoing fight to chow time. When Haynesworth hears a whistle, "I stop in my tracks and look around. It's not just a noise to me—it captivates me. That was my life."

Haynesworth and Burke text each other almost every day. Sometimes they just check in. Other conversations are more serious—for better and for worse. Burke told Haynesworth when her dog died and shared the news that she was going to be a grandmother. On January 3, 2017, Burke got a check-in text from Haynesworth. It was the thirty-third anniversary of the rape. "I needed to hear from you today," she wrote. "Thank you." He texted back, "Thinking about you on this day and wishing you peace." Burke said, "We are a family. We both say that. So we stay connected to each other."

Two weeks after the anniversary of the rape, on January 17, 2017, Richmond held a National Day of Healing. The event took place in the chapel of Richmond Hill, a Christian community center built on the highest point in the city, overlooking the James River Falls.[13] Burke visited Richmond Hill's website, which provided a place to submit a personal story. Inspired, Burke wrote about Haynesworth's case. The following day, she received a call from one of the directors of Richmond Hill asking if she and Haynesworth would speak at the event. Burke hesitated before texting Haynesworth, not wanting to impose, but he responded immediately that he would be glad to do it.

That night, before an audience of a hundred people, they talked about their shared experience through the prism of faith. Haynesworth said that his faith never wavered; it was his conviction that he was a child of God that had sustained him, allowing him to believe that the truth would eventually come out and he would be released. For Burke, it had been a zigzag journey. After the rape, she lost her faith. Years later, married with two children and a good life, she slowly rebuilt it. Then came the awful revelation of the misidentification and the questions returned: "Why Thomas? Why me? Faith is so many things. There is faith in yourself, religious faith, faith in the justice system. After the DNA process and the exoneration, I had totally lost faith in all of these things."

Yet on the day that Burke met Haynesworth for the first time, faith was what he wanted to talk about, to get her to understand not only how he survived, but who he was and what he could offer her. "I cannot forgive with my love, I can forgive with God's love," he had told her. "My love is not perfect, but God's love is perfect. I can give that." The wildly improbable existence of their relationship and its restorative power, Burke told the audience, had given her something to believe in.

Epilogue

IN APRIL 2017, Healing Justice held its third retreat at the Aqueduct in Chapel Hill, North Carolina. The first afternoon, a warm Friday, was full of hugs and exclamations as the participants were introduced to and reunited with one another. There were good reasons to celebrate—it was the organization's second birthday, and Jennifer Thompson brought a cake. Thomas Haynesworth and Janet Burke could not attend, and Sarah had come down with pneumonia, but Thomas Webb was there, along with Christy Sheppard, Jerome Morgan, and a diverse group that included exonerees, victims, and family members, some of whom were attending for the first time.

Thompson and Katie Monroe invited me to come and observe. Watching the participants brought back vivid memories of my time with Kash Register, the improbably named client who changed my life.

In the years since Register was exonerated, I have stayed close to him and to his mother, Wilma. My children refer to Register and Wilma as members of an extended family, which they are. At the conclusion of every conversation, we always say, "I love you."

Shortly after his exoneration, Register sued the Los Angeles Police Department. In January 2016, he won a settlement of $16.7 million—the largest judgment the city has ever paid out to an individual exoneree. The money has not changed Register, except to make him exceptionally generous. He and Wilma continue to live in the same small apartment where he grew up, while they take their time looking for a house. The first thing Register did when he got his settlement was give some of the money away: to Loyola's Project for the Innocent, to the individuals who helped him, to me. When I was struggling financially, that money made it possible for me to finish this book.

Register and Wilma are deeply private people. It is hard to imagine them at a restorative justice retreat. They have their own way of healing. But they were very much on my mind and in my heart during the days I spent at the Aqueduct. Without them, I would not have been there. Without them, there would be no book.

At the retreat, I was able to reconnect with the people I had come to know through visits and telephone conversations. It was a reunion and a chance to catch up. Sheppard's advocacy work is continuing, Morgan's barbershop is in the black, and Webb had received the news, several months earlier, that the state had finally agreed to compensate him: $175,000, tax free. Webb planned to use part of the money to repay his ex-wife the money she had spent on the DNA testing. He also hoped to buy a new car and even afford a down payment on a small house.

But he found that his feelings were oddly mixed: "This is the most money I have ever had in my entire life, and I am still working through what to do next. I am not depressed and anxious about it. I don't feel like time is ticking, but I do feel that emptiness that comes from achieving your goal and it's kind of done. I have spent the majority of my life dealing with this, and now that it is really over, the thought occurred to me, what now? What is my purpose? I am waiting for the next door to open."

There was sorrow, too: it was just over a year since Darryl Hunt's death. On the first morning of the retreat, Saturday, April 22, the retreat participants gathered in a circle in the middle of the meadow outside the Aqueduct to plant a slender green sapling. It came from the Survivor Tree, an ancient elm that marked the southern boundary of the Oklahoma City National Memorial and Museum. Nearly a hundred years old, the elm was only forty feet tall and it listed sideways, the two main branches jutting in opposing directions. Since the late 1970s, its roots have been buried in concrete, which had been poured to build the parking lot for the employees who worked in the Alfred P. Murrah Federal Building.

On April 19, 1995, Timothy McVeigh parked a rented truck with four thousand pounds of explosives in front of the Murrah Building. When the truck exploded, it took part of the building with it, and 168 lives. Fifteen children in the second-floor day-care center died.

As cars in the parking lot burned, the elm remained standing. Afterward, there was talk of cutting it down to collect the evidence—including human remains—that clung to its branches. But a community of people urging its preservation prevailed. Over the years, hundreds of cuttings had been taken from the Survivor Tree and replanted.[1]

Thompson was determined to have a sapling to plant at the retreat, but the cuttings were not easy to obtain and permission was needed to plant one out of state. Thompson explained, "You had to get in line on this particular day in April on the anniversary and if you were not there, you could not get one. But if there is one person I know who would take her tiny little behind to Oklahoma City and stand in line, it's Christy Sheppard." A few months later, Sheppard sent Thompson a picture of her ten-year-old daughter, Addison, holding a cutting from the Survivor Tree as she stood facing the memorial. On the plane to North Carolina, Sheppard carried the potted sapling in her lap like a baby.

Now Sheppard knelt in the meadow to place the sapling in a small hole that had been dug in the ground. Each retreat participant took turns shoveling dirt over its roots. Sheppard poured in three shovels of earth: one for herself, one for her cousin Debbie Carter, and one for her aunt Peggy. Others did the same, filling the space around the sapling with earth to acknowledge loved ones who were absent—the old, the sick, the murdered, the dead.

Thompson said, "This tree is in memory of Darryl Hunt and all those we couldn't save and all those we won't save. But it is also in honor of all of us here and all of us who have survived. This tree will shelter us, provide shade, and endure, and we will watch it grow.

"We are still standing," Thompson continued, "and our roots are deep."

Acknowledgments

THIS BOOK WOULD NOT have been possible without the willingness of exonerees, crime victims, family members, prosecutors, defense attorneys,
Innocence Project lawyers, judges, probation officers, community activists, academics, and reporters to talk to me at great length. For many people, the process involved multiple interviews and requests for follow-up.
For the exonerees, crime victims, and their advocates and families, the
interviews were not only time consuming, they were fraught and draining.

Nor would the book have been possible without the National Registry of Exonerations, which Samuel Gross and Maurice Possley have scru-
pulously maintained and updated over the years. It is a rich repository of
data and powerful narratives, with more than two thousand cases meticu-
lously documented, coded, and interpreted to give the user a sense of the
racial, gender, and geographic implications of the wrongful convictions
as well as their primary causes. Sam and Maurice, you were unfailingly
patient and responsive to my numerous requests for help and clarification.
Thank you.

The MacDowell Colony and Mesa Refuge gave me the time, space,
and support to write parts of this book in spectacularly beautiful parts of
the country while being well cared for and in the company of writers, mu-
sicians, photographers, composers, poets, painters, sculptors, and film-
makers I have come to count as friends. Those residencies, and a grant
from the Mountain School, inspired me to keep going by affirming that
the work was important.

To the survivors of wrongful conviction: Marvin Anderson, Janet
Burke, Shannon Coleman, Thomas Haynesworth, Sarah, Katie Monroe,
Beverly Monroe, Jerome Morgan, Christy Sheppard, Jennifer Thomp-
son, Thomas Webb, and Anthony Wright, thank you for trusting me with

your stories. I hope I have done you a small measure of justice. Jennifer and Katie, your willingness to let me inside the Healing Justice circle gave me so much, including a deeper understanding of restorative justice. I am grateful. To the participants in the April 2017 retreat, thank you for welcoming and accepting me.

To the advocates in *Haynesworth v. Commonwealth of Virginia*: Shawn Armbrust, Alice Armstrong, Ken Cuccinelli, Michael Herring, and Peter Neufeld, thank you for taking the time to explain your remarkable group effort to cross the courtroom divide to free an innocent man.

To Mark Rabil, without your willingness to share your thoughts and experiences, I could not have understood Darryl Hunt's wrongful conviction and its cascading impacts. Thank you for talking to me.

To everyone in Pennsylvania who guided me on an unforgettable tour of the state's criminal justice system, thank you for sharing your personal knowledge and hard-won experience. In Philadelphia and the suburbs: Marissa Boyers Bluestine, Marc Bookman, Shannon Coleman, Jim Figorski, Stewart Greenleaf, Tom Hogan, Daylin Leach, Kathleen Martin, Jack McMahon, H. Charles Ramsey, Andrew Wellbrock, Anthony Wright, and Aaron Zappala. In Pittsburgh and its environs: Jay Costa, Lawrence Fisher, Noah Geary, Steve Hoenstine, Mike Manko, John Rago, Drew Whitley, and Stephen Zappala. In New York: Rebecca Brown, Nina Morrison, and Peter Neufeld. In Washington, DC: Jim Trainum.

To the advocates in Louisiana who spoke to me about Jerome Morgan's case and the Real Gentlemen Barbershop: Morgan's attorneys, Emily Maw and Kristen Wenstrom; his advocate in and out of prison, Kelly Orians; and RGB seed funder Jason Flom.

To the RISE founders and participants in Massachusetts: Janet Connors, Allyson Lorimer Crews, Maria D'Addieco, Bobby Fitzpatrick, Page Kelley, Jennifer Pucci, Laura Santana, Patti Saris, and Leo Sorokin, all of whom I had the pleasure of interviewing and many of whom I had the pleasure of meeting in person. Allyson and Maria, I am so appreciative of your allowing me to visit with some of the RISE participants after a restorative justice workshop.

To Alicia Garza, Nancy O'Malley, and Eva Paterson, in Oakland, California, thank you for giving me your accounts of the restorative justice meeting that brought together representatives from the Alameda County District Attorney's Office and the Black Lives Matter protestors.

To the reporters: Frank Green and Shaun Hittle, thank you for taking me behind the scenes of your work investigating the Haynesworth and Webb cases.

To the experts: Eric Butler, Fania Davis, John Douglass, Brandon Garrett, Richard Leo, and Howard Zehr, thank you for explaining difficult legal concepts, restorative justice practices, and putting all of it in a larger context.

To Ramon Chalkley III and Bob Pool, for telling me difficult stories. To Rand Eddy and Larry Helman, for important information about Thomas Webb's case.

To my diligent, thoughtful, and empathic agent, Emma Patterson, who has continued to believe in me. To my editor, Rakia Clark, and the Beacon team, I am so lucky. You were behind this book from day one and offered help, encouragement, and excellent editing along the way. Any mistakes are mine.

To my beautiful children, Carter and Ella. Finally, and especially, to Kash Delano Register and Wilma Register. You opened my heart and my mind. I love you.

Notes

Introduction

1. Robert J. Norris, *Exonerated: A History of the Innocence Movement* (New York: New York University Press, 2017).

2. Ashley Powers, "Witness' Sister Helps Free Man Convicted in 1979 Killing," *Los Angeles Times*, November 7, 2013.

3. Bill Whitaker, "Prosecutor Laments Role in Wrongful Death Row Conviction," *60 Minutes*, October 9, 2015.

4. Lara Bazelon, "Justice After Injustice," *Slate*, September 30, 2015.

Chapter One: A Rapist in Richmond

1. Under Virginia law, all files and records in Haynesworth's case were expunged, meaning that they are sealed from public view, after the Court of Appeals granted a writ of actual innocence. Virginia Code Ann. Section 19.2–327.13. The description of the rapes, sexual assaults, and other attacks for which Haynesworth was charged are taken from the three separately written opinions written by Judge Elder (joined by Judge Petty), Judge Beales, and Judge Humphreys, all of whom dissented from the Virginia Court of Appeals's decision, Haynesworth v. Commonwealth of Virginia, 59 Va. App. 192 (2011). The dissents begin on page 198 and continue through page 224. Additional facts and details were obtained from interviews with Janet Burke on May 19, 2015, December 17, 2015, and February 23, 2016; with Thomas Haynesworth on June 16, 2016, and February 22, 2016; Haynesworth's lead counsel, Shawn Armbrust, on June 1, 2015, and December 1, 2015; with Richmond, Virginia, common-wealth attorney Michael Herring on February 23, 2016; and with former attorney general Kenneth Cuccinelli III on March 17, 2016, and September 26, 2016.

2. Watkins v. Sowders, 449 U.S. 341 (1981) (Brennan, J., dissenting).

3. Felix Frankfurter, *The Case of Sacco and Vanzetti: A Critical Analysis for Lawyers and Laymen* (Boston: Little, Brown, 1927), 30.

4. United States v. Wade, 388 U.S. 218 (1967).

5. *Watkins v. Sowders*; Summitt v. Commonwealth, 550 S.W.2d 548 (1977).

6. Karen Kafadar, "Statistical Issues and Reliability of Eyewitness Identification as a Forensic Tool," University of Virginia (2016), available at https://www.nist.gov/sites/default/files/documents/2016/11/22/statistical_issues_and_reliability_of_eyewitness_id_as_a_forensic_tool.kafadar.legalfact.pdf (summarizing studies).

7. Gary L. Wells, "Eyewitness Identification: Systemic Reforms," *Wisconsin Law Review* 615 (2006). As Wells described in his article, there is vigorous debate over which is the preferred method: sequential or simultaneous. He concluded, "In particular, there is some concern that the rate of accurate identifications could be lower using the sequential lineup. However, there does not appear to be any evidence that the sequential procedure produces a worse ratio of accurate to mistaken identifications than does the simultaneous procedure." Wells, "Eyewitness Identification," 625. Matthew A. Palmer and Neil Brewer, "Sequential Lineup Presentation Promotes Less-Biased Criterion Setting but Does Not Improve Discriminability," *Law and Human Behavior* 36, no. 247 (2012); Dawn McQuiston-Surrett et al., "Sequential vs. Simultaneous Lineups: A Review of Methods, Date, and Theory," *Psychology, Public Policy, and Law* 12, no. 137 (May 2006); Gary Wells et al., "Double-Blind Photo Lineups Using Actual Eyewitnesses: An Experimental Test of a Sequential Versus Simultaneous Lineup Procedure," *Law and Human Behavior* 39, no. 1 (February 2015).

8. Elizabeth F. Loftus, *Eyewitness Testimony* (Cambridge, MA: Harvard University Press, 1979), 189–90; see also Roy S. Malpass and Jerome Kravitz, "Recognition of Faces of Own and Other Race," *Journal of Personality and Social Psychology* 13, no. 330 (1969): 333. In this classic study, Malpass and Kravitz showed photographs of black and white people to students at Howard University, which was predominantly black. The researchers conducted the same experiment at the University of Illinois, which was majority white. The black and white students who participated in the study recognized faces of their own race better than faces of the other race. Even the white students who attended Howard University were susceptible to this bias, making two to three times as many false identifications when attempting to identify black faces than when attempting to identify white faces.

9. Elizabeth F. Loftus, James M. Doyle, and Jennifer E. Dysart, *Eyewitness Testimony: Civil and Criminal*, 4th ed. (Newark, NJ: Lexis-Nexis, 2007), 103: "It is well established that there exists a comparative difficulty in recognizing individual members of a race different from one's own"; Otto H. Maclin, "Racial Categorization of Faces," *Psychology of Public Policy and Law* 7, no. 98 (2001). Studies show that people who primarily interact within their own racial group, especially if they are in the majority group, will better perceive and process the subtlety of facial features of persons within their own racial group than persons of other racial groups.

10. United States v. Telfaire, 469 F.2d 552, 559–61 (D.C. Cir. 1972). The chief judge of the US Court of Appeals for the District of Columbia and author of the concurring opinion in *Telfaire* was my grandfather, David L. Bazelon.

11. New Jersey v. Cromedy, 727 A.2d 457, 467–68 (N.J. 1999).

12. People v. Boone, 2017 WL 6374286, New York Court of Appeals (December 14, 2017).

13. David E. Aaronson, "Cross Racial Identification of Defendants in Criminal Cases: A Proposed Model Jury Instruction," *Criminal Justice* 23, no. 4 (2008).

14. Ibid; see also Ashley Southall, "To Curb Bad Verdicts, Court Adds Lesson on Racial Bias for Juries," *New York Times*, December 15, 2017.

15. Payne v. Commonwealth, 65 Va. App. 194 (2015).

16. Samuel P. Gross et al.: "Of all the problems that plague the American system of criminal justice, few are as incendiary as the relationship between race and rape. Nobody would be surprised to find that bias and discrimination continue to play a role in rape prosecutions." "Exonerations in the United States 1989–2003," *Journal of Crime and Criminology* 95 (2003): 548; Sherrilyn A. Ifill, *On the Courthouse Lawn: Confronting the Legacy of Lynching in the Twenty-First Century* (Boston: Beacon Press, 2007), describing an attendance of thousands, including women and children, and the practice of immortalizing lynchings with photographs and keepsakes.

17. Lisa Lindquist Dorr, *White Women, Rape, and the Power of Race in Virginia: 1900–1960* (Chapel Hill: University of North Carolina Press, 2004); Amy Louise Wood, *Lynching and Spectacle: Witnessing Racial Violence in America, 1890–1940* (Chapel Hill: University of North Carolina Press, 2011), for a description of the social acceptability of public lynching in the Deep South as a way to terrorize and repress the black community as well as its role as a form of public entertainment.

18. David Garland, "Penal Excess and Surplus Meaning: Public Torture and Lynchings in Twentieth Century America," *Law and Society* 39 (2005): 793, 796, for a description of public executions "taking place in the first decades of the twentieth century, in long-settled regions of the world's most advanced capitalist nation, in front of well-dressed crowds who traveled in excursion trains and automobiles, clicked Kodak cameras, and drank Coca-Cola"; Carol S. Steiker, "Remembering Race, Rape, and Capital Punishment," *Virginia Law Review* 83, no. 693 (1997).

19. Dan T. Carter, *Scottsboro: A Tragedy of the American South*, rev. ed. (Baton Rouge: Louisiana State University Press, 1979).

20. McCleskey v. Kemp, 481 U.S. 279 (1987).

21. Samuel P. Gross, *The First 1,600 Exonerations*, National Registry of Exonerations, 2015, www.law.umich.edu/special/exoneration/Documents/1600 _Exonerations.pdf.

22. A copy of Eric Allan's letter is on file with the author.

Chapter Two: Convicting the Innocent

1. The National Registry of Exonerations began collecting exoneration data in 1989, the first year that DNA exonerations happened in the United States. According to cofounder Sam Gross, the registry will publish a "shorter and less complete list of pre-1989" cases in 2018. He continued, "As for reports on our data, most are posted online and can be found on our website under 'Resources.' The most complete list is still [the report called] *Exonerations [in the United States], 1989–2012*, when we had 873 cases. The latest general report on the website is *1,600 Exonerations*, but the *Race [and Wrongful Convictions]* report is based on 1,900 exonerations. *Exonerations in 2016* is the latest yearly report that focuses on the exonerations in that year that were known as of late Feb. 2017."

2. The National Registry of Exonerations moved its operations from the University of Michigan Law School to the University of California at Irvine's

Newkirk Center for Science and Society. Gross, *The First 1,600 Exonerations*; Samuel R. Gross, Maurice Possley, and Klara Stephens, *Exonerations in 2016*, National Registry of Exonerations, March 7, 2017, https://www.law.umich .edu/special/exoneration/Documents/Exonerations_in_2016.pdf.

3. "San Francisco Crime Lab: Promoting Confidence and Building Credibility," *Report of the Civil Grand Jury* (2016), http://civilgrandjury.sfgov.org /2015_2016/201516_CGJ_Final_Report_Crime_Lab_6_1_2016.pdf, accessed July 4, 2017.

4. Rebecca Cohen, "Forget CSI: The Real Crime Labs Are a Total Mess," *Mother Jones*, April 20, 2015, recounting crime-lab scandals in San Francisco, California; St. Paul, Minnesota; Houston, Texas; Cleveland, Ohio; Omaha, Nebraska; Oklahoma City, Oklahoma; Nassau County, New York; "and the entire state of North Carolina"; Deborah Baker, "More Than 20,000 Drug Cases Compromised in Dookhan Scandal Are Dismissed," *WBUR News*, April 19, 2017; Crimesider Staff, "6,000 Drug Cases Linked to 'Rogue Chemist' at Mass. Lab to Be Dismissed," *CBS News*, November 30, 2017.

5. Gross, *The First 1,600 Exonerations*.

6. Jan Hoffman, "4.1 Percent Are Said to Face Death on Convictions That were False," *New York Times*, May 1, 2014, http://www.nytimes.com/2014/05 /02/science/convictions-of-4-1-percent-facing-death-said-to-be-false.html? _r=0. Conservative estimates put the number of those wrongfully convicted of any felony at somewhere between 2 and 8 percent.

7. US Department of Justice, Bureau of Justice Statistics, *Prisoners in 2015* (Washington, DC: USDOJ, December 2016), available at https://www.bjs.gov /content/pub/pdf/p15_sum.pdf.

8. See Beth Schwartzapel and Hannah Levintova, "How Many Innocent People Are There in Prison?," *Mother Jones*, December 12, 2011, http://www .motherjones.com/politics/2011/12/innocent-people-us-prisons/.

9. Stephanie Clifford, "Brooklyn Prosecutors Revisit 3 Convictions in Fatal 1980 Fire," *New York Times*, December 16, 2015.

10. Maurice Possley, "Amaury Villalobos," National Registry of Exonerations, updated February 23, 2018.

11. Maurice Possley, "Clarence Elkins," National Registry of Exonerations, June 2012.

12. Elkins v. Summit County, Ohio, 615 F.3d 671, 673 (6th Circuit 2010).

13. Sara James, "Killer Instinct," *Dateline, NBC News*, January 2, 2009.

14. "Statement of Six People Who Were Wrongly Convicted on Their Experiences in Solitary Confinement," Hearing Before the Senate Judiciary Sub-Committee on the Constitution, Civil Rights, and Human Rights, June 19, 2012.

15. Stacey Frey, "'Since the Injection, No More Nightmares,' Clarence Elkins Gives Update After Shot to Treat PTSD," *Fox 8*, May 17, 2017.

16. Gross, *The First 1600 Exonerations*.

17. Milke v. Ryan, 711 F.3d 998 (9th Cir. 2013).

18. Milke v. Mroz, 236 Ariz. 226 (Court of Appeals of Arizona, 2014).

19. Shaila Dewan, "Duke Prosecutor Jailed; Students Seek Settlement," *New York Times*, September 8, 2007.

20. Pamela Colloff, "The Guilty Man," *Texas Monthly*, June 2013, http://www.texasmonthly.com/the-culture/the-guilty-man/.

21. Adam M. Gershowitz, "Prosecutorial Shaming: Naming Attorneys to Reduce Prosecutorial Misconduct," *UC Davis Law Review* 42, no. 1059 (2009): 1061–64. There is a smattering of other examples, including Washington-Burleson County, Texas, prosecutor Charles Sebasta, who was disbarred after a disciplinary committee found that he lied, presented perjured testimony, and committed other misconduct to wrongfully convict Anthony Graves. Graves, who was convicted of killing six people, spent sixteen years on death row before he was released in 2010. Maurice Possley, "Anthony Graves," National Registry of Exonerations, updated February 2, 2016.

22. Gross, *The First 1,600 Exonerations*.

23. Steve Mills, "Cameron Todd Willingham's Case: Expert Says Fire for which Father was Executed was not Arson," *Chicago Tribune*, August 25, 2009.

24. Spencer S. Hsu, "FBI Admits Flaws in Hair Analysis over Decades," *Washington Post*, April 18, 2015.

25. "Microscopic Hair Comparison Review Project," National Association of Criminal Defense Attorneys, https://www.nacdl.org/haircomparison, accessed July 4, 2017.

26. Spencer S. Hsu, "D.C. to Pay $9.2 Million in Wrongful Conviction," *Washington Post*, February 28, 2015.

27. Maurice Possley, "Kirk Odom," National Registry of Exonerations, March 2, 2015.

28. Spencer S. Hsu, "Kirk Odom, Who Served 20 Years for 1981 D.C. Rape, Is Innocent, Prosecutors Say," *Washington Post*, July 10, 2012.

29. Possley, "Amaury Villalobos."

30. Stephanie Clifford, "Brooklyn Prosecutors Revisit 3 Convictions in Fatal 1980 Fire," *New York Times*, December 16, 2015.

31. Gross, *The First 1,600 Exonerations*.

32. Ken Burns, Sarah Burns, and David McMahon, "Central Park Five," PBS Distribution, 2013.

33. Maurice Possley, "Shawn Whirl," National Registry of Exonerations, January 26, 2017.

34. Samuel R. Gross and Michael Shaffer, *Exonerations in the United States, 1989–2012*, National Registry of Exonerations, June 22, 2012.

35. ABA Standing Committee on Legal Aid and Indigent Defense, "Gideon's Broken Promise: America's Continuing Quest for Equal Justice," American Bar Association, December 2004.

36. Anderson Cooper, "Defenseless: Inside NOLA Public Defender's Decision to Refuse Felony Cases," *60 Minutes*, April 16, 2017.

37. Derwyn Bunton, "When the Public Defender Says, 'I Can't Help,'" *New York Times*, February 19, 2016.

38. "The Crisis of Counsel in Alabama," Equal Justice Initiative, https://eji.org/alabama-inadequate-counsel-death-penalty-cases, accessed July 4, 2017.

39. Hinton v. Alabama, 134 S. Ct. 1081, 1087–90 (2014).

40. Maurice Possley, "Timothy Cole," National Registry of Exonerations, updated March 10, 2015.

41. *Race and Wrongful Convictions in the United States*, National Registry of Exonerations, March 7, 2017.

42. Ibid.

43. Gross, Possley, and Stephens, *Exonerations in 2016*.

44. Gross, *The First 1,600 Exonerations*.

Chapter Three: A Broken System

1. Herrera v. Collins, 506 U.S. 390, 428 (Scalia, J., concurring).

2. Gross, Possley, and Stephens, *Exonerations in 2016*.

3. Jeffrey S. Gutman, "An Empirical Reexamination of State Compensation for the Wrongly Convicted," *Missouri Law Review* 82, no. 369 (2017): 373n14.

4. Vickie Welborn, "Judge Denies Glenn Ford Compensation," *Shreveport Times*, March 27, 2015.

5. "In a Landmark Decision, Texas Forensic Science Commission Issues Moratorium on the Use of Bite Mark Evidence," Innocence Project, February 12, 2016.

6. *Exonerations by State*, National Registry of Exonerations, https://www.law.umich.edu/special/exoneration/Pages/Exonerations-in-the-United-States-Map.aspx, accessed July 4, 2017.

7. Gross, Possley, and Stephens, *Exonerations in 2016*.

8. Ibid.

9. Jed S. Rakoff, "Why Innocent People Plead Guilty," *New York Review of Books*, November 20, 2014.

10. Gross, Possley, and Stephens, *Exonerations in 2016*.

11. Commonwealth v. McGarrell, Petition Requesting Exercise of Extraordinary Jurisdiction and/or Writ of Mandamus, E.D. Misc. Docket No. 2011 (June 8, 2011).

12. Ibid.

13. Commonwealth v. McGarrell, 87 A.3d 809, 810–11 (Saylor, J., dissenting).

14. Nicole C. Brambila, "Disorder in the Court: Troubled Attorneys Often Take On Capital Cases," *Reading Eagle*, October 25, 2015.

15. Death Penalty Information Center Fact Sheet for Pennsylvania, https://deathpenaltyinfo.org/innocence?inno_name=&exonerated=&state_innocence=38&race=All&dna=All, accessed December 23, 2017.

16. State v. Nieves, 746 A.2d 1102, 1104–06 (Pa. 2000).

17. Aja Beech, Philadelphia district attorney, "Pennsylvania Innocence Project Seek Justice Through Improved Conviction Review," WHYY.org, May 19, 2014.

18. "Former Philadelphia Prosecutor Accused of Racial Bias," *New York Times*, April 3, 1997.

19. *State v. Nieves*.

20. Maurice Possley, "William Nieves," National Registry of Exonerations, https://www.law.umich.edu/special/exoneration/Pages/casedetail.aspx?caseid=3507, accessed July 4, 2017.

21. *Exonerations by State*, National Registry of Exonerations.

22. Commonwealth v. Walker, 92 A.3d 766, 769 (Pa. 2014).

23. Philadelphia District Attorney's Office, "Conviction Review Unit Announced," press release, April 15, 2014.

24. Chris Palmer, "Justice on Hold: To Philly DA's Conviction Review Unit, No One Is Innocent," *Inquirer*, November 18, 2016.

25. Paul Solotaroff, "The Trials of Tony Wright: How DNA Exonerated a Convicted Murderer," *Rolling Stone*, March 2, 2015.

26. Paul Solotaroff, "Finally Free: Inside Tony Wright's Murder Exoneration," *Rolling Stone*, August 29, 2016.

27. Lara Bazelon, "Pennsylvania's Shame," *Slate*, October 12, 2016.

28. The facts of David Munchinski, the misconduct of Solomon and Warman, and the twisting, turning path of his case through the Pennsylvania state and federal courts is chronicled in two published opinions, Munchinski v. Wilson, 807 F. Supp.2d 242, 248–59 (W.D. Penn. 2011), and Munchinski v. Wilson, 694 F.3d 308, 313–26 (3rd Cir. 2012). It is also set forth in some detail in the Memorandum and Opinion of the trial judge in Munchinski's civil lawsuit, David Munchinski v. Gerald Solomon and Ralph Warman in their Individual Capacities, Memorandum and Trial Order, Case No. 2:13-cv-1280-DSC (July 2017).

29. Janice Crompton, "Sticking Up for the Weak: Lawyer Gaining Reputation for Taking on Bullies for the Weak," *Pittsburgh-Post Gazette*, April 9, 2006.

30. Order, Commonwealth v. David Munchinski, Case Nos. 755 and 755 ½ Court of Common Pleas, October 1, 2004.

31. Joe Mandak, "Judge Grants Bond to Pa. Suspect in '77 Deaths," Associated Press, September 30, 2011.

32. Peter Hall, "Federal Appeals Court Upholds Mandatory Retirement at 70 for Pennsylvania Judges," *Morning Call*, April 30, 2014.

33. *Munchinski v. Solomon*, 618 Fed. Appx. 150, 156–57 (3rd Cir. 2015).

34. *David Munchinski v. Gerald Solomon and Ralph Warman in Their Individual Capacities*, Memorandum and Trial Order, Case No. 2:13-cv-1280-DSC (June 27, 2017).

35. Order Scheduling a Pretrial Settlement Conference for 8/8/2017, Case No. 2:13-cv-1280-DSC (July 5, 2017).

36. Plaintiff's Response to Motion to Amend Order to Permit Interlocutory Appeal Filed by Defendants Ralph Warman and Gerald Solomon, Case No. 2:13-cv-1280-DSC (August 11, 2017).

37. Whitley v. Allegheny County, 2010 WL 892207, at *37 (W.D. Pa. 2010) (unpublished decision).

38. Bazelon, "Pennsylvania's Shame."

39. *Exonerations by State*, National Registry of Exonerations.

40. New Jersey Senate Bill No. 1219 (2013).

Chapter Four: The Road to Damascus

1. John Rago, "A Fine Line Between Chaos & Creation: Lessons on Innocence Reform from the Pennsylvania Eight," *Widener Law Review* 12 (2006): 359.

2. Pennsylvania Advisory Committee, *Report of the Advisory Committee on Wrongful Convictions* (September 2011), https://deathpenaltyinfo.org/documents/PAwrongfulconvictions.pdf, accessed July 4, 2017.

3. "Report Would Create Roadblocks to Justice," Pennsylvania District Attorney's Association, press release, September 20, 2011.

4. Pennsylvania Independent Committee, *Independent Report of Law Enforcement and Victim Representative Members of the Advisory Committee on Wrongful Convictions* (September 2011), http://www.phila.gov/districtattorney/pdfs /Law_Enforcement_Report.pdf, accessed July 4, 2017.

5. Jake Blumgart, "The Brutal History of Frank Rizzo, the Most Notorious Cop in Philadelphia History," *Vice*, October 15, 2015.

6. Pennsylvania Senate Judiciary Committee Meeting Transcript, Allegheny County Courthouse, February 11, 2015.

Chapter Five: Life After Conviction

1. "Timeline of Events in the Case of Thomas Haynesworth," Innocence Project, February 3, 2011, https://www.innocenceproject.org/timeline-of -events-in-the-case-of-thomas-haynesworth/, accessed July 4, 2017.

2. Maurice Possley, "Marvin Anderson," National Registry of Exonerations, updated May 14, 2014, https://www.law.umich.edu/special/exoneration /Pages/casedetail.aspx?caseid=2995.

3. "Black History Month: Marvin Anderson, a Case of Race and Injustice," Innocence Project, February 18, 2015, https://www.innocenceproject.org/black -history-month-marvin-anderson-a-case-of-race-and-injustice.

Chapter Six: The Path to Exoneration

1. Frank Green, "Scientist's Legacy: Freedom for Two," *Richmond Times-Dispatch*, February 18, 2003.

2. Elizabeth P. Bruns, "Cruel and Unusual? Virginia's New Sex Offender Registration Statute," *William & Mary Journal of Women and the Law* 171, no. 2 (1995).

3. Possley, "Marvin Anderson."

4. Anthony Brooks, "Virginia Case Review Revives DNA Debate," *NPR News*, January 25, 2006.

5. Michael D. Shear and Jamie Stockwell, "DNA Tests Exonerate 2 Former Prisoners," *Washington Post*, December 15, 2005.

6. According to the National Registry of Exonerations, "By the end of 2013, 10 other men—Julius Ruffin, Curtis Moore, Victor Burnette, Arthur Whitfield, Willie Davidson, Philip Thurman, Thomas Haynesworth, Calvin Wayne Cunningham, Bennett Barbour, and Garry Diamond—also had been exonerated as a result of the testing of evidence in Burton's files." Possley, "Marvin Anderson."

7. Maria Glod, "In DNA Reprieves, Guilt from Another Source," *Washington Post*, March 22, 2011.

8. Josh Israel, "Ken Cuccinelli's Legal Appeal and How He Helped Undermine Virginia's Protections Against Adult Sex with Minors," *ThinkProgress*, April 3, 2013.

9. Robert McCartney, "For Cuccinelli, Losing Big Cases Won't Work Forever," *Washington Post*, June 30, 2012.

10. John Collins Rudolf, "A Climate Skeptic with a Bully Pulpit in Virginia Finds an Ear in Congress," *New York Times*, February 22, 2011.

11. Barbara Jean McAtlin, "Written in Blood, Stamped in Unfairness: Virginia's Infamous 21-Day Rule," *Justice Denied—the Magazine for the Wrongly Convicted* 2, no. 2 (November 2000).

12. *Turner v. Commonwealth*, 56 Va. App. 391 (2010) (en banc).

13. *Carpitcher v. Commonwealth of Virginia*, 273 Va. 335 (2007).

14. Frank Green, "Despite Backing Haynesworth's Case Poses Challenges," *Richmond Times-Dispatch*, August 22, 2011.

15. Frank Green, "Thomas E. Haynesworth Freed on Parole," *Richmond Times-Dispatch*, March 22, 2011.

16. Frank Green, "Entire Court of Appeals to Consider Haynesworth Case," *Richmond Times Dispatch*, July 10, 2011.

17. John Schwartz, "Cleared of Rape but Lacking Full Exoneration," *New York Times*, September 24, 2011.

18. Berger v. United States, 293 U.S. 552 (1935).

19. Haynesworth v. Commonwealth of Virginia, 59 Va. App. 197 (2011) (en banc).

20. Ibid.

Chapter Seven: The Myth of Happily Ever After

1. Jon Schuppe, "The Wrong Man: The Wrongful Conviction of Thomas Webb III," *NBC News*, August 31, 2016.

2. Ibid.

3. Carmel Perez Snyder, "Governor Signs Law Allowing Tort Claims in False Convictions," *Oklahoman*, May 30, 2003.

4. Schuppe, "The Wrong Man."

5. John Grisham, *The Innocent Man: Murder and Injustice in a Small Town* (New York: Doubleday, 2006).

6. Sara Rimer, "Life After Death Row," *New York Times*, December 10, 2000.

7. Gore v. State of Oklahoma, 119 P.3d 1268 (2005).

8. Monroe v. Angelone, 323 F.3d 286 (4th Cir. 2003).

Chapter Eight: Reframing Harm and Accountability

1. Howard Zehr, *Changing Lenses: Restorative Justice for Our Times*, twenty-fifth ann. ed. (Scottdale, PA: Herald Press, 2015).

2. Ibid.

3. Antjie Krog, *Country of My Skull: Guilt, Sorrow, and the Limits of Forgiveness in the New South Africa* (New York: Three Rivers Press, 2000).

4. Promotion of National Unity and Reconciliation Act 34 of 1995 (South Africa).

5. Desmond Tutu, Truth and Reconciliation Commission, *Truth and Reconciliation Report*, vols. I–VII (Cape Town: Truth and Reconciliation Commission, 1998).

6. Sherwin Bryce Pease, "TRC Is an Example of Forgiveness: Clinton," *SABC News Live*, February 25, 2016.

7. Children, Young Persons and Their Families Act of 1989 (New Zealand).

8. Fred W. M. McElrea, "Twenty Years of Restorative Justice in New Zealand," *Tikkun*, January 10, 2012.

9. Restorative Welcome and Reentry Circle (Stories Matter Media, 2013), available at https://www.youtube.com/watch?v=uSJ2GPiptvc.

10. Ibid.

11. Sascha Brodsky, "Is Discipline Reform Really Helping Decrease School Violence?" *Atlantic*, June 28, 2016; Emmanuel Felton, "More Teachers' Union Leaders Come Out Against New Student Discipline Policies," *PBS NewsHour*, December 27, 2016; Mackenzie Mays, "Restorative Justice? Teachers Say McLane High School Classrooms Are Spiraling Out of Control," *Fresno Bee*, December 21, 2016.

12. Kale Williams, "Alameda County DA Drops Charges Against the Black Friday 14," *SF Gate*, December 4, 2015.

13. Josh Hafner, "How Michael Brown's Death, Two Years Ago, Pushed #BlackLivesMatter into a Movement," *USA Today*, August 10, 2016.

14. "Black Friday 14," Office of the District Attorney of Alameda County, press release, December 4, 2015.

15. Keith Kamisugi, "Alameda County DA Drops Charges Against the 'Black Friday 14,'" Equal Justice Society, press release, December 4, 2015.

16. Milton J. Valencia, "Drug Violators Get a Chance to Change Lives, Avoid Prison," *Boston Globe*, October 27, 2015.

17. Sentencing Memorandum as to Robert Fitzpatrick, United States v. DiNunzio et. al., 14-cr-10282-PBS (March 13, 2017).

18. Judgment and Order, United States v. DiNunzio et. al., 14-cr-10282-PBS (March 27, 2017).

19. Defendant's Sentencing Memorandum (Redacted), United States v. Santana, 14-cr-10246-PBS (November 21, 2016).

20. Judgement and Order, United States v. Santana, 14-cr-10246-PBS (December 1, 2016).

21. Judge Leo T. Sorokin, District of Massachusetts, Statement to the United States Sentencing Commission in Advance of Testimony on March 15, 2017.

Chapter Nine: "Restorative Justice in Its Purest Form"

1. North Carolina's General Statute Section 148–82 et seq. (2013).

2. North Carolina's General Statute Annotated Section 15A-284.52 (2008).

3. A thorough account of Darryl Hunt's case can be found in his attorney's account. Mark Rabil, "My Three Decades with Darryl Hunt," *Albany Law Review* 75, no. 1535 (2012).

4. "Darryl Hunt," National Registry of Exonerations, Summary Courtesy of the Innocence Project, updated November 6, 2016.

5. Michael Hewlett, "Writing Book Helped Woman Find Closure," *Winston-Salem Journal*, April 19, 2012.

6. Phoebe Zerwick, "Murder, Race, Justice: The State v. Darryl Hunt," series, *Winston-Salem Journal*, 2003; "Sundance Will Show Documentary About Darryl Hunt," *News & Record*, December 6, 2005.

7. Max Blau, "The Tragedy of Darryl Hunt: How Exonerated Man Came to Take His Own Life," *Guardian*, March 19, 2016.

8. North Carolina Innocence Inquiry Commission, http://innocence commission-nc.gov.

9. William L. Holmes, "Darryl Hunt Walks Out of North Carolina Death Row a Free Man After 18 Years," Associated Press, February 7, 2004.

10. Jennifer Thompson Cannino and Ronald Cotton with Erin Torneo, *Picking Cotton: Our Memoir of Injustice and Redemption* (New York: St. Martin's Press, 2009).

11. Stephanie Denzel, "Gregory Taylor," National Registry of Exonerations, updated October 16, 2014.

Chapter Ten: Bittersweet Reunions

1. Shaun Hittle, "After 32 Years and a Wrongful Conviction, New Suspect in Rape Is Charged," *Oklahoma Watch*, July 14, 2014.

2. Shaun Hittle, "Mississippi Man Charged in 1982 Rape Case," *Oklahoma Watch*, July 15, 2014.

3. State of Oklahoma v. Gilbert Duane Harris, Case No. CF-2014–1222, Oklahoma State Courts Network Docket; Jessica Bruha, "Rape Case Dismissed Due to Statute of Limitations," *Norman Transcript*, May 8, 2015.

Chapter Eleven: The Retreats

1. The final days and weeks of Darryl Hunt's life are chronicled by Phoebe Zerwick, the journalist who covered Hunt's case for more than ten years for the *Winston-Salem Journal*, in "The Last Days of Darryl Hunt," *Atavist* (Fall 2016).

2. Ibid.

3. Maurice Possley, "Jerome Morgan," National Registry of Exonerations, updated June 13, 2017.

4. State of Louisiana v. Jerome Morgan, Case No. 367–809, Master Calendar (Criminal District Court Parish County of New Orleans).

5. State of Louisiana v. Jerome Morgan, Case No. 2014-K-0276 (Court of Appeal for the Fourth Circuit), May 23, 2014.

6. State of Louisiana v. Jerome Morgan, Case No. 367–809 (Criminal District Court Parish of New Orleans) Oct. 10 and Oct. 16, 2013 (evidentiary hearing transcript).

7. *State of Louisiana v. Jerome Morgan*, Court of Appeal for the Fourth Circuit.

8. *State of Louisiana v. Jerome Morgan*, Master Calendar (Criminal District Court Parish County of New Orleans).

9. Whitney Benns, "American Slavery Reinvented," *Atlantic*, September 21, 2015.

10. *State of Louisiana v. Jerome Morgan*, Criminal District Court Parish of New Orleans, October 10 and October 16, 2013 (evidentiary hearing transcript).

11. Ibid.

12. John Simerman, "Orleans District Attorney Cannizzaro Prosecuting Witnesses Who Recanted in 20-Year-Old Murder Case," *Advocate*, March 14, 2015.

13. Beau Evans, "Wrongfully Convicted Men Dissect Criminal Justice, Race," *Times-Picayune*, May 27, 2017.

14. "Innocent Man Tells Leon Cannizzaro He Won't Bow Down," available at https://vimeo.com/146500783.

15. Ken Daley, "DA Cannizzaro Halts Prosecution of Jerome Morgan, Ending Decades-Long Case," *Times-Picayune*, May 27, 2017.

Chapter Twelve: The Reformers, Part I

1. Report by the Oklahoma Death Penalty Review Commission (2017).

2. Ibid.

3. Katie Fretland, "Scene at Botched Oklahoma Execution of Clayton Lockett Was a 'Bloody Mess,'" *Guardian*, December 14, 2014.

4. Glossip v. Gross, 135 S. Ct. 2726 (2015) (Breyer, J., and Sotomayor, J., dissenting).

5. Andrew Buncombe, "Charles Warner Execution: Oklahoma Inmate's Last Words Are 'My Body Is on Fire,' as State Carries Out First Death Penalty in Nine Months," *Independent*, January 16, 2015.

6. *Glossip v. Gross.*

7. Tamara Logsdon Hawkinson, "Four Men Hanging," *This Land*, July 20, 2012, http://thislandpress.com/2012/07/20/four-men-hanging/.

8. Christy Sheppard, "Richard Glossip Case: We Can't Be Cavalier About Death Penalty," *Oklahoman*, September 12, 2015.

9. Ibid.

10. Bruce Prescott, "Newly Discovered Evidence in the Glossip Case," press conference, September 14, 2015, available at https://vimeo.com/139307395.

11. A detailed explanation of the botched execution of Charles Warner and the events leading up to the near-execution of Richard Glossip is provided in In the Matter of the Multicounty Grand Jury, State of Oklahoma, Supreme Court of Oklahoma in the District of Oklahoma County, D.C. Case No. GJ-2014–1, May 19, 2016.

12. Ibid.

13. Rick Green, "Governor's Legal Counsel Resigns Four Months After Testifying Before Grand Jury," *Oklahoman*, February 11, 2016; Mark Berman, "Oklahoma Corrections Director Resigns After Problems with Executions," *Washington Post*, December 4, 2015.

14. Ohio Legislature 132nd General Assembly, Senate Bill 162.

15. Proponent Testimony of Christy Sheppard, Senate Bill 162, October 21, 2015.

16. "Oklahoma Bipartisan Death Penalty Review Commission Formed, Supported," *Capital Beat OK*, March 16, 2016.

17. *In the Matter of the Multicounty Grand Jury*, State of Oklahoma.

18. Josh Sanburn, "Oklahoma Votes to Add the Death Penalty to Its Constitution," *Time*, November 9, 2016.

19. Paul Hammel, "Nebraskans Vote Overwhelmingly to Restore Death Penalty, Nullify Historic Vote by State Legislature," *World-Herald Bureau*, November 9, 2016.

20. Report by the Oklahoma Death Penalty Review Commission (2017).

21. Sean Murphy, "Panel Recommends Keeping Moratorium on the Death Penalty," Associated Press, April 25, 2017.

22. Report by the Oklahoma Death Penalty Review Commission (2017).

23. Graham Lee Brewer, "Joe Allbaugh Named Permanent Director of the Oklahoma Department of Corrections," *Oklahoman*, July 7, 2016.

24. Patrick McGuigan, "Allbaugh Discusses Death Penalty with Coalition Opposed to Executions," *CapitolBeat OK*, February 17, 2017.

25. "Plenty for Oklahoma to Consider in Commission's Death Penalty Report," editorial, *Oklahoman*, April 27, 2017.

26. Graham Lee Brewer, "Panel Finds 'Serious Flaws' in Oklahoma Death Penalty Process," *News OK*, April 25, 2017; "Panel Recommends Keeping Moratorium on Oklahoma Executions," Associated Press, April 25, 2017.

27. Stewart Greenleaf, SB 1134, Senate Co-Sponsorship Memorandum, January 19, 2016.

28. Stewart J. Greenleaf and Tedd C. Nesbit, "It's Time to Fix PA's Testing Law," op-ed, *Penn Live*, April 18, 2017.

29. Senate Judiciary Committee Hearing on SB 1134, http://judiciary.pasenategop.com/042417/.

30. Paul Solotaroff, "The Trials of Tony Wright: How DNA Exonerated Convicted Murderer," *Rolling Stone*, March 2, 2015.

31. "District Attorney: Release Anthony Wright," Change.org petition, https://www.change.org/p/district-attorney-release-the-man-wrongly -convicted-of-murdering-my-aunt, accessed February 1, 2018.

32. Copies of the emails from Shannon Coleman to Jennifer Selber dated June 2, June 18, June 27, and July 15, 2016, are on file with the author.

33. Shannon Coleman, "Help Anthony Wright Transition Back into Society After 23 Years of Wrongful Imprisonment," Change.org petition, https://www.change.org/f/help-provide-anthony-with-the-money-to-support-himself -in-his-freedom, accessed February 1, 2018.

34. L. Felipe Restrepo and Timothy R. Rice, Annual Report—Reentry Program, July 7, 2014, https://www.ussc.gov/sites/default/files/pdf/training /annual-national-training-seminar/2014/memo_star.pdf.

35. Senate Judiciary Committee Hearing on SB 1134, http://judiciary .pasenategop.com/042417/.

36. Marissa Boyers Bluestine, "Philly Has More Work to Do in Freeing the Innocent," *Philadelphia Inquirer*, August 28, 2016.

37. Chris Palmer, "Philly DA's Reforms Unit Dedicated to Reviewing Innocence Claims," *Philadelphia Inquirer*, February 8, 2017.

38. Dave Davies, "Krasner Jumps into Philly DA Race," *Daily News*, February 8, 2017.

39. Ibid.

40. Alice Speri, "Meet Philadelphia's Progressive Candidate for DA: An Interview with Larry Krasner," *Intercept*, May 16, 2017.

41. Jeremy Roebuck and Chris Brennan, "Philly DA Seth Williams: Brought 'Shame' To Office, Won't Run for Reelection," *Philadelphia Inquirer*, February 10, 2017.

42. Docket in United States v. Rufus Seth Williams, No. 17-CR-00137-PD.

43. Jeremy Roebuck, David Gambacorta, and Chris Brennan, "D.A. Seth Williams Indicted on Corruption, Bribery-Related Charges," *Philadelphia Inquirer*, March 21, 2017.

44. Harrison Jacobs, "The Inside Story of How Trump United a City of Activists to Elect the Most Progressive District Attorney in a Generation," *Business Insider*, November 12, 2017.

45. Speri, "Meet Philadelphia's Progressive Candidate for DA."

46. Maurice Possley, "Shaurn Thomas," National Registry of Exonerations, June 20, 2017.

47. Ibid.

48. Tom Jackman, "Man Cleared of Murder Conviction After 24 Years Behind Bars, with Help of an Ex-Cop," *Washington Post*, May 23, 2017.

49. Ryan Briggs and Max Marin, "Leaked List Shows Krasner Firings Targeted Top Staff, Porngate Prosecutors," *Philadelphia Weekly*, January 5, 2018. My sister, Dana Bazelon, became an assistant district attorney in Philadelphia several weeks after Krasner took office, advising him on policy.

50. Chris Palmer, "DA Krasner Promised Change. His First Full Week Showed He Meant It," *Philadelphia Inquirer*, January 13, 2018.

51. Ryan Briggs, "Sources: Philly DA Krasner to Name New Heads of Two Key Units, City & State of Pennsylvania," January 10, 2018; "Dallas District Attorney and Innocence Project Move to Reverse Conviction Based on False Bite Mark Testimony," Innocence Project, October 12, 2015.

Chapter Thirteen: The Reformers, Part II

1. Mike Perlstein, "Former Inmates Freed, Reunited as Business Partners on a Mission," WWL-TV, February 6, 2017.

2. Miller v. Alabama, 567 U.S. 460 (2012).

3. Montgomery v. Louisiana, 136 S. Ct. 718 (2016).

4. Nina Feldman, "Getting Out of Prison It's Hard to Find a Job. Why Not Help Ex-Prisoners Start Their Own Businesses?," *The World*, PRI, September 2, 2016.

5. "Our Fellows: Kelly Orians, 2015 Black Male Achievement Fellow," Echoing Green, http://www.echoinggreen.org/fellows/kelly-orians.

6. "PitchNola 2017: Education Presented by Capital One: Increasing Equitable Educational Outcomes for All New Orleanians," Propeller, http://gopropeller.org/pitchnola/pitchnola-2017-education-presented-by-capital-one/.

7. Morgan and Rideau's pitch script is on file with the author.

8. "Three Solutions Tie for First at Inaugural $10,000 Education Pitch," Propeller, http://gopropeller.org/news/1461/.

9. Bill Capo, "Burglars Ransack Center for Former Prisoners Starting Over," WWL-TV, July 11, 2016.

10. Stephanie Denzel, "Douglas DiLosa," National Registry of Exonerations, updated March 2, 2017.

11. Dan McCarthy, "How the Man Who Signed Katy Perry and Lorde Is Challenging Wrongful Convictions," *Pacific Standard Magazine*, October 19, 2016.

12. Jason Flom, "An Innocent Teenager Sentenced to Life in a Living Hell: The Incredible True Story of Jerome Morgan," *Wrongful Conviction* podcast, season 3, episode 5, July 10, 2017.

13. Connect VA, National Day of Healing, January 17, 2017.

Epilogue

1. "Witness To Tragedy, Symbol of Strength," Oklahoma City National Memorial and Museum, https://oklahomacitynationalmemorial.org/press -room/press-kit/survivor-tree.

Index

About the Author

LARA BAZELON is an associate professor at the University of San Francisco School of Law, where she directs the criminal defense and racial justice clinics. She was a deputy federal public defender for seven years in Los Angeles and is the former director of the Loyola Law School Project for the Innocent. A contributing writer for *Slate*, Lara's opinion pieces and essays have also been published in the *New York Times*, *Washington Post*, *Atlantic*, and *Politico*, among other media outlets. She was a 2016 Mac-Dowell Fellow and a 2017 Mesa Refuge writer-in-residence, where she was named the Jacob and Valeria Langeloth Fellow for excellence in writing about criminal justice.

Bazelon focuses on systemic breakdowns inside and outside the court-room and what can be done to repair the harm. Her writing confronts barriers based on stereotypes, misinformation, and the impulse to see the world as separated into sides with no possibility for dialogue or mutual understanding. Her published work includes long-form investigative pieces about crime, harm, and healing, as well as personal essays that ex-plore the complexities of the modern-day family. As the coparent of two children, she has written about the breaking apart and re-creation of her own family in search of a post-divorce narrative that does not follow a traditional script. In all her work, she asks that her readers open their minds to unexpected—even unlikely—ways of thinking about problems that may not be so intractable after all.

An East Coast transplant, Bazelon lives in the Bay Area. *Rectify* is her first book.